Why Companies Fail

Why Companies Fail

The 10 Big Reasons Businesses Crumble,
and How to Keep Yours Strong and Solid

MARK INGEBRETSEN

CROWN
BUSINESS
NEW YORK

Published by Crown Business, New York, New York.
Member of the Crown Publishing Group, a division of Random House, Inc.
www.randomhouse.com

CROWN BUSINESS is a trademark and the Rising Sun colophon is a registered trademark of Random House, Inc.

Portions of chapter 6 dealing with the satellite broadband industry and its competitors were adapted from an article by Mark Ingebretsen, commissioned by the *IEEE Spectrum* magazine, used with permission.

Portions of chapter 9 dealing with protecting the food supply from terrorism and how companies can communicate with their publics in the event of a disaster were adapted from an article by Mark Ingebretsen that appeared in *Agri Marketing* magazine, January 2002, used with permission.

Portions of chapter 9 dealing with alternative dispute resolution appeared in a slightly different form in an article by Mark Ingebretsen published in *PM Network* magazine, used with permission as follows: Reprinted from *PM Network*, Project Management Institute, Inc., August 2002. Vol. 16, Number 8. Copyright © 2002 by Project Management Institute, Inc. All rights reserved. Unauthorized reproduction or distribution of this material is strictly prohibited.

Printed in the United States of America

Library of Congress Cataloging-in-Publication Data
Ingebretsen, Mark.
    Why companies fail : the 10 big reasons businesses crumble, and how to keep yours strong and solid / Mark Ingebretsen.
        p.   cm.
    Includes index.
    1. Success in business. 2. Business failures. 3. Industrial management.
    I. Title.
    HF5386 .I373   2003
    658—dc21   2003004196

ISBN 0-7615-6374-1
10 9 8 7 6 5 4 3 2 1

First Edition

To Karen and Amanda

Contents

Acknowledgments

My thanks to the many people who took the time out to speak with me regarding this book. Your invaluable insights helped make *Why Companies Fail* possible.

Preface

Foul-Ups, Faux Pas, and Abject Failures

Some years ago, a major U.S. food producer poured millions of dollars into a pineapple-processing facility, set deep within the tropical forests of Mexico. It was a convenient location, or so the planners thought. The cannery lay upstream from where the pineapples actually grew. So come harvest time, barges could simply ferry the fruit to the cannery. The only problem, it turned out, was that during harvest season, the river's current typically became so strong that no barge could make any headway against it. This meant the pineapples had no hope of reaching the processing facility, and a mistake that could easily have been avoided ended up wreaking havoc with the company's operations.

In a similar vein, during the 1980s, Apple Computer executives tried to enter the Japanese market, but their efforts kept hitting a brick wall. One reason, they finally realized, was that the manuals and other accompanying literature packaged with their computers were printed in English.[1] Though this was not exactly an oversight, it was a blunder for Apple to think that Japanese customers would purchase a computer whose manual they couldn't understand.

The history of business is rife with examples of similar foul-ups and cultural faux pas. There's the famous example of the Chevy Nova, which was introduced in Latin America despite the fact that its name in Spanish translates as "It doesn't go." More recently, when Kimberly Clark debuted its pre-moistened adult version of the baby wipe, its reported slogan was "Sometimes wetter is better."[2] To find even more examples of blunders, just look at the lengthy list of products that have long since vanished from supermarket shelves: Panda Punch, Hagar the Horrible Cola, and Gimme Cucumber hair conditioner.[3]

The Blue Light Dims

These failures—though costly, to be sure—are not the catastrophic blunders and deadly mishaps that typically bring down companies. And for that reason, they are not the types of failures that I will analyze in this book.

Instead, I will focus on the kind of missteps made by Kmart, to single out just one company. In another era, Kmart eclipsed Sears as the nation's largest retailer. Its customers were as loyal as Wal-Mart's, surveys revealed. And yet, when Kmart filed for bankruptcy in January 2002, some in the media said it had been on a downward spiral for years. "It's hard to remember when Kmart Corp. wasn't in turnaround mode," said *Business Week* commentator Joann Muller.[4]

Kmart's problems may have begun during the mid 1980s when the company first fell victim to what *Fortune* writers Ram Charan and Jerry Useem called the "strategy du jour." What they meant was that Kmart's management tended to embrace whatever quick-fix ideology seemed popular at the time. And then, instead of sticking with that strategy, they reputedly moved on, adopting whatever the leading gurus had begun to preach next. Starting in the late 1980s, say Charan and Useem, Kmart executives were intent on becoming a diversified retail conglomerate. Accordingly, they bought newly fashionable big-box retailers, the so-called category killers that were designed to dominate a particular line of merchandise. Kmart's big-box acquisitions included Sports Authority, OfficeMax, and Borders Books. Later, these acquisitions were sold when the company decided that instead of becoming a conglomerate, it would focus on discounting merchandise to its core customers.[5] Meanwhile, Kmart's ambitions grew. After CEO Charles Conway took the helm in the spring of 2000, he announced a $1.4 billion two-year IT shopping binge. The high-priced effort was aimed at revamping the retailer's creaky supply chain–management systems—a decision likely inspired by similar highly successful moves made by rival Wal-Mart.[6] For a time, Kmart even tried to go head to head with Wal-Mart. It engaged in a vicious price-cutting war of attrition with the Godzilla of retailers, which it stood little chance of winning. This was just one more strategic blunder that moved Kmart closer to Chapter 11. Or, according to some, it formed part of pattern that led inexorably to disaster.

The Arrogant and the Innocent

When companies' managers engage in a long series of costly missteps, we are all left to wonder: What were they thinking? But as James C. Collins relays in his book *Good to Great: Why Some Companies Make the Leap and Others Don't*, in many cases, managers at failed companies prefer to plunge ahead blindly, rather than think through the consequences. Which is to say, they truly *weren't* thinking. "When you look at companies that get themselves into trouble," he writes, "they're often taking steps of great lurching bravado rather than quiet, deliberate understanding."[7]

The first years of the new century have revealed all too many painful examples of lurching bravado on the part of companies. As shareholders, as employees, as customers, or simply as individuals who must function in this economy, we have all suffered the consequences of such mistakes. When large numbers of companies edge precariously toward failure—such as is happening now in the telecom and biotech sectors—the layoffs and other ripple effects quickly spread throughout the economy. The resulting pain seems even worse when the failures—at least, in hindsight—seem so easily preventable.

The truth is that companies that fail because of lurching bravado are the exceptions. Most managers agonize over their companies' day-to-day successes and failures. They are well aware of their responsibilities to customers, shareholders, and employees. For managers, a highly competitive breed, nothing could be worse than facing defeat and losing control of a company they worked for years to create. When their companies do fail, it is usually not because of deliberate neglect but rather through an unfortunate chain of events, a failure to recognize steps that should have been taken—in short, honest but still catastrophic mistakes.

A Fascination with Failure

If success smells sweet, what must failure smell like? You only have to ask Nicholas Hall, reportedly the veteran of three failed start-ups and the founder of a Web site on the subject called startupfailures.com. "It really stinks," he told a *Wall Street Journal* reporter.[8] And perhaps the worst moment, he alluded, comes when you realize the dream has ended.

Following the death of the dream comes the nasty publicity, and often the litigation, the calls from irate creditors, the moments of terror and self-doubt. And all that's just for starters. Worst of all might be the loss of privacy and dignity that results when news surfaces that a business is about to crash and burn. When that happens, suddenly your life becomes an open book, the butt of jokes, a continuing story on the nightly news.

Our society rewards success perhaps better than any other does. But it also ruthlessly punishes failure. Worse, we cruelly fixate on failure. While all of us would like to believe we're more interested in success than failure, the opposite is often true. Failure dominates our conversations. It dominates the news. When the president makes a speech, political pundits tear it apart, looking for flaws. Likewise, any time a major corporation issues an announcement, armies of analysts and business journalists deconstruct it. What kind of positive spin are they trying to put on their information? What are its real chances for success? What are they hiding?

Clearly, failure fascinates us. Spectacular failures have the power to hold an entire nation spellbound—sometimes for months. Think back on celebrity trials you've watched or the Clinton sex scandal. Night after night, we heard the latest details on the news and the jokes on TV talk shows.

Even when we don't understand how a failure occurred, we're able to derive lessons from it. Few of us, for example, understand the Byzantine accounting methods Enron allegedly used to justify its earnings. But when we learned of the mind-numbing salaries and perks received by some of its former executives, the lesson became clear. Power corrupts; those who fly high, fall far; pride goeth before the fall.

In fact, the exploits of Tyco, Enron, Andersen, Worldcom, ImClone, and others that have been reported on nightly business news shows are nothing new. They are the modern equivalents of ancient Greek morality plays—the popular mass medium of that era—which depict the punishments suffered by those who stray from the righteous path. They are warnings disguised as entertainment.

Warnings well taken. Those charged with running companies, whether large or small, know all too well that failure can be only one or two missteps away. Cross a fine line, and at the slightest hint of trouble, the predators and then the scavengers will soon arrive.

Lessons Learned from Corporate Shock Troops

Most managers hope they will never experience the kind of sensationalized company failure that makes the nightly news. But failure remains an inevitable danger of running a business. And that's why this book was written. It's an attempt to look beyond the details of business failures and to discover a fundamental lesson: How do smart people, working for successful companies, fail to heed the warning signs of disaster and, as a result, bring their companies and their careers to the brink of ruin?

To find answers to that question, this book taps into a wide array of sources, from magazine articles and studies published in academic journals to interviews that I have conducted over many years with dozens of business executives, consultants, and analysts. Some of those interviewed have made tragic mistakes themselves. Others were the victims of such mistakes. Yet others were hired to save floundering companies before they went belly-up.

Some of the most valuable interviews were conducted with turnaround managers and consultants. These people are charged with rescuing failing companies. The interviews were coordinated with the cooperation of their profession's principal organization: the Turnaround Management Association. As you might guess, turnaround managers are in a unique position to understand just where and how mistakes occur within companies. That is because they operate in a time-critical environment. When a turnaround manager arrives at a floundering company, creditors, suppliers, customers, and employees are already aware of the serious problems that exist. One turnaround manager likened the situation to that of an emergency medical technician (EMT) arriving at an accident scene to treat the wounded. The EMT's first task is to quickly stop the bleeding and stabilize the patients for the trip to the hospital. In the same way, a turnaround manager must stop a company from hemorrhaging money. Then, over the longer term—normally, a matter of several weeks—the turnaround manager must allay the fears of the company's stakeholders, creditors, employees, and customers. This individual must also earn their trust and enlist their help in reviving the company.

To accomplish the latter, turnaround managers need to quickly learn all they can about a company's operations, where the firm is succeeding and where it's failing. Then—often in a marathon session—they must create a viable plan for the company's recovery.

And that's the easy part. Executing the plan is where the real challenge lies. One turnaround manger, Randall Wright Patterson of BBK, Ltd., compared rescuing a failing company to saving a row of burning houses. "If you try to fight the fire from the beginning of the row, you'll simply follow the fire and you'll never put it out," he explains. "Sometimes you have to let the first three or four houses burn. During that time you design and put in place a plan of action to save the runaway business, a 'fire wall' per se, to save the remaining houses on the block."

A Guide for Firefighters

How do companies reach that dismal point of sacrificing large parts of themselves in order to save the rest? In so many cases, experts tell us, the warning signs were clearly present long beforehand. I will tell you exactly what those signs are and why they are often tragically ignored. Although this is a work of business journalism and not a how-to book in the strictest sense, it contains strategies that experts have devised to detect mistakes in the earliest stages or, failing that, to take quick action when problems occur.

Certainly, the root forces causing companies to fail are many and varied. The actual circumstances are often unique. Nevertheless, the effects tend to be the same, regardless of the reason for failure or the size of the company involved.

This book first describes general reasons for and consequences of business failure, followed by specific causes. Finally, it examines overall strategies that veterans have devised to safeguard a company from future missteps.

In the first part, I discuss the consequences of failure. Chapter 1 explores what happens when a company spirals out of control, leaving management with few recourses but bankruptcy. Chapters

2 and 3 reveal some hidden common elements that cause businesses to fail.

The 10 Deadly Sins

In the second part of the book I take a more detailed look at the 10 most common reasons why companies fail. These problems have been identified by people who study company failures or who have experienced them firsthand. Though the list is not definitive, each mistake has led to crippling company failures in the past.

Letting Stock Price Dictate Strategy

How many dot-coms were launched with all the best intentions, only to find themselves going public far too quickly in order to cash out investors while the boom was still in progress? Similarly, how many companies have cannibalized their own future operations in order to achieve the short-term performance numbers needed to satisfy an ever-more-fickle investment community? Letting stock price dictate strategy is the first deadly sin because it leads to so many others. The perceived need to build earnings leads to misbegotten alliances that result in failed synergies. It results in overly aggressive accounting that will only turn around and haunt the company when it is discovered. Likewise, it results in quality shortcuts in the company's product or service that alienate customers.

Growing Too Fast

Many companies contain the seeds of their own destruction within their business plans. Like armies that advance beyond their capacity to supply themselves, they pursue a growth strategy that inevitably leads to saturation. For brick-and-mortar companies, this can simply mean overbuilding too many stores or apartment complexes within a given region. It can also manifest in sales. Companies unable to demonstrate a record of ever-growing earnings often pursue a path of ever-growing revenues instead. In lieu of actual revenues, companies may also adopt strategies to boost market share. Airlines, for example, built new hubs or sought merger candidates in hopes that the increased passenger load might eventually lift the bottom line. This strategy proved especially popular with dot-coms. Web sites merged or created subsidiaries in order to gain visitors they hoped would someday be converted into paying customers.

Ignoring Customers

During the 1970s and 1980s, the poor quality of U.S. manufactured goods allowed aggressive, nimble, and well-capitalized Asian firms an inroad into a lengthy list of bedrock American industries. Today, lapses in quality on the part of New Economy companies are causing them to fail. Excite@Home is but one example. Plagued by problems, its broadband Internet service folded, leaving thousands of customers summarily disconnected.

Ignoring Paradigm Shifts

In a world where knowledge and technological know-how may double many times within a single generation, companies must look into the near and the distant future for signs of trends they must reckon with if they are to remain profitable. Companies must also devise ways to adapt their products and services to reach as yet undefined customer groups. Most important of all, they must gear their strategy to the singular fact that massive change is the norm, and that earth-shattering upheavals are part of the "new normal." The September 11 attacks tragically revealed how events can change everything, sometimes overnight.

The corporate battlefield is littered with examples of companies that have failed to adapt. Whittle Communications, once a company that pioneered new media—everything from magazines customized for large advertisers to TV news programs beamed into high school classrooms—failed to capitalize on the explosive growth of online media. And so the company folded—ironically, on the eve of the biggest new communications medium since the debut of the printing press, the Internet.

Fighting Wars of Attrition

The multibillion-dollar meltdown in the telecom sector is but one example of how companies in a race to build market share and colonize new territories find that the product or service they plan to offer has been commoditized by the marketplace. When that occurs, companies frantically wrestle to become low-cost producers. As in a real war of attrition, when companies become locked in a death struggle with competitors, their resources fall into a black hole. The longer the quagmire persists, the less likely the company will develop new products to differentiate itself out of an attrition war. Instead, the common strategy is to dump products or services furiously onto the marketplace, even though this racks up ever-higher losses in the process. Big companies aren't the only ones to find themselves locked in wars of attrition. Take a look at retailing at the coffee shop level. "In the major cities in the United States there's a coffee shop on every corner, there's more coffee shops on every corner than banks," explains Toronto-based turnaround expert Mel Zwaig. "They're labor-intensive and I can't figure out how they make money. That's a small bubble, but it's a bubble that will burst." Some companies have managed to thrive in wars of attrition. And they've done so through a process of constant innovation and differentiation. Coke and Pepsi have fought what is perhaps the business world's most protracted trench war. Yet both companies—while gaining or losing fractions of a point from quarter to quarter—have managed to reward investors with relatively consistent performance. And they've done so by continually introducing new products.

Ignoring Liabilities, Threats, and Crises

Litigation once nearly destroyed America's small aircraft industry. It now threatens to topple powerful brokerage firms because of the conduct of their analysts. Even an organization as powerful and steadfast as the Catholic Church has shown itself to be frighteningly vulnerable to an onslaught of litigation. No one knows how many hundreds of millions of dollars it may be forced to pay out, due to the rash of alleged abuses by its priesthood.

Indeed, perhaps nothing can bring a company down with such amazing speed as misconduct. The classic example, of course, being Arthur Andersen. Though relatively few employees were the subject of the Justice Department's allegations, the suspicion of improprieties caused massive customer defections. To quell losses, the company was forced into fire sales of many of its operating units.

Firms can also be completely innocent, yet suffer from potential liabilities. However, through a well-wrought strategy they can emerge from potentially ruinous episodes unscathed, and on occasion in a stronger position than before. Consider Johnson & Johnson in the 1980s, when it, not once but twice, fell victim to terrorist tampering of its Tylenol brand pain reliever. The Johnson & Johnson case illustrates that while companies can't protect themselves from all dangers, they can, through responsible action and open, honest communication with the public, regain charge of the situation. The public, always quick to condemn bad behavior on the part of companies, will reward genuine displays of concern and action taken to protect customers' well-being. Recently, Johnson & Johnson was voted America's most trustworthy company.

Over Innovating

Pioneers face arrows, and the leading edge all too often translates into the bleeding edge. These may be well-known business axioms, but companies continually choose to ignore them. The entire New Economy revolution was built on the idea that consumers would radically change their habits within months of the introduction of a new product or service. And while this was the case with some Internet products, such as online brokerage firms, the companies that hoped to entice consumers into buying their pet supplies, wine, and garden tools over the Internet quickly found themselves out of business. Inevitably, in a society where technology continues to grow exponentially, some companies will position themselves too far along the consumer-adoption curve. Witness Iridium. Its global satellite phone service, reminiscent of *The Man from Uncle* TV show, enjoyed unprecedented buzz. Nevertheless, what the company discovered after its multibillion-dollar constellation of low earth-orbit satellites was circling the earth is that relatively few people—save perhaps yachtsmen, journalists, and explorers—were willing to pay a high price for the chance to communicate from any spot on earth to anywhere else. Meanwhile, the vast armies of global business travelers congregating in cities—where the satellite phones didn't work especially well—found that they could call home with relative ease using a rented cell phone or a new brand of phone that could patch into the different cell phone networks utilized in the United States, Europe, and Asia.

Poor Succession Planning

Successful companies go to great pains to demonstrate that they have built long-term continuity into their management team. Key promotions are announced with a degree of fanfare, allowing rumors to circulate that the person chosen is being groomed for the eventual top position. When companies do look outside for top talent, the process is often made deliberately long and complex to signal to investors and other stakeholders that it is the subject of much deliberation. When hiring decisions are a surprise, by contrast, it signals trouble. Wall Street likes to know who is and who will be in charge. This is one way of affirming its long-term earnings forecasts. When a company appears indecisive about how its chain of command functions, it becomes like an unstable government during a coup. No one can confidently predict the outcome. An equally damning sin occurs when a company names a new head and then fails to rally support behind the new person. Consider Maytag, the stalwart supplier of washing machines and other quality big-ticket consumer appliances to millions of consumers worldwide. The company chose as its CEO Lloyd Ward, who it was reported found himself at odds with the board. Management had deliberately looked outside its own ranks for a candidate with strong marketing skills, who could help the Newton, Iowa, company compete as the number of global-scale appliance makers dwindled. Ward, a Pepsi veteran lauded as a marketing genius, seemed an ideal choice. Dynamic, charismatic, and stylish, he was featured on the cover of *Business Week* as the first African American to occupy the top executive suite of a major U.S. corporation. Yet a profit downturn led to Ward's demise. Former CEO Leonard Hadley[9] was compelled to reassume the top job, following Ward's departure. Only with the appointment of former Whirlpool CFO Ralph Hake[10] and a series of cost-cutting and other strategic measures did the company again curry favor in the eyes of Wall Street.

That same Fortune 500 company drama plays out daily in countless family-owned businesses, where faulty succession planning can lead to losses, premature sales, or even bankruptcy. Turnaround experts in family businesses often assume a role not unlike a family psychologist, working closely with diverse family members, uncovering long-standing family disputes, and creating agreement among parents and siblings to ensure a firm's long-term survival.

Failed Synergies

In the 1980s leveraged buyout firms sought to unearth "hidden value" within companies by selling them off one division at a time. Often those divisions were cobbled together a decade or more beforehand, when it was believed that diversified conglomerates provided the best protection against the vagaries of the business cycle. During the 1990s, companies were meshed together for different reasons: for example, to quickly build market share in a fast-growing sector such as the Internet. As always seems to be the case with alliances and mergers, what looks good on paper can turn into a devilish conundrum as the two organizations' cultures resist converging.

The prime example, of course, is AOL Time Warner, a controversial match-up to begin with. The company sought to create a vertically integrated media monolith that someday would allow consumers to watch CNN via AOL TV, while downloading pages of the latest *Sports Illustrated* online. Then, of course, a slowed economy and the dot-com bust pushed down AOL Time Warner's stock price. Analysts called for divestiture of everything from the media giant's cable properties to its core online service. Similarly, Daimler Chrysler began as a marriage of two highly successful and innovative auto companies, each significantly occupying a distinctly different niche. As the merger was consummated and a power struggle evolved between the German executive team and its U.S. counterparts, both the Mercedes and the Chrysler franchises reportedly suffered.

Some companies do understand how to bring together disparate units into a whole that is greater than the sum of its parts. Witness Cisco Systems, a company that in 2000 had plans to acquire a new firm almost every two weeks. In the future, synergies may not take the form of actual mergers or acquisitions. Instead, partnerships between companies will become increasingly important. Smaller firms will increasingly be faced with the task of working with diverse partners, whether on temporary projects or as subsidiaries.

Arrogance

This book saves the worst corporate sin for last, because it is all too common. Moreover, the public has grown accustomed to arrogance on the part of corporate chieftains, even as they steered their companies aground. Shareholders and others are also increasingly hostile to executives who reward themselves with generous salaries and huge stock options, while their companies lose millions and render thousands jobless.

Indeed, examples of arrogance in the face of failure dominated the news during 2002. As proof, think of Enron—the poster child of bad corporate behavior—and the seeming contempt some of its executives displayed for their employees and shareholders. When Enron began firing employees in droves, for example, it still reportedly managed to find $200,000 to fund its luxury box at the formerly named Enron Field.

Or look at Polaroid, a company founded on the idea of instant photography. Management was unable to shift its focus sufficiently when customers instead opted for digital cameras, with devastating consequences. Polaroid reportedly canceled healthcare benefits for the company's retirees in the wake of its Chapter 11 filing. At the same time, management reportedly petitioned the bankruptcy court for permission to dole out roughly $19 million in bonuses to keep key executives from leaving.

Webvan is yet another example. It hoped to change the way Americans buy groceries, by having customers complete their shopping lists online. The groceries would then be home delivered. The future didn't happen fast enough for Webvan. Traditional supermarkets proved to be strongly entrenched competitors. But before it ceased operations, the company reportedly agreed to pay its resigning CEO, George Shaheen, $375,000 per year for life. Never mind the fact that Webvan's stock price declined 99 percent during his tenure.[11]

Thanks to the highly publicized incidents of executive gluttony, Americans have grown to distrust big business to a degree not seen since the rebellious 1960s. And they are furious about it. Americans, after all, had been promised a New Economy and a new age of boundless prosperity. Yet it turned out to be all smoke and mirrors. Worse, while the nation faced a deadly threat from terrorism, the rampant greed displayed by America's corporate elite appeared in stark, shameful contrast to the sacrifices made by brave rescue workers in Lower Manhattan and by U.S. soldiers in Afghanistan.

Business leaders likewise have every reason to be angry at the wanton missteps and displays of arrogance by their colleagues. All companies suffer a kind of guilt by association because of the actions of this group.

Moving beyond these sensational examples, turnaround experts claim that management in countless smaller companies exhibits arrogance as well: the boss who deliberately sidesteps the law, the key manager who carries on affairs with coworkers. And though it's easy to cite examples of arrogance, it's not always so easy to determine the root cause. Is the motive simply greed, or does it go deeper than that? And in either case, how does the company's culture allow an attitude of arrogance to spread throughout the organization?

The final chapter of the book, chapter 14, examines probable causes for business failures in the years ahead, when all companies must run on Internet time. Analysts forecast that companies will succeed or fail based on their ability to forge seamless bridges between their various constituents, even as those constituents are constantly reshaped. The crucial test of success in the years ahead may well be management's ability to create those partnerships across broad geographic and cultural boundaries.

Such skills are a far cry from the product or service focus most companies employ today. They require that management focus on

the company's core values and on the potential of the relationships its people have developed. No doubt by the time such skills
become firmly implanted within an organization, new threats will
emerge.

Thus, the greatest skill of all that management must cultivate
now and in the future is the ability to foresee the signs of failure
and take appropriate steps.

Comprehensive Strategies

Finally, an appendix examines strategies that have been devised to
help companies reduce the risk of failure—whatever its cause. I
detail ways that management can regain control of the company's
bureaucracy and culture, as well as keep vital channels of communication open. Among the items discussed in detail are the commitments that management must make, what management must
be prepared to concede, and how difficult the job is likely to be.
The goal is to build a bulletproof yet nimble organization. And
while this is no simple task, it is dwarfed by the challenge of rescuing a company that failed to guard itself against failure. Why do
companies fail? For uncountable reasons. But as you will see in
the first chapter, the result of their failure is often very similar, a
deadly spiral downwards that takes hold of owners and employees and families and communities.

1

The Deadly Spiral

May 22, 2002: Shares of the Gap clothing company plummeted roughly 15 percent just one day after the surprise resignation of CEO Millard Mickey Drexler.[1] And that was on top of the company's lengthy market-cap erosion. From a high of more than $30 in May of 2001, the clothing retailer's stock had plummeted to less than $15. The slide was both a symptom and a cause of a snowballing chain of events that commonly occurs when a company is widely perceived to be in trouble. A major analyst cut the retailer's rating from *strong buy* to *neutral,* which some on Wall Street say is really a code word for "sell immediately." Many no doubt complied. Meanwhile, the business press openly speculated whether Drexler had the right talents to lead a complex company that included other mall mainstays such as Banana Republic and Old Navy. As Gap chairman Don Fisher said during a conference call to announce Drexler's leaving, what the company really needed was "a person that can manage the divisions without micro-managing."

For the 57-year-old Drexler, the resignation announcement seemed a dramatic reversal of fortune. During the 1990s, he was widely credited with transforming the Gap into a 4,200-store American icon. And although Drexler has since gone on to head a smaller retailing rival, J. Crew, at the time his leaving seemed but

1

another example of a seemingly all-too-frequent occurrence in the no quarter–given realm of upper management. When a company falls on bad times, the old guard that built the firm often finds itself compelled to hand over the reins. Many times, outsiders must be brought in to provide a fresh perspective when serious problems occur. But another possibility is that shareholders and creditors—seeing their investment erode—naturally seek a quick fix. And in such cases, the management quickly becomes if not a scapegoat, then a target.

Whatever the case, an executive-suite shake-up can be a wrenching, humiliating experience for those who are its victims, especially when it involves leaders who are cast out of companies they helped build—and all the more so if the affair takes place in a media fishbowl. To get an idea of just how wrenching the experience can be, consider that the people who rise to the top of organizations are by nature hardened, competitive types. They are not accustomed to failure. Yet at some point comes the sad realization that all the years of effort may have been in vain.

And what a long, hard road it's been. No one builds a successful company without pouring in enormous amounts of energy, soul, and emotional commitment. Fame and fortune may be fleeting, it is true. But to be suddenly left out in the cold when problems occur can destroy a career.

What Will Your Kids Think?

In truth, nothing about a business failure is pretty. As anyone who's been through the process can relate, when a company falls on hard times, employees, their families, suppliers, creditors, and customers all find themselves swept up into a suddenly stressful world—one that quickly consumes vast amounts of everyone's waking day. Liquidators may arrive unannounced to claim computers, furniture, and other supplies. Employees, fearing they'll come to work only to find the doors padlocked shut, begin carting out important files and personal belongings. Meanwhile, the founders stand by helplessly as they watch their hard-earned wealth hemorrhage. As stock options, bonuses, and the like turn into lost promises, the founders' dreams transform into nightmares.

Tom Cage,[2] founder of a Stanford, Connecticut, dot-com, watched his company eat through $2 million in funding. When the additional funding he'd banked his business plan on didn't materialize—a casualty of the NASDAQ crash—Cage's company dwindled from 21 to 5 employees. The worst part of the whole ordeal, he remembers, was telling his two sons. Both became teary at the news.[3]

Like a grave family medical crisis, dealing with the business failure quickly becomes all-consuming. An army of specialists with whom the company has had no previous contact suddenly seizes control of events, in the same way that doctors, counselors, and insurance companies step in to dominate the life of a gravely ill patient. Also, tragically, at a time when a company is most in need of focus, its managers spend precious hours assuaging nervous inquiries from everyone with some stake in the firm. Employees, meanwhile, become easily distracted from their work. Instead, they spend their day trafficking in rumors and frantically mailing resumes.

And just like a medical crisis, a company's death spiral will tend to begin slowly and then accelerate toward an end game. Indeed, the earliest seeds of disaster may have taken root months or even years earlier, or they may exist within elements of an organization's culture that, like faulty genes in an otherwise healthy patient, predispose the firm to fail. As with gravely ill patients, the company often reaches a critical and irreversible stage in its downward spiral once these symptoms become manifest. Then management and other interested parties become aware of the problem and the crisis ensues.

Denial, Anger, Bargaining, Depression, and Acceptance

Once the realization occurs that the company may indeed fail, turnaround expert Randall Wright Patterson of BBK, Ltd. believes that managers of financially-troubled businesses go through a series of traumatic emotional changes. In fact, he believes the changes are similar to those that dying patients go through, as outlined by Elisabeth Kübler Ross, M.D., in her classic book *On Death and Dying*. Those stages begin with denial and progress through anger, bargaining, depression, and acceptance.

As an example, Patterson says, denial might first surface when subordinates question the company's latest results or when a banker points to a disturbing decline in sales. Management, particularly if it adopts an autocratic and isolated posture, might respond in typical fashion, "I don't know what everybody's talking about. There's a little blip in the economy, combined with the seasonality of our business. Everything is fine."

Anger on management's part, the next stage, sometimes manifests as a defensive posture, particularly when the level of criticism becomes amplified. Perhaps a banker openly questions management's projections, or a key customer cites the firm's precarious position as its reason for leaving. Here, says Patterson, a typical response is "I can't believe my suppliers are putting me on COD. We've been paying them on time for over 75 years. So I'm six months past due. What's the big deal?"

Bargaining is a last-ditch effort on management's part to regain mastery of events—events that sadly are often destined to remain out of managers' control. Usually, Patterson says, this stage shows itself as a variation of denial, because the remedies that management contemplates are beyond its means. The CEO might tell himself, "If only my banker would lend me another $1 million, all my problems would be solved," or "If only I could find a salesman who knows how to sell, that would solve all my problems." On some level, the manager may recognize that these remedies are mere exercises in fantasy. The bank, now fully aware of the company's problems, is unlikely to lend the cash, nor is a crack salesperson liable to rescue a firm so near to closing its doors. But management steadfastly goes through the motions, thinking that if familiar tactics and procedures are used, all will ultimately be well.

The phrase "rearranging the deck chairs on the *Titanic*" vividly illustrates the futility of the bargaining phase.

At some point, management comes to this sad realization: Bargaining, too, has failed. Then depression sets in. Perhaps by this time a general alarm has been raised, both inside and outside the organization. Phone calls from unpaid suppliers become a major irritant during the business day. Bankers demand revised business plans, and customers question whether the company will be able to fulfill its obligations. Management's response at this stage frequently is to hole up, to isolate itself. Secretive closed-door meetings take place throughout the day. These, of course, only exacerbate employee concerns and further fuel rumors. As the depression stage progresses, managers begin to avoid the office and the problems they know they'll encounter there. Often they arrive late, leave early, or disappear entirely.

According to Kübler Ross, the acceptance stage is marked by a sense of forthright preparedness for the inevitable. With managers of an ailing business, acceptance may come following an intervention by creditors or, in some cases, by junior members of the management team. A meeting may take place between, say, the banker or silent partners. During that meeting, an ultimatum is given: Either take dramatic steps, or all the loans are called. In a successful intervention, the top management, no doubt exhausted by the long ordeal, accepts the fact that it can no longer effectively run the company and that some form of outside help is needed. Anxious to preserve a portion of its vested interests in the company, management then steps aside.

Patterson says that roughly 80 percent of referrals he receives come from either bankruptcy attorneys or lenders. "Basically, the company is in default on a loan document," he explains. "The banker says, 'I might let you go this one last time, but only if you hire a turnaround professional.'" Because of lender liability considerations, creditors generally do not demand that a company hire a particular turnaround firm. Instead, they may recommend several suitable firms, leaving the final decision up to management.

Regardless of how it occurs, when outsiders enter the picture, a new chapter in the company's failure cycle commences. Often, management is quickly replaced at this point. Alternately, the turn-around expert functions as a consultant, ferreting out the problems in the organization. Whether the original management team stays or goes, the firm must quickly decide on one of several courses—the most common choice, but certainly not the only possible one, is to enter bankruptcy proceedings.

The Bankruptcy Whirlwind

Most business owners are only vaguely familiar with the bankruptcy process—and are likely quite happy to remain that way. But, as the Securities and Exchange Commission (SEC) explains on its Web site,[4] bankruptcy is actually a process designed to protect a company from its creditors. It's lengthy and messy. Worse, its outcome is seldom clear at the onset.

Indeed, bankruptcy is to business what divorce is to marriage. Once the proceedings begin, the normal channels of communication abruptly halt. Instead, decisions flow through formal channels, such as committees and lawyers representing the various stakeholders. And often for good reason. Suspicions reign supreme during any bankruptcy proceeding. Business owners are naturally anxious to learn what rights and protections they'll receive. Creditors and stockholders will likewise want to know how their interests are being protected, as well as what remnants of their investment will flow to them once the reorganization is complete.

For good or ill, the bankruptcy process provides easy answers to at least some of these questions. And indeed, this is one reason why companies opt for bankruptcy. It brings order to an otherwise chaotic process, while, of course, buying the company time to re-group. When a reorganization occurs, secured creditors—that is, those to whom the company has pledged its assets as collateral—are first in line to receive some form of reimbursement. Next come the unsecured creditors. This group might include banks, as well as suppliers and bondholders. Stockholders are third in line. The rationale behind this order is that secured creditors knowingly entered a low-risk/low-reward investment. Suppliers and bondholders had assumed more risk in return for a higher payout. Third in line are stockholders, who essentially bought an ownership stake in the company and thereby assumed the highest risk of all.

Thus the payout goes from low to high risk. All too frequently, the high-risk investors—the shareholders—end up with nothing. The company is normally under no legal obligation to aid shareholders. Therefore, it will likely focus its efforts on assuaging creditors who do possess legal rights. Legal obligations aside, this strategy of shutting out shareholders is in stark contrast to the way companies are apt to treat them during better times. As you'll see in chapter 4, many companies bend over backward to satisfy stockholder expectations. And ironically, many run into trouble as a result.

Stocks on the Rocks

Business professors at the University of Massachusetts and Philadelphia University examined 154 corporate bankruptcy filings that occurred from 1984 through 1993. Shareholders received nothing in 93 cases, they found.[5] Which is not to say that shares of failed companies suddenly evaporate. Instead, many are delisted from the major exchanges after failing to meet their minimum price-level requirements. Shares of companies in bankruptcy are often relegated to the over-the-counter market, where they may reside in obscurity for months, if not years. The volume of shares traded each day slows to a trickle. This is because analysts normally stop covering them. Institutions may be forbidden from buying them. Likewise, mutual funds more often than not shy away from taking large positions in a stock that might prove difficult to sell.

Speculators and penny stock aficionados dominate what trading does take place. Their hope is that the stock will move pennies based—perhaps—on some rumor. While Enron was mired in bankruptcy proceedings in early May 2002, its shares still traded at roughly 20 cents each. Turnaround strategist Bill Brandt, told *Business Week* online that there's a mystique surrounding stocks of companies in their death throes, which accounts for much of their volume.

One instance where shareholder values stand a better chance of holding up during a bankruptcy, according to *Business Week* online, is when the company opts for Chapter 11 to guard itself from lawsuits. This occurred when a building-products firm reportedly faced possible asbestos-related claims. Shares, which at first lost 60 percent of their value, gradually traded from $5 to $7.[6]

Of course, the rapid decline of shareholder value during a bankruptcy proceeding affects management as well. Witness the unfortunate employees of Enron, who had invested their retirement savings in that company's stock. To those company's employees, with dreams of paying off the kids' college education via their stock options, the idea that those shares are now utterly worthless only adds to the trauma during a bankruptcy process.

Dangerous Debts

Exactly how the actual payments come to be made during the bankruptcy process can depend on the kind of reorganization that's agreed upon by all the parties involved and by the court. Certain key suppliers may receive payments before others, so that they will continue to furnish the goods needed by the company in order to stay in business. In other cases, new stakeholders may step in and supplant the traditional payout schedule. Some lending companies, for example, specialize in bankruptcy financing. Their loans—which generally can be as much as $15 million—are normally used to cover day-to-day operations. The term for this is *debtor-in-possession (DIP) financing*. Such loans are secured by existing company assets, meaning DIP lenders get first dibs on inventory or receivables in the event of a default. Because of the risks they face, DIP lenders may charge credit card–like interest rates of 13 percent or more, while their upfront fees can run as high as 4 percent.[7] At times, DIP lenders' principal value added is that they assume the risk of unloading distressed assets in the event of default.

Chapter 7 Versus Chapter 11

How payouts get made may also depend on the form of bankruptcy the failing company elects to enter. Briefly, the two major types of bankruptcy used by businesses are Chapter 11 and Chapter 7. (Two other forms, Chapter 13 and Chapter 12, allow individuals and family farmers, respectively, to reorganize their debts.)

The two forms of business bankruptcies have stark differences. Chapter 11 allows a company to remain in business, while it puts together a reorganization plan. The intent is that the company will be able to return to profitability once the reorganization is complete. All the while, creditors are kept at bay.

Another important facet of Chapter 11 is that management, whether it consists of the original team or an interim turnaround group, continues to run day-to-day operations. But while management maintains a free hand with respect to routine business matters, all important decisions—such as the sale of a division—are ultimately made by the bankruptcy court, which in a sense functions like the board of directors.

In contrast to Chapter 11, where the company remains a viable business with hopes of continuing operations indefinitely, in a Chapter 7 bankruptcy, the company ceases all operations. When this happens, the bankruptcy court appoints a trustee to tie up loose ends. With the company's doors padlocked shut, the trustee initiates a fire sale of its remaining assets.

Following the post-2000 crash, the dot-com industry was rife with such sales, particularly in areas such as Northern California. A cottage industry of expert liquidators quickly sprang up to dispose of the companies' usually minimal assets. One *Business Week* online article jokingly described the men who organize these sales as akin to "cleaners" in organized crime, those semi-mythical characters seen in movies like *Pulp Fiction,* who remove evidence from grizzly crime scenes.[8]

Despite funds recouped through such fire sales, with Chapter 7 filings even secured creditors may not receive complete reimbursement. Once assets are sold, lawyers and others handling the bankruptcy get paid first. The secured creditors are next in line. However, if the company's assets won't cover all of the secured creditors' claims after a partial payment, they must wait in line with unsecured creditors for whatever is left. Meanwhile, stockholders are often not even notified at all when Chapter 7 proceedings take place. The reason for this is that by the time a company reaches Chapter 7, its stock has likely been rendered effectively worthless.

Chapter 7 obviously is a last resort. More common with small businesses than with large, it may occur when the business owners, due to death or other reasons, are unable to continue to run the company and the company has no hope of returning to profitability.

The Lesser of Two Evils

Of the two forms of bankruptcy, Chapter 11 is normally the more popular choice. It allows management to retain some control and ultimately recover from its losses in order to fight another day. Creditors, too, have a vested interest in the company continuing to operate and take in some income. Should that happen, the chances increase that they will receive some payback of money owned. Furthermore, if the restructuring proves successful, suppliers and creditors might hope to resume a profitable relationship with the company.

That said, the outcome of a Chapter 11 filing will become known only following a protracted process that to all involved may seem overly bureaucratic and hamstrung by legal provisions. The process is ruled over by something called the U.S. Trustee, which is the bankruptcy arm of the Justice Department. Its chief task at the onset of bankruptcy proceedings is to appoint a committee to represent unsecured creditors such as bondholders, banks, suppliers, and so forth. The committee is called, appropriately enough, the Official Committee of Unsecured Creditors. It's possible, too, that the Trustee will appoint other committees as well. One committee might be formed to look out for the interests of shareholders. Another special committee might fight for the interests of secured creditors, such as employees or subordinated bondholders.

Management, working with these committees and other stakeholders, drafts a rough outline of a plan that spells out how the company will be reorganized and how creditors will be paid. All relevant stakeholders normally have a chance to sign off on this plan. But as frequently happens, one or more groups may posture for a larger share of the pie and thus reject the plan. If that does occur, the committee may still approve the plan if it believes that it's the best deal that all parties are liable to receive. The court must also ensure that the plan passes legal muster. When the court finally gives its blessing, management must file a more detailed plan, referred to as Form 8-K, with the SEC. Only then can payouts be made.

Stratospheric Legal Costs

As you can see, in bankruptcies the devil is definitely in the details. Throughout the protracted negotiations, each of the stakeholders in the company naturally wants to receive the maximum payout from the company in the shortest period of time. While management, hoping to return the company to profitability, wants to hold on to as many of its assets as possible. During the process, the SEC may also play a somewhat limited role. It may insist that the court create a special committee to represent shareholders, and it may pass judgment on disclosure documents. Also, as was demonstrated time after time in 2002, the SEC may initiate investigations on its own if it suspects fraud. Add lawyers, representing the major parties, and it's a prescription for a long and expensive fight—one that can sometimes take years.

Indeed, legal and other administrative expenses are paid out before the company's other creditors receive so much as a dime. And in the case of widely held public companies, these expenses can be horrendous. For example, each shareholder may need to receive at least a copy of the reorganization plan, along with a court-approved disclosure statement, plus ballots if the plan is to be voted on by shareholders. Regardless of whether shareholders vote or not, they still have the right to file an objection to the plan, and they must receive instructions on how to do so. Finally, should any payouts be made, new shares may need to be issued, as well as new bonds.

Going Out of Business Sale

Besides reorganizations, in which present management is able to retain some control of the company's destiny, Chapter 11 can also be used as a basis for liquidation or for the sale of the company in its entirety. There are certain advantages to having the courts stand watch over these more radical remedies. Take the case of a sale of the company, for example. On the one hand, the process will likely take longer under court supervision than it would if management had found a buyer itself prior to Chapter 11 filing. However, a court-approved sale can allow the company to change hands free of liens and other claims from its past. The same is true of liquidations, in which the assets are sold off and the company is permanently shut down. Court-sanctioned liquidations take longer than fire sales, making them impractical in some cases. But by using Chapter 11, management at least gets a chance to organize the sale itself, should that prove advantageous. More important, under court auspices, management can normally emerge from the liquidation free of further liability.[9]

A Silver Lining

As time-consuming and expensive as a bankruptcy process appears, U.S. laws actually make it easier for a company to file for bankruptcy than do those of any other industrialized nation. U.S. laws are tilted in favor of debtors, whereas laws of many other nations favor creditors, explains Mel Zwaig, a turnaround expert based in Toronto, Canada. The U.S. bias, he says, goes far back into the nation's history. The Pilgrims and other early colonists were refugees from Europe's debtor prisons. Others came as indentured servants. It's easy to see why early lawmakers sought to curb common abuses by creditors. (And why the U.S. democracy was deemed radical at the time by other nations.) By contrast, England's former colonies, such as Canada and Australia, have largely retained the mother nation's system of laws, which embodies elements of the debtor prisoner concept, says Zwaig. "As a creditor, I'd rather practice in Canada," he admits. But the U.S. laws possess certain advantages to both debtors and creditors. Specifically, U.S. laws give bankrupt companies more flexibility in how they restructure than may be the case in other nations. The result, theoretically, is that the company stands a better chance of recovering and in the process providing more reimbursement to its creditors.

But differences between U.S. and Commonwealth bankruptcies have diminished over the years, Zwaig says. Laws in Canada, for example, have been tempered somewhat to give creditors and debtors more incentives to cooperatively work out solutions. The result is that the success rate for bankruptcies in the United States and Canada remains about the same, roughly 30 percent. "Regardless of the regime," Zwaig says, "if there is a debtor and a group of creditors that sincerely believe they can restructure a company, it will happen." The key is forging and maintaining certain crucial cooperative relationships.

Alternatives to Chapter 11

One way to do that is to seek alternative ways to file for bankruptcy if management can find them. A half-way measure is the prepackaged bankruptcy plan, in which a company that needs to file Chapter 11 contacts major stakeholders and tries to negotiate a plan before it even approaches the court seeking bankruptcy relief. Resorts International and TWA are said to have used prepackaged bankruptcies. The obvious advantage is the time savings. If everyone can be brought on board, the actual bankruptcy process can be sped along, greatly reducing the company's burn rate.

Companies can usually save even more time and money if they can find an alternative to a Chapter 11 filing. In fact, the possible options increase exponentially if this is done. Bankruptcy proceedings are rigidly constrained by their need to adhere to legal procedures. On the other hand, a good negotiator can hammer together a deal that will benefit everyone. Payments can be deferred or discounted. Asset and debt swaps are also possible.

The key to making such complicated deals work in a short amount of time is to have on board a strong negotiator. Turnaround managers or interim managers may play this role. Operating under the designation "assignment for the benefit of creditors," they lay out the situation to creditors: Accept this much in settlement or risk losing it all. Skilled interim managers receive a handy sum for their efforts, a minimum of $75,000 or 7.5 percent of the company's assets that they succeed in selling. But they earn it. Interim managers' value lies in the fact that they can work discreetly with individual creditors. Whereas formal bankruptcy proceedings, especially when they involve large companies, take place in a fishbowl.

As skilled negotiators, interim managers also have a good sense of what kind of settlement each creditor will likely accept.

And they understand the channels for selling off assets, everything from the company's own receivables, to bonds, to the office furniture. It's not as easy as it sounds. The market for distressed bonds, for example, is sorely limited. Pension funds and other institutions may be prohibited from buying these bonds. And banks are typically loath to carry debt of failing companies.

The Boom in Gloom

That said, an entire industry exists around those who trade in the assets of dying companies. Among them are bond brokers and hedge funds that traffic in so-called distressed securities—a growing field, as it turns out. Zurich Capital Markets tracks no less than 50 funds that specialize in distressed securities. In 2001 the monitoring group found that seven had a 100-percent compound return over a five-year period. One firm was up a reported 267 percent. Similarly, in 2001, the Van Hedge index, which tracks the performance of distressed hedge funds, said that average returns for the group rose 16 percent for the year.[10] During a period when other investments experienced one of the worst performance records ever, distressed funds proved there's a boom in gloom.

The boom attests to the fact that distressed asset traders perform a valuable service. However it came about, debt is a far more common cause of business failure than are operational problems, according to some who counsel failed businesses.[11] Operations problems can be solved through rapid reorganization. But just as individuals can be weighed down by credit card debt for years, companies can spiral downward due to an unsustainable debt load. Management becomes preoccupied with short-term measures aimed at meeting the next loan payment. Over the medium term, debt can dictate strategy to the company's long-term detriment. In the wake of customer defections and legal action following its Enron audit, Anderson was forced to seek buyers for many of its lucrative regional units.[12] As one analyst noted, buyers were able to purchase Andersen's market share for just half their worth.

A typical distressed asset transaction might involve a hedge fund locking up bonds at 40 cents on the dollar. By doing this, the fund manager is betting in part that the company won't enter Chapter 11, in which case interest payments will end, pending the reorganization. A correct bet can yield above-market interest yields, as those yields may be pegged to the bond's face value. Moreover, if the company does turn itself around, the bonds will most likely appreciate in value. But of course, the high return brings with it a high degree of risk. A failure can wipe out the investor's principal.

Carrion On

In her book *The Vulture Investors,* Hillary Rosenberg recounts how this special breed of distressed asset investors can score big by purchasing debt from troubled companies.[13] The roots of vulture investing go back to the Great Depression, as business failures swept through the nation. But roughly four decades later, a bankruptcy filing by Penn Central railroad—one of the largest up to that point—propelled the field into the modern era. As creditors sorted through the remnants of the once-mighty railroad, they discovered a tangled heap of bonds and other assets, unprecedented in size. In fact, the sheer size of the Penn Central debacle succeeded in drawing in more vulture investors than had ever converged on any firm before. Rosenberg believes the bankruptcy proved that vulture investors could make money. Some years later, vulture investors circled above REITs (real estate investment trusts). At the time, the specialized partnerships that invested in everything from shopping malls to trailer parks were dying slow deaths because of skyrocketing interest rates. In the process of reorganizing the REITs' crushing debt, still more vulture capitalists made money. A decade later, energy and steel companies were dropping like flies—the former due to once again plentiful supplies; the latter due to antiquated plants that couldn't compete with cheap foreign imports. Today, of course, endless new areas have opened up to vulture investors following the 2000 tech wreck.

The Power of the Purse

Vulture investors typically choose not to meddle in company operations, allowing management or surrogate turnaround managers to do their job. Instead, they focus on their own area of expertise, which is reconstituting a company's finances. In fact, a symbiotic relationship can develop between a distressed securities buyer and a troubled company's management team. Both develop a strong vested interest in pulling a company out of its quagmire. Management's leverage—such as it is—stems from the fact that it needs cash to sustain the business. Thus, it can enter a pact with a vulture investor to defer interest payments for a time, in exchange for a plan spelling out the money's use. A retail chain might use the money to pay off a key supplier, for example, in order to ensure that company store shelves remain stocked. In exchange for the interest concession, a vulture investor might ask for a percentage of ownership in the reorganized company.

Often, skilled vulture investors may ultimately gain the final say. They accomplish this by acquiring enough of the company's bond debt to earn a prominent place at the bargaining table during bankruptcy proceedings. In some cases, vulture investors are even able to dictate the terms or at least block proposals they don't like. If a suitor comes into the picture, offering to buy the company for a price unacceptable to the vulture capitalist, that individual can veto the bid. Likewise, vulture investors can convince other smaller creditors to sell out or vote with them. The alternative is to be marginalized during the negotiations process.

Sometimes creditors hold a big-enough stake in the company to block a reorganization plan they don't like—perhaps in the hope of securing a higher payout for their own investors. When this happens, a distressed securities expert who is a skilled negotiator can step in to either buy out the debt or convince the maverick debt holder to vote with the group.

The Eternal Cycle

Don't begrudge vulture investors their profits. Just like carrion in the wild, they perform a valuable service by making efficient use of assets that might otherwise languish. Thanks to their efforts, inventory that would decay to the point of worthlessness can still be made to retain some value. Bonds that might not have been worth the paper they were printed on can at least partially reimburse their original holders. And while there is no denying the pain suffered by those who lose their jobs because of the harsh measures needed to fix a broken company, often many more people are able to continue working, thanks to these harsh reorganization efforts.

The key to successful vulture investing, it seems, is seeing the difference between the value of a company's assets and the market value of its debt. Often the former is understated. But the real secret is in seeing where and how the two diverge. Author Rosenberg relays the strategy of one successful vulture investor, who said that a business failure is simply one more stage in that company's cycle, just as illness or death is an inevitable part of being alive. During their life cycles, companies may progress through several stages, just as all living things do. Skilled investors can view these cycles in terms of the value of their assets—again, seeing just where both the perceived and the real values diverge. In its early stages, a company might appear undervalued to everyone but the most sharp-eyed analysts, for example. Later, when its value peaks, the company might be deemed ripe for a break-up or an acquisition. Owners like to sell at the top. Some time later, as its value declines, the company will invariably need to be rescued in some way.

Failure at the Speed of Thought

Companies, unlike individuals, can enjoy a life span that extends well over a century. But few do, according to David Nadler, a consultant to troubled companies such as Lucent and Xerox and author of the book *Champions of Change: How CEOs and Their Companies Are Mastering the Skills of Radical Change*. Only the rarest of companies can find ways to create value afresh in a rapidly changing business environment. One company that has succeeded is 150-year-old Corning. And it does so, Nadler says, because it has committed itself to innovation and has resisted defining itself by its products. Instead, Corning defines itself by the ways in which it develops products.

For the great majority of companies, however, death indeed often comes like a thief in the night. All too often, the victim fails to foresee change and fails to deal with it once it occurs. Examples of this are readily available. "I'm a student of history when I'm not doing restructurings or forensic work," explains Mel Zwaig. "There's a company in Canada that manufactured pianos for almost a century. In 1934, if you read their minute book, someone [at a board meeting] suggested that they take on a line of radios." The company's board rejected the idea, however, because it thought that radios were just a passing fad.

"Twenty years later," says Zwaig, "the board rejected taking on a line of TVs for exactly the same reason. And 10 years later, the 100-year-old company went out of business. Because people weren't buying the pianos that they used to buy. That is what I'm referring to as stale management."

The difference now, of course, is that it no longer takes a decade for management myopia to wreck a company. As witnessed with Enron and Anderson, within weeks, even days after rumors of failure surface, the company effectively loses control of events.

Nadler believes that this is because the clock speed of business has ramped up dramatically.[14] In an environment where information rules, all companies operate in a kind of fishbowl. Thus, word of a poor earnings report or questionable accounting practices will quickly reverberate from one critical community to the next—from investors, to customers, to suppliers. One false step and you're headlining the evening news.

Winning by Spinning

Little wonder that just as an industry of specialists stands ready to bury, salvage, or mine the assets of a failed company, a parallel army of consultants can also be hired to help companies tell their story during a crisis. Such firms help diminish one of the more traumatic parts of a business failure: facing the cameras. Not only is the company gone and the owner's money with it, but the management team must now face the music while friends and peers watch.

One firm that specializes in helping companies cope is Des Moines–based Wixted Pope Nora Thompson & Associates. The company coaches clients whose business may make them especially prone to disasters. Several major airlines form part of its client list, along with many of the nation's nuclear power plants. Cofounder Eileen Wixted, who covered corporate disasters as a TV newscaster, believes that companies should never face the cameras alone. When relaying bad news, particularly if the news will affect others, have someone stand beside you on the podium. "Always coordinate your communications efforts with the proper agencies," she explains.[15] If that were a hospital facing closure, for example, the proper agencies might include local health officials to ensure that care will remain available in the community. "People feel more reassured when they know many organizations are working together."

In the post–market crash, post-9/11 world, Wixted says, "90 percent of the work we're doing right now is fire drills." These intense, often multiday exercises prepare company managers at all levels for crisis episodes. And great pains are taken to simulate the tense atmosphere of a real crisis. Managers emerge from strategy planning meetings only to find reporters at the ready with cameras and tough questions.

In fact, says Wixted, it's vital that companies understand the varying audiences they must reach in times of crises, as well as how the information needs of each audience differ. Members of the public want to know what the effect of a business failure or a crisis will be on them and what steps have been taken to minimize the impact. Likewise, the company's employees want to know who's looking out for their interests. If management doesn't fill the information void, rumors surely will. And management typically doesn't fill the void. "The tendency is to circle the wagons during a crisis, when in fact the opposite is necessary," Wixted says. "Because in the absence of communication, people think the worst."

How this information is communicated during a crisis can be as important as what is being said. Details must be relayed with compassion, clarity, and, above all, honesty, or the media and the public will quickly sense that they are being deceived. Different media, too, require different means of relaying the same information. A TV interview, for example, will demand a succinct statement, backed by facts. A lengthier newspaper report will require the executive to have far more facts on the situation at the ready.

To err when confronting the public can be devastating. Former secretary of state Al Haig will forever be remembered for his "I'm in charge," statement following the assassination attempt on President Ronald Reagan. The idea of a former military chieftain proclaiming himself personally in charge of the White House during the highly uncertain period following a crisis horrified many Americans and all but ruined Haig's subsequent political career. Perhaps the most important lesson that corporate heads take from their seminars with crisis consultants at Wixted Pope Nora Thompson is the subtle art of grace under pressure.

A Far Better Alternative

An appearance on the evening news is often the low point in the long, drawn-out ordeal of a company failure. Worse, it is frequently the low point that follows long months of frantic efforts to save the firm, and it can lead to a dismal recognition that failure is indeed now inevitable—an acceptance akin to the endgame thoughts of a patient during a protracted illness.

There is an alternative to facing the glare of TV cameras to explain why a company is putting hard-working people out of a job and why families and the community at large must suffer the consequences of a business failure. That alternative is to understand that the signs of a failure within an organization are apparent months or even years before TV news crews show up at the company's doorstep. This alternative also puts the burden on management to recognize the signs when they occur and to take remedial action. Companies that get past the crisis stage have developed a hard-won ability to do just that. Sadly, this ability is absent in companies that fail. The next two chapters look at some generalized and common reasons that cause companies to fail, reasons which are often in management's power to recognize and prevent.

CHAPTER

2

Early Warning Signs

One day you're a hero; the next day you're a goat. Back in 2000, America Online ranked high on the hero side of the ledger. It had craftily positioned itself at the very epicenter of the Internet revolution. Here was a company with millions of customers, all of whom paid roughly $20 per month, and just for the privilege of connecting to AOL's tidy universe of proprietary content. A vast sea of ever-growing revenues seemed to await the company. Management could concoct infinite ways to entice AOL's customers into buying everything from athletic shoes to symphony tickets—all through personalized pop-up ads. Moreover, with the mammoth acquisition of Time Warner, AOL seemed assured of keeping its customers entertained with quality content. A wireless AOL and an AOL Interactive TV would create vast new universes of possibilities.

And yet a few short months after the AOL-Time Warner merger, a *Forbes* magazine article[1] openly pondered whether AOL was destined to replay Henry Ford's mistakes with the Model T. Just as the iconic car had offered dependable transportation to the masses, AOL's dial-up networking provided millions with an easy on ramp to the information highway. And just as the Model T eventually lost out when competitors introduced cars with more options, AOL might be left in the dust if its customers couldn't be upgraded to a broadband connection.

True enough, the company had made valiant efforts to do just that. The Time Warner acquisition was in part motivated by the formidable array of cable systems the old-line media company possessed. In fact, the merger had sparked protests from competitors and a federal regulatory review precisely because Time Warner was then the nation's second-largest cable service provider and by extension the number two cable broadband service. But cable systems could reach only a limited number of viewers. Meanwhile, the Baby Bells' copper wires collectively invaded virtually every home in the nation. And increasingly, those homes were switching to DSL technology as a broadband alternative. In order to compete, AOL would need to patch together an expensive nationwide DSL network of its own, while convincing its legions of current dial-up customers to make the switch.

In all likelihood, AOL will prevail, just as Ford, after abandoning the Model T, went on to achieve new successes in the then rapidly changing auto market. But the story illustrates an important point: One strategic misstep can threaten even the most successful companies.

In fact, as you'll read in this and the next chapter, the research into why companies fail is full of scary examples that reveal how otherwise well-managed, forward-thinking, high-growth companies—companies that at one time changed an industry and then grew to dominate it—suddenly and unwittingly lost their way. Xerox, once a generic term for the photocopying process (known as xerography), was reduced to a much beleaguered version of its former self. Lucent, which possessed one of the most enlightened research facilities in the corporate world, saw its stock price nosedive from a high of $60 in late 1999 to a fall 2002 low of under $1.

Falling Icons

Or take Kmart. It showed that Americans would happily buy their lawn mowers and TVs at the same supermarket-style store where they bought shampoo and aspirin, rocking the department store industry to the core as a result. In the 1980s Kmart nearly toppled America's then most powerful traditional retailer: Sears. Years later, it found itself wedged between a rock and a hard place or, more specifically, between soccer-mom-favorite Target and deep-discounter Wal-Mart.

Or look at the Gap. During the '90s, its yuppie-utilitarian clothing lines became the uniform for a generation hooked on *Seinfeld* and *Friends*. With a global brand image on par with behemoths like McDonald's and Pepsi, it was a fixture within virtually every mall in the industrialized world. Following a phenomenal five-year growth sprint that saw average annual earnings climb by 30 percent, the Gap racked up $877 million in profits during 2000. However, by 2002, the company had lost $7.8 million on $13.8 billion in sales. Analysts reportedly relegated the Gap's debt to junk bond status.[2] One of the Gap's more serious sins, according to one business journalist: It ignored its aging customer base by trying—and failing—to lure younger customers.

Dismal Numbers

The previous examples represent a few of the more spectacular flameouts that managed to draw headlines. And in fact, business failures, whether large or small, are an inevitable part of the capitalist system. In any given year, the number of business failures totals roughly 40 percent of the company formations that take place during the same time period.[3]

However, the aggregate statistics suggest that business failures became pervasive at the turn of the new century. And their number continues to grow. In 2001, some 257 public companies filed for bankruptcy, according to a study by PriceWaterhouseCoopers authored by Carter Pate, a founding member of the Turnaround Management Association. He estimates that only 100 of these companies will emerge successfully from bankruptcy, if typical averages apply.[4] The number of bankruptcies, however, representing some $256 billion in combined assets, compares ominously to the

113 public companies that on average have filed for bankruptcy between 1986 and 2000. During the first quarter of 2002, *Fortune* magazine noted that the failure rate continued unabated, with 67 public companies "going bust." Noting that some of those companies were large, household-name, Fortune 500 firms, a *Fortune* magazine commentator said, if the failures continued unabated, the magazine might have trouble filling out its annual list of the 500 largest companies.[5]

Yet the bankruptcies by public companies, large or small, represent a small fraction of the nearly 11,000 private companies that PriceWaterhouseCoopers predicted would file Chapter 11 in 2002. And again, based on historical averages, only about a third of these will emerge from the proceedings successfully, the authors said. Picture the turmoil resulting from bankruptcy within just one of these companies and multiply that by 11,000. Only then do you get a true picture of the huge effect failures have on employees, families, and communities.

The unusually high number of recent failures in part reflects two unforeseen events: the 2001 recession, including the dot-com bomb, and the September 11 attacks. But despite these events, the business climate at the turn of the century was said to be healthier than during previous recessions, according to the PriceWaterhouse-Coopers study. Inflation remained manageable. And interest rates and unemployment stood at lower levels than they had during the nation's last major recession at the beginning of the '90s, factors which would seem to make the failures themselves more alarming.

What Lies Beneath

So what, then, are the reasons behind these thousands of business failures? According to Pate, many stem from strategic moves companies undertook that could have been avoided, whether or not a recession had occurred. Many companies, for example, became accustomed to a lengthy boom period. Then, when the economy softened, they found themselves unable to apply the brakes.

Other companies didn't bother to save for a rainy day. Quite the contrary, they over-leveraged themselves and overinvested in new technology. Still other companies went on a buying binge during the boom times and then discovered that the synergies they'd hoped to achieve through acquisitions simply never materialized. Worse, the new units were not so easy to absorb. Yet other companies failed after they resorted to what Pate calls "creative financing and complex investing," occasionally of the kind Enron became famous for.

Are these the reasons that first come to mind when we learn that a business has failed? Hardly. Fierce foreign competition was not a major factor cited for their failure. Nor did ill-conceived government regulations, wrenching changes in the economic climate, or hostile labor relations bring the companies down. Instead, the report implies that many companies simply imploded. The collapse, like that of the Soviet Union, resulted from internal forces. If we look more closely, it becomes evident that all of these causes are in reality management blunders: mergers that weren't thought through, expansion plans that proved too optimistic, a lack of fiscal controls—all ultimately traced back to executive row.

"A Shortage of Good Judgment"

And this is hardly an unusual situation. When you delve into the literature on why companies fail, you discover that analysts over the years have reached much the same conclusion. For the most common reason why companies fail, look no further than a firm's management team. The Turnaround Management Association, for example, polled its members, people whose job it is to quickly move in and repair companies in trouble. The poll found that while 22 percent of turnaround professionals cited increased competition as a reason for business failures, a full 58 percent put the blame on faulty management decision making.[6] Other studies have similarly found that internal, rather than external, causes are behind up to 90 percent of company failures.[7]

Peter Tourtellot, a turnaround manager himself who served as chairman of the group in 2001–2002, notes one of the most common mistakes—one that's so obvious, companies simply overlook it. "Usually, we find that troubled companies don't listen to their customers," he says. "You could say that in almost every troubled situation, communication is lacking."

Writing in the early '90s, several years before the tech boom substantially raised the level of management hubris, business journalist Bruce G. Posner cited some of management's most notorious faux pas.[8] "What kills companies," he said, "has less to do with insufficient money, talent, or information than with something more basic: a shortage of good judgment and understanding at the very top." Posner cited some specific examples that I hope won't sound too familiar. Here are four:

Falling in Love with the Product.   If the management team that created the product likes it, legions of customers surely will, too, or so the thinking goes. The faulty logic here, according to Posner, is that customers need a compelling reason to change their buying habits. Lacking that, they'll continue to behave as usual.

One Tiny Piece of a Huge Market Will Make Us Rich.   This is the idea that propelled thousands of Western companies into China. "If just 1 in 1,000 Chinese buys our washing machines," management thinks, "we'll sell a million of them." It's never that simple.

We've Got the Money, We'll Find a Way.   This was precisely the trap that ensnared so many dot-coms. Remember Pets.com? It earned $66 million from its IPO and spent much of that money on TV advertising. We all thought the ads were cute—even when they cost millions to air during the Superbowl. Kevin Scott and Greg Grand, two analysts with AMR Research, believe that instead of pouring funds into TV, the company would have been better off acquiring mailing lists of pet owners, preferably those already comfortable with shopping for pet merchandise outside traditional stores.[9] But instead the company fell victim to the widely believed Internet myth that the first outfit to lay claim to a slice of online real estate would own it, forever, as surely as Pets.com owned a definitive category Web address. With that myth firmly embedded in its business plan, the company embarked on a mission, trying to convince Americans they were better off buying their pet supplies online. Pets.com closed shop a mere 10 months after its IPO.[10]

The Emperor's New Clothes Syndrome.   Managers wax on about their openness to new ideas. But at the same time, says Posner, they send signals, unconscious or otherwise, that theirs is the only opinion that really counts. Turnaround expert Peter Tourtellot concurs. And he suggests that companies over the years promote cadres of yes men to ever-higher positions. This happens because upper management likes being told it *is* on track. Being a part of the organization for years, the acquiescent hires are finally promoted to their level of incompetence. At that point they become fearful of losing their jobs. Which makes them even less likely to constructively criticize the company's leadership. As a remedy, a Stanford University professor once suggested that company heads hire people they *don't* get along with, so that they'll be sure to hear opposing views.

How to Win Over the People from Missouri

Argumentative people can perform the same function. Indeed, argumentative people are exactly the kind of people turnaround expert Randall Wright Patterson seeks to win over when he rushes in to save a company. In fact, they rank among the most valuable of what he considers to be the four basic types of employees found within a failing company. Patterson calls these four groups the soldiers, the people from Missouri, the destructive dissenters, and the constructive dissenters. As Patterson explains:

> The soldiers are the guys that when you show up, they stand at attention and say, "Reporting for duty; anything you want me to do, I'll be on your team." It's a very, very small group.

Instead, the vast majority are the people from Missouri (known as "The Show Me State"). They listen to you and say, "Nice story, but let's see what you can do. If you work the magic, then maybe I'll join your team."

The destructive dissenters are those who say, "That'll never work." But they never offer a reason, and they may even try to sabotage the efforts to save the company.

The constructive dissenters are also those who say, "That'll never work." The difference is that when asked why, they will usually offer reasons why they believe it won't work and provide useful insight to the problem. These are the people you need to work closely with. If you can turn these constructive dissenters into soldiers, the people from Missouri will begin to join the team.

Employee Triage

But, says Patterson, "You must get rid of the destructive dissenters immediately." To figure out who the most valuable employees are, when Patterson and his colleagues move in to save a company, they create a matrix that incorporates questions like "What's the person's value to the firm and what's the probability of that person leaving?" As an example of how the process works, he said:

> We had a person on a scale of 1–10 who was extraordinarily valuable to the company. If we lost him, the turnaround would not have worked. He was also very loyal, so his probability of leaving on a 1–10 scale was low. Other people may have been less valuable to the company, but with a higher probability of leaving. So they were the ones who the turnaround management team had to focus their efforts on.

Big Problems for Small Business

Such are the Byzantine organization dynamics that come into play with large companies. Smaller companies may face similar problems, but they typically fail because of far more basic reasons. Two business professors from Middle Tennessee State University, Troy A. Festervand and Jack E. Forrest, conducted an extensive review of everything that had been written academically about small business failure; they isolated three principal, if seemingly obvious, causes: finance, management, and marketing.[11] Some 80 percent of small businesses failed because they were undercapitalized, the pair said. Few people realize just how quickly lack of cash can wreak havoc with operations. Companies on a capital starvation diet waste all their time searching for additional funds, and they're forced to pay higher interest rates to lenders once they find the capital.

So, is management still to blame for most small business failures? Yes, say Festervand and Forrest. "Because management often tends to underestimate start-up and operating costs, cash flow becomes a problem even before the firm opens its doors."[12] Here, the remedy is to work through the financial data in excruciating detail even before the venture launches—and to seek professional help, when necessary. Sadly, many failing small firms ignore this advice. Instead, they spend profligately during their launch phase, while ignoring the need to watch over receivables.

So once again, it comes down to planning: "The keys to managerial success are the development of managerial expertise and adherence to a master plan," Festervand and Forrest relay.[13] By contrast, the two found that unsuccessful companies lacked both focus and goals.

The third problem area, according to Festervand and Forrest—marketing—also reflected a lack of focus on management's part. Smaller firms failed to access both the market and the competition, and their products or services bombed as a result. The remedy here is as simple as the problem: Perform market analyses regularly.

Merging and Purging

Whether discussing management-related failures in small companies or large, another point that analysts appear to agree on is that company-quashing problems rarely crop up overnight. Instead, they tend to fester, either unnoticed or ignored. Dominic DiNapoli, in his book *Workouts & Turnarounds II,*[14] which is devoted to ways to fix ailing companies, cites poor management information systems as the reason so many fail. Managers, in other words, failed to develop effective channels of communication within their organization. The result: The people at the top are literally flying blind.

But poor planning on the part of top management was also to blame. DiNapoli found that poor planning is particularly at fault when it comes to mergers and acquisitions. On occasion, management failed to foresee the economic downturn (though many did forecast it) and paid too high a multiple for companies that would later drain resources.

The '90s boom period created a kind of collective madness of crowds, which led many companies into ill-conceived acquisitions. As the boom continues, DiNapoli notes, more and more money is put in play to chase deals. At the peak of the cycle, buyers searching for a strategic fit may be outbid by financiers who hope to gain from the company's assumed growth prospects. Further, they use this rationale "to justify prices that would exceed the most extravagant synergy gains that an industry player could expect from a merger."[15] Financial buyers are willing to pay more, too, because they hope the acquisition will bolster the company's stock price in a manner that can be translated into a quick gain. Such a gain is entirely detached from the company's actual prospects.

Inevitably, as we have seen all too often of late, the stock price declines once the initial excitement surrounding the deal wears off. The stock price continues to drop until it finally reflects the company's true value. Although the financial buyers have made their money, the company and its shareholders are left in effect to pay the bill. Indeed, says DiNapoli, one of the most common causes of failure is when companies over-leverage their assets, in other words: they carry too much debt.

Living on the Edge

So, you can blame management there as well. Whether out of greed, arrogance, or blindness, management backed the deal and paid the price. Which again begs the question, What were they thinking? Is there a common denominator behind these fatal mistakes on management's part? The answer is yes, according to industrial psychologist Mortimer R. Feinberg, who advises CEOs of Fortune 500 companies. Feinberg is coauthor, along with consultant John Tarrant, of the book *Why Smart People Do Dumb Things*.[16] Indeed, the fact that people are intelligent makes it all the more likely that they'll make mistakes. According to Feinberg, something akin to a genetic time bomb exists within highly motivated, intelligent people, programming them to fail. In some, the flaw impels them to push the envelope beyond acceptable limits. We've seen this happen with far too many public figures. Remember Gary Hart? Once he practically chided reporters to discover whether he was having an affair. Of course, the affair was discovered, ruining his bid for the White House. Afterward, journalists and others wondered why Hart took the seemingly insane risks of having an affair when he was under the media microscope and then, even more insanely, bragging about it.

The reason, says Feinberg, is due to a kind of operant conditioning. Business leaders, like politicians, must take risks if they are to succeed. But it's not the penchant for risk-taking alone that causes the reckless move. Instead, it's the successful person's spectacular ability to brush aside the dangers. Such a skill would have rewarded these people in the past, naturally inclining them to push the envelope yet again. But, more important, successful people are by nature great salespeople—so great they can even sell themselves on the idea that the risks are minimal. And so they plunge ahead.

No Real Entrepreneurs

Failures may also occur because a company's management forgets they must think like entrepreneurs. Business journalist and investor

Stewart Alsop provides what he believes is an example of this phenomenon. "What I didn't calculate was the stupidity of some management decisions," he wrote in *Fortune* magazine, after he'd poured money into Webvan.[17] Recall that Webvan was one of many dot-com firms that sought to radically change the behavior of consumers. In this case, the company hoped to home-deliver groceries that customers ordered over the Internet. Even though the company had just six months' cash remaining, management reportedly embarked on a rebranding campaign. This and other management moves that Alsop discovered eventually convinced him that "there were no real entrepreneurs running this company. Real entrepreneurs never let money out the door for any reason," unless it moves the business forward. The mistakes were particularly damning to the company, he notes, given that Webvan was after all in the grocery business, one of the most competitive and tightly margined sectors in the country.

The Bunker Mentality

Failures on a grandiose scale rarely occur in a vacuum, some believe. Instead, they may arise because a management team acts to reinforce each other's decisions, even as they gravitate further and further from reality. Thus, dubious management decisions, when they are widespread and consistently reinforced, may also amount to a kind of denial on the leadership's part that true problems exist within a company. All too often, notes Tourtellot, this is because management shuts itself off and adopts a "bunker mentality" as a shield against all the bad news.

DiNapoli agrees, saying that eventually this bunker mentality becomes a fixture of the organization's structure. When an organization adopts a rigid design it in effect puts obstacles in the way of efficient communication, he says. This in turn compels managers to formulate decisions without input. And the irony is that this input is easy to come by. Subordinates are more than willing to share it. They need only be asked.

Based on his own experience helping failing companies, Tourtellot notes, "I'm amazed at how little management understands that their employees know what's happening and know what needs to be done before they do. You can find out anything you want about a company by just talking with its employees."

The Culture of Complaints

In fact, when large rifts appear between management and its employees, these provide a clear early warning sign that a company is in trouble—all the more so, if those rifts become a permanent part of the organization's culture. And if that's the case, the culture itself can doom a company to fail.

Jana Matthews, coauthor with Katherine Catlin of *Building the Awesome Organization,* surveyed dozens of companies to find out why some created successful cultures and others dismal ones. Like Tourtellot and DiNapoli, she found that in the case of unsuccessful cultures, communication with the top invariably was cut off. Isolated as a result, employees spent unproductive hours trying to second-guess management's motives. With successful cultures, on the other hand, people readily saw their own goals in tandem with the company's. Everyone was on the same page.[18]

That, of course, begs the question: If management has effectively cut itself off, how can it hope to discover the problems it must ultimately face up to? Are there signs management should look for? Indeed there are commonsensical signs, says Matthews. As examples, she says that certain signs indicate a company's in trouble, among them: Employees are more apt to dwell on gripes and problems than on constructive ideas. Put another way, the destructive dissenters whom turnaround expert Patterson identified are doing most of the talking within the company. And their ranks may even be growing. Gripes might center on salaries, but that's just for starters. Rampant griping has the effect of Balkanizing or factionalizing a company.

Heading for the Exits

Meanwhile, many of the company's employees simply don't seem to be working up to their potential. In short, people no longer experience the excitement that was prevalent when the company was in its earlier rapid-growth phase. Instead, like married couples in crisis who spend more time than normal discussing their relationship, employees inside companies with failing cultures spend an extraordinary amount of time in meetings, often with little to show for it. Meanwhile, many of the company's most prized employees simply leave, Matthews says, to the extent that one of the early warning signs of a company in trouble is a spike in turnover. When there are too few good people, or what Matthews calls "awesome people," working in a company, it tends to slide further into its malaise. Patterson and others created the aforementioned matrices to determine the value of key employees within a company. But Matthews offers what is perhaps an easier way. Simply make a list of the people working for you now whom you would classify as awesome. If it's a short list, then you're in trouble. Next, think back on the quality people who recently turned down job offers from your company and those who've quit the company for jobs elsewhere.

Who Does What?

These endemic cultural problems inevitably make it more difficult for work to get done in an organization, says Matthews. And again, the signs of this are not difficult to recognize once you know what to look for. Organizations with failing cultures tend to hammer away at the organization chart, changing the company's chain of command to little effect.

Interestingly, one of the first personnel-related areas that turnaround manager Tourtellot addresses when he begins work within a failing company is defining the lines of authority. And to do that, he uses a form of team-building:

I find that if you start team building, you start delegating, you give people responsibility, they usually respond. And if they know what kind of box they're to work in, that is, within this parameter they can make any decision that they want, but outside that parameter they've got to come and ask for help. And most people respond pretty well to that.

Death by a Thousand Cuts

All too often, management lacks the courage to take what are really not-so-bold steps on its own. Nor is management in failing organizations prepared to ask itself these hard questions—even when executives are fully aware that the answers will pinpoint problems rooted in their own behavior and, consequently, in the company's culture. "They're in that denial phase," says Tourtellot, "and egos start playing a part. Many of these companies don't have a good adviser. Don't even have a good board of directors."

In the process of ignoring problems, management moves down a path leading to disaster via a series of small steps, according to Berkeley professor Raymond E. Miles and Pennsylvania State University professor Charles C. Snow, coauthors of the book *Fit, Failure & the Hall of Fame: How Companies Succeed or Fail.* Any one of those small steps might hardly seem noteworthy. In fact, by itself, each step might seem to make perfect sense. Nevertheless, wrong assumptions beget more wrong assumptions, with wrenching consequences. Miles and Snow cite as an example Harley-Davidson. Up until the 1980s the iconic motorcycle manufacturer insisted on making its own parts. This greatly added to costs and led to production inefficiencies and delays and finally to quality shortfalls. It took a heroic turnaround effort, built around an ambitious just-in-time supply chain management system, to rescue the company. The rescue was aided by the company's fiercely loyal customers and some helpful government intervention.

From the 1920s to the 1950s, Ford Motor Company made a similar mistake, if on a much grander scale, say Miles and Snow.

The company integrated vertically, from owning iron mines to steel companies, to production facilities and dealerships.

"What is interesting about managerial mistakes such as those at Ford and Harley-Davidson is that managers are not doing anything wrong," Miles and Snow claim. Integrating vertically, even to the amazing extent achieved by the two companies, appeared to make perfect sense at the time. Instead, the authors say, such systems frequently fail later on because managers have done too many step-at-a-time things right!"[19] If management can't be depended on to find fault with itself, then the company's stakeholders must look for other ways to detect warning signs. As you'll discover in the next chapter, no shortage of ways exists.

CHAPTER 3

More Early Warning Signs

The year 2002 proved a rude awakening for American investors. Not only had they endured a 24-plus-month bear market and the demise of the New Economy dream, but by midway through the year, painful daily news reports informed them that even Wall Street's top analysts weren't able to unravel the inordinately complex finances of the nation's corporate behemoths. What hope then did everyday investors have of ever reading between the lines of companies' financial statements? Case in point: Tyco, a company once lauded by analysts as a new-style conglomerate, built to weather whatever punishing economic cycles Wall Street could throw at it. One of the reasons the Street liked Tyco, according to *New York Times* commentator Alex Berenson, was that its chief executive officer, L. Dennis Kozlowski, and chief financial officer, Mark Swartz, together constituted a kind of Fortune 500 dream team. The two had personally overseen Tyco's mind-numbing 1,000 acquisitions over the previous three years.[1] Yet by late spring Tyco had lost a considerable amount of its luster, according to Berenson. You could blame it on Kozlowski's resignation under fire and the investigations he faced. Part of the blame could also be due to the Wall Street witch-hunt that was in full swing by June 2002, as, one by one, companies were rumored to have doctored their finances. Wall Street's worst fears came to pass in late June, when it was discovered that the nation's second-largest long-distance provider, Worldcom, had misreported its performance to the tune of billions.

Numbers to Live and Die By

One of the most commonsensical ways to analyze a company's prospects and glean an early warning of trouble is to follow its stock price. The market's cold-hearted assessment, whether justified or not, directly affects management's ability to leverage the company's market cap when borrowing or to raise more money via follow-on stock offerings.

There are dangers to using stock price as an early-warning indicator to be sure. In the short term, as much as 80 percent of a stock's price may be reflective of prices within its sector, many analysts believe. And in a nervous bear market, the price of widely held companies is apt to be strongly influenced by the fear du jour. Far better, then, to focus on investors' long-term view of a stock. Is the share price rising steadily or declining? And is it rising or declining faster or slower than the market as a whole? Whatever the direction, is the momentum sustainable? Finally, beyond the obvious, what does that tell us about a company?

To find out, it helps to look at the advice offered by long-term investment gurus. That advice would seemingly be in sync with the long-term goals of management and shareholders, since all concerned wish the company well in the years ahead.

One adviser who has created a large following by urging investors to focus on companies with solid long-term growth prospects is William J. O'Neil, founder of the financial newspaper *Investor's Business Daily*. O'Neil's book *How to Make Money in Stocks* advises investors to seek companies with a demonstrated record of earnings. How much money should the company make? O'Neil first answers that question in the short term. On a quarterly basis, he says, the percentage increase should be significant and not be the result of special circumstances, such as the sale of a subsidiary. Instead, it should follow a trend of *accelerated quarterly earnings* increases over 10 quarters. Likewise, for 5 years *annual earnings* per share should steadily increase, ideally by 25 percent or more.[2]

It's important to note that O'Neil advises investors to seek high-growth stocks, as opposed to companies locked in cyclical industries. But because he adopts a multiyear time horizon, the company's earnings growth is less likely to be the result of industry expansion and also less likely the result of aggressive accounting methods and other short-term methods of boosting performance on paper. (The latter work for only so long.) Which is to say, the profit growth is more likely to be the result of good management. More specifically, the growth likely results from management focused on new products or new ways of organizing the supply chain.[3]

New products rarely emerge in a vacuum, so a successful company will have competitors. However, the company should be a leader—again, judged by earnings growth—within its sector. It can take years for a company to reach this stage. During that period preceding the growth phase, the company's stock price may appear to languish. But the ultimate reward for management comes when investors discover the company and, seeing management's diligent efforts to provide solid long-term growth, bid up its stock ever higher.

It's important in using this analysis that O'Neil's other criteria, such as the company's standing in relation to its competitors be weighed along with earnings growth. That's because O'Neil's own analysis functions as a benchmark for some. The result being that companies plan their operations so that their performance paints a perfect picture of a high-growth company. As you'll see in chapter 4, companies can fail by doing just that.

However, notwithstanding, using O'Neil's portrait of a successful firm, it's also possible to extrapolate and paint a picture of a company headed for trouble. Not surprisingly, according to O'Neil, diminished earnings growth is a critical early warning sign. "Two quarters of major earnings deceleration may mean trouble," he writes.[4]

This can be the result of both the industry maturing and the company maturing. In either case, the onus is on management to redirect the company, rather than allow it to be trapped in a cyclical or slow-growth path.

Concurring with this idea that a business, if it is to remain vibrant, must continually seek new products and new markets is Peter Drucker, perhaps the world's best-known management guru. He counsels managers to set aside time every few years to reflect on the company's strategic long-term direction and to always be prepared to abandon unworkable markets when necessary. Drucker calls this process *organized abandonment.* Managers should ask themselves if they would still enter into the same markets that may have led to success in the past. And if the answer is no, they need to seek opportunities elsewhere.[5]

The Dead Cat Bounce

While growth investors keenly watch for signs that a company's moment in the sun is about to either begin or wane, those of another investment school—so-called bottom feeders—wait for companies to descend much further down the steep slope toward failure before making their move. The bottom feeders typically wait for a firm's stock price to reach a low-enough point that the company becomes an attractive candidate for a buyout or a breakup. What bottom feeders bet on is that other investors will see this as a possibility and bid up the shares. The merger or a similar rescue may or may not take place. But that hardly matters to bottom feeders, since their intent is to tag along for the brief run-up following a period of crushing news that drove the stock to its low. In investment parlance this brief run-up is known as the dead cat bounce, after the idea that even a dead cat will bounce if it falls hard enough. And, of course, following the bounce it falls back down and may go even lower. When a company's management sees this occurring, it's a sign that the investment community has written the company off for dead.

Enter the Contrarians

Yet another more optimistic group of investors—so-called contrarians—offers a better way of discerning whether a company's failings are apt to be cataclysmic or whether management has a chance to turn the situation around.

Ideally, contrarians like to buy up shares when all the bad news is already known about a company. To hide their moves, they may build their positions gradually as the stock trades within a narrow range, so that their purchases do not show up as a blip in volume. A contrarian's entry signals his faith that management may be on the ropes but will be able to lift itself from where it is now. In so doing, the company may never be as large as it once was, but it will still advance a great deal from its low point.

Like Public Opinion Polls

The advantage of looking at stock price movements as an early warning sign is that the opinions are clearly delineated and easy to come by. A company's stock price can be easily graphed on any number of financial Web sites, and analysts' reports can be purchased online. However, both the stock price and the analyst reports are only opinions. (Lately, the accuracy of the latter has come under question.) Also, many smaller companies are tracked by just one or two analysts. And some receive no coverage at all, which tends to dampen the stock's performance. There are many examples where a stock languishes for years, while the company remains healthy. In such cases, the company may simply be off Wall Street's radar screen. Its stock may be held largely by insiders, who are profiting in other ways. To find out whether such companies are healthy or not, you have to dig deeper and look for specific causes.

The Fortune list

In May 2002 a pair of *Fortune* writers, Ram Charan and Jerry Useem, devised their own list of reasons why companies fail.[6] It's worth looking at this list in some detail, because it overlaps some of the categories found in this book.

Growth Junkies

At the top of the list, Charan and Useem claimed, were companies that have fallen victim to their own success. Lucent and Worldcom were but two examples the authors cite of firms that had reached the top and then found themselves floundering. But you could easily add Compaq, Xerox, and a host of others. Turnaround expert Peter Tourtellot offers one theory why this can occur in small companies. Oftentimes, "companies hit walls," he says. "With some companies it's $50 million [in sales], in some companies it's 75 million. When they hit a wall, they plateau, and they can't get to the next level."

Like Carter Pate (author of PriceWaterhouseCooper's study on business failure, mentioned in the previous chapter),[7] Charan and Useem say that many times the reason large, top-of-the-heap companies crash is because their entire strategy is built around growth. And when this strategy appears to work for awhile, management sees no reason to abandon it—just like the old adage, "If it ain't broke, don't fix it." Pate said that this addiction to growth caused businesses to fail for the obvious reason that it causes companies to become overextended.

By contrast, the two *Fortune* writers claim that the problem with companies addicted to growth is that even as the old engine responsible for a company's rapid growth continues to work without noticeable problems, a competitor somewhere is in the process of building a more powerful or more efficient engine that will render the original obsolete.

Management Myopia

So, related to the first reason for why companies fail is the number-two reason, say Charan and Useem. They fail to wake up and smell the coffee. Polaroid, for example, got into trouble because it failed to diversify sufficiently beyond its instant film process, which had propelled the company to greatness. The same fate may befall Kodak and for the same reason. In a world where people want to e-mail photos to friends, digital cameras make far more sense than plain old film.

Yet not all companies fall into this trap. Back in the mid '80s, Intel founders Andy Grove and Gordon Moore realized that their company's core business in memory chips was being attacked by cheaper Asian imports. Their solution: Transform the company into a maker of microprocessors. The Wintel desktop monopoly resulted. But few management teams are so enlightened.

One-Man Shows

Like others studying business failures, Charan and Useem found that an insular and sometimes arrogant management team is a third important reason why large companies fail. Needless to say, examples of both highlighted the news during 2002. In March, for example, several months before the extent of Worldcom's troubles became known, CEO Bernard J. Ebbers summoned his managers from around the globe to the company's headquarters in tiny Clinton, Mississippi. They were on hand to learn Ebbers's plan for rescuing the company. "What they heard instead," according to one account, "was their boss thundering about the theft of coffee."[8] According to the story that appeared in *Business Week*, Ebbers had tried to match up the number of discarded coffee filters with bags of coffee when he discovered the theft. From now on, he told managers, they would need to do the same. And they would need to monitor lights to make sure these were shut off at the end of the day. Finally, he directed them to turn up their office thermostats by four degrees come summer.

It was all part of a cost-cutting strategy that few in attendance at the meeting believed would do much to help save the $40-billion company from its growing problems, such as cascading debt and sluggish forward growth.

That kind of approach has since enraged shareholders of many firms, who charge that the company's top managers were as grossly overpaid as they were incompetent. Indeed, shareholders had many reasons to feel they were not being treated fairly. While in bankruptcy, Kmart, for example, authorized payment of $362,000 per month in retirement benefits to some 242 of its executives,[9] which caused Kmart's creditors, to whom the company owed a reported $6 billion, to protest to a Chicago bankruptcy judge.

Noting the high salaries that came despite poor performance, *LA Times* writer John Balzar observed that creditors and shareholders aren't the only ones enraged at the seemingly arrogant attitudes of America's corporate giants. "Consumers are mad, and some are declaring petty war against the mighty corporation, against the shenanigans, the double-dealing, the get-rich-quick schemes, the fraud, the self-serving deals." Those investors felt that they themselves had been robbed. And, indeed, many had seen their retirement savings dwindle by one-third or more. So they were striking back in any number of ways, whether by sabotaging fruit at a grocery store or stealing music via an Internet site.[10]

Small companies, too, can become victims of an insular management. According to Tourtellot:

> You find this [type of insular management] usually in family companies with second or third generation. But it also happens when an entrepreneur starts a company and he has the belief that—because he started the company—he's the only one that really understands the business. And what happens to those folks is that it works for a while because the company is small, and you have very few people. But when you get bigger and you have more

people and you don't know how to delegate, and you don't know how to team build, then you start driving away your good people. And you end up having people who are "yes" people, and that's not very helpful to the company. When you walk into a situation like that, then you have what we call a one-man show. A very dominant person keeps everything to himself, and all the people that are working for him really can't manage because of this.

Risk Takers

A management that listens only to itself is also perhaps more prone to take risks, which is yet another reason the *Fortune* writers believe companies fail. One heady, high-risk tactic that companies employed was turbocharging a company's numbers and gleefully reporting good news even when the news was untrue. Blame the surge in stock prices and Wall Street's merciless fixation with performance, notes a Boston University business professor. "Through the 1980s and 1990s, we constructed an architecture that emphasized reporting good news to the extent where CEOs could not be frank," she says. As a result, companies that needed to take corrective action failed to do so, lest that action alert the Street to the company's problems. So, instead of taking care of business, management tweaked the numbers some more.[11]

In fact, the New Economy actually encouraged this form of risk taking because it was based on the idea that the old rules no longer applied. So, breaking those rules amounted to an act of liberation. A common theme among many Internet stock cheerleaders was that dot-com companies were really in the business of creating an entirely new species of economy—cutting out the middleman, speeding the flow of information, and aggregating buyers and sellers into groups that would have been impossible in the pre-Internet era.

Priceline.com was often held up as an example of how Internet companies were said to be changing the very dynamics of commerce. Priceline, for those who don't know, operates a kind of reverse auction for airline tickets. It has even succeeded in getting a patent on the process. Users input a price they are willing to pay for, say, a flight from New York to London. Priceline finds an airline willing to sell them a ticket at or near that price. The company devised plans to expand its reverse-auction concept into other areas, such as mortgages, insurance, and automobile sales.

Out with the Traditional Yardsticks!

Because companies like Priceline were supposedly pioneering ways to get business done, all the stuffy old rules for evaluating a company—and the risks it might be taking—no longer applied, or so pundits said. How could someone use traditional measures of the value of a stock when the underlying company was reinventing capitalism on the fly? For this reason, no one was particularly bothered that the numbers posted by Internet players blew out the normal measures used by fundamental analysts. Amazon.com, even after the August–September 1998 crash, was selling for about 16 times sales. Again, that is sales, not profits. Amazon had yet to generate profits. If every business enjoyed valuations like that, the corner magazine store, with a yearly gross of, say, $100,000, would be worth $1.6 million, even if it consistently lost money.

So the real question to Internet stock pundits became this: If the traditional measures are too scary to use, how else can you determine Amazon's value? Michael Murphy, editor of the *California High Technology Stock Letter,* devised one solution. He looked at something he called "growth flow." Simply defined, growth flow is a measure of earnings per share plus research and development per share. To calculate growth flow, you divided research-and-development spending by the number of shares outstanding. The theory behind using growth flow as an indicator is that the more a company spends on research and development, the more it invests in its own future.

Other analysts came up with equally ingenious methods. Buyout value was one method used. Still other analysts sought to redefine the price-to-sales ratio, a traditional fundamentalist measure. This valuation method was based on the idea that all Internet companies were brand new. Most new companies lose money. Therefore, the important thing to focus on was not earnings but sales. How much had sales grown over the years? Amazon.com provides an illustration. At one point during the late 1990s, it had a sales growth rate of something like 838 percent, which meant that maybe the stock was not such a bad buy after all, even if it was selling for 16 times sales. Indeed, in 1998, when star analyst Henry Blodgett, who was working for CIBC Oppenheimer at the time, announced that Amazon's price might hit $400, the announcement set off a fevered buying frenzy that may have acted to fulfill the forecast.[12]

Another popular method used to predict an Internet stock's value was something called discounted future price. Here, the financial software maker Intuit, selling some time ago at a pre-crash price of $39, or 32 times earnings, provides an example. Let us suppose that analysts predicted that Intuit would grow by 20 percent annually over the next several years. Current earnings were something like $1.21 per share. Compound that amount by 20 percent annually. Result: By 2004, Intuit should earn about $3.12 per share. Now multiply that figure by 32 (the accepted pre-crash Street multiple). By that reckoning, Intuit should sell for just under $100 per share by 2004—reason enough to buy the stock at $39. Use a more conservative multiple, say, 22 times earnings, and the price comes out to around $69 per share. That still made $39 look like a bargain.

The Advancing Borg

Another way management took huge risks during the boom was through acquisitions, say Charan and Useem (chapter 12 also deals with acquisitions). Again, in the rush to capitalize on the boom era, many companies realized that the fastest way to beat the competition was to join it. Adherents to this idea pointed to network equipment giant Cisco Systems, which accrued billions in sales in part by acquiring many smaller companies. From 1993 to around 2000, Cisco is said to have gobbled up 51 firms. And plans reportedly called for it to ingest 25 more within the coming year. Little wonder that Cisco received the nickname "the Borg," after the fictional *Star Trek* aliens that assimilated entire races in their quest to dominate the universe.

Cisco was uncannily able to not only quickly assimilate the firms it acquired but to mine huge value from their operations in a relatively short time. Often as a result it found immense value in companies it acquired. In 1993, for example Cisco paid $75 million for Crescendo Communications. It later created a division around the now digested Crescendo that less than a decade later produced nearly $7 billion in sales.

In fact, Cisco proved so successful at its acquisition strategy that some claimed it had succeeded in remaking itself several times as a result. Little wonder that other New Economy companies actively studied its methods. What they discovered was that long before an acquisition was consummated, teams within Cisco had the company up on its radar screen. Sometimes the team would arrange for Cisco to purchase a small stake in the targeted firm, as a way of scrutinizing its operations more closely.

The intense study allows the networking giant to pounce with lightning speed while a deal is being struck. In 1999, for example, Cisco shelled out $7.2 billion for Cerent Corp., a fiber optics equipment maker. Before the acquisition even became final, a Cisco assimilation team moved in with Borg-like efficiency, working one on one with Cerent employees. Each employee received a new job title and a new bonus plan. (T-shirts and mugs were also distributed.) As a result, two months after the deal was announced, only a handful of Cerent's 400 employees had left the company.

Cisco demonstrated that it was a class act even during the 2001 downturn. When it announced layoffs of 11 percent of its workforce, a total of 5,000 jobs, it softened the blow by giving employees a full six months of salary and benefits.

Uncivil Wars

All too often, however, the assimilated companies aren't properly integrated when a company makes an acquisition. Witness AOL Time Warner. *Vanity Fair* writer Nina Munk describes the bitter infighting that occurred as top executives in the newly merged firm squabbled, while the company's stock plummeted 70 percent in value and management was forced to write off some $54 billion. Monk noted that, "The company is hobbled by a massive $28 billion of debt, a shaky credit rating, and a loss of confidence on Wall Street. Its shareholders are angry; its employees have lost faith; some of its big partners in various joint ventures and subsidiaries are looking to get out."[13]

Similarly, controversy surrounding the Hewlett-Packard Compaq merger threatened to tear both companies apart before the union even occurred. By a two-to-one margin, employees voting through HP's 401k plan, recorded their disapproval of the deal, linking their protest with that of Walter Hewlett, son of the company's founder. Some critical of the merger wondered if HP's colorful CEO Carly Fiorina could hope to be successful at uniting the two huge computer makers, given her track record upon joining the company. As one anonymous employee noted, "She came in with an attitude that this is a country club, and I'm going to shake it up."[14]

A Slave to the Street

The rift over the Compaq merger at HP likely played some role in the company's stock decline during the period. However, in other cases, Wall Street will often reward an acquisition strategy that appears to make sense on paper, just as it will reward—for a time— a company that obediently makes its numbers, no matter how shaky those numbers eventually turn out to be.

Indeed, companies that blindly follow the whims of the Street also risk failure, says *Fortune* (see chapter 4). Companies that resorted to overly aggressive accounting methods have found this coming back to haunt them. Although the exploits of Andersen, Worldcom, and others have lately received considerable attention, those who studied boom-and-bust cycles while these were in progress have noticed that a large incentive existed within companies to put the best possible face on operations by being overly zealous in their financial statements.

UCLA business professor and IPO expert Ivo Welch and his colleagues studied hundreds of newly IPOed companies during the '90s boom period and discovered that many used a rarified form of accounting to add bounce to their balance sheets. The method, known as positive accrual, allowed companies to account for expenses as bills are paid, while stating earnings based on receivables—instead of basing earnings on when payments were actually received. Using positive accrual, earnings might appear to exceed cash flow. "There's quite a lot of earnings management going on," Welch says ruefully.

Some companies tended to continue using this rarefied accounting practice for three months or more following an IPO—roughly the amount of time needed for VCs, investment banks, and management to legally sell their own shares. It's at this point, Welch says, that share prices tend to plummet as the public gleans the real numbers for the first time.

Management by Drifting Around

Companies with the best of intentions can also fall into failure if they otherwise lack direction. Rather than pursuing a consistent goal, they allow their strategy to drift. Newton, Iowa–based Maytag, for example, after acquiring a host of businesses sufficient to place itself squarely in third place among white goods makers, then sought a CEO with the marketing savvy to promote its various brands. Those inside and outside the company, thought they had an ideal choice in Lloyd Ward, brought in from Pepsi. Ward, the first African American to lead a Fortune 500 company, was likewise widely lauded in the press. But his flamboyant style reportedly clashed with the company's conservative rural Iowa roots. He debuted the company's new Neptune washers with a gala celebration in New York—a significant departure from the image of the company's sanguine Maytag repairman. The loss of several key distributors, including Circuit City, which got out of appliance retailing, and Montgomery Ward, which ceased operations, only further squeezed profits. The stock took a hit. Meanwhile, Wall Street analysts lamented that the company had too few products in the development pipeline.[15] After Ward quit, his successor, seeking to boost revenues, bought rival appliance-maker Amana. While the company appears to be back on track, its waffling cost shareholders dearly. "Management went into lock-down mode," said one consultant close to the company.

Cry Foul

Management indecision is one thing. The company failures that Americans will remember most during 2002 had more to do with an arrogant, dangerous mindset at the executive level. Transcontinental corporate jets and mansions on a scale not seen since the Gilded Age became as much a part of the CEO lifestyle as the hundreds of millions in stock options that virtually assured that a company's leaders would make money, regardless of whether the company itself did. Again, the boom times of fast, easy money fueled this attitude, as venture capitalists and investment banks fattened up young dot-com companies and sent them to market, oftentimes before they were ready, if only to reap huge profits from the companies' IPOs.

During the height of the tech boom, the Internet IPO process became a well-oiled machine. From company management, to venture capitalists, to underwriters, to the brokers who sold shares to the public, it was run by a relatively small group of inner players. And huge profits could be had all along the food chain. The techniques used to create Internet companies had changed little since the earliest years of OTC trading. The difference now was that the business of raising capital, developing a company, and then selling its shares could all be tied together seamlessly, thanks to the Internet. The resulting synergies became even tighter, because the IPOed companies themselves were intended to do business on the Internet.

Ultimately, the reason opening-day IPO shares exploded in price was that getting those shares was nigh impossible. Not only were floats kept deliberately small, as noted, but large portions of the shares actually made available were promised to institutions and other powers-that-be on the Street. Because of these thin floats, the few shares actually available to retail traders tended to be gobbled up quickly, and the resulting price rise benefited the institutions. Having received the shares at the actual offering price, institutions faced far less risk than retail investors did and enjoyed a much greater opportunity for profit.

Ultimately, companies built on a house of cards topple quickly. Meanwhile, more and more IPOs selling garden supplies, pet food, and groceries online continued to pour from both traditional and nontraditional investment banking sources. Supply inevitably reached saturation levels—another sure sign of a bubble about to burst. In the months before a market crash occurs, "there is a rise in prices sufficient to encourage an influx of new supply," writes stock market analyst Martin Pring. Stock markets, for example, will debut new issues to investors at an ever-faster rate, he says. At some point there simply will turn out to be fewer companies worthy of going public. And it's at that point that everyone's standards get lowered, and increasingly companies based on nothing more than concepts get offered to an investing public bent on making a quick killing. In the end, says Pring, rather than simply falling, stock value in essence evaporates.[16]

Concept companies were a long tradition in the OTC market. During the '20s, it was the trusts; during the '60s, it was aerospace and electronics companies. Internet firms were simply a new twist on an old idea.

To be sure, a few of those Internet companies succeeded fabulously and did change the way all of us live. But many others simply vanished. Still others were remanded to the clearance room of bulletin board stocks.

Poor Governance

One of the principal reasons such largess was permitted was because of ineffective boards, say *Fortune*'s Chanan and Useem, citing the last of their 10 reasons why companies fail. Indeed, many would echo that view. *Business Week* proclaimed that faulty corporate governance had prompted the worst crisis in corporate America since the trustbuster era of a century ago. Noting that during the '90s boom, both corporate heads and boards held progressively larger equity stakes in the company, the magazine mused that in theory this should have aligned the board and top management with shareholders—with everyone pushing for a company's long-term success. Instead, the unintended consequence was that whether through actual stock ownership or option grants, "many executives and directors realized that their personal wealth was so closely tied to the price of the company stock that maintaining the share price became the highest corporate value."[17]

In fact, such a conflict of interest can take place whenever an organization puts its own interests ahead of customers' or shareholders'. During the mid-'90s, for example, the National Association of Securities Dealers (NASD) was forced to launch its damage-control efforts following a series of investigations by the SEC and the Justice Department over alleged price fixing and other abuses by NASD member firms. These investigations and the resulting charges and lawsuits led to cries of foul play in the business press. Here was a sure sign that Wall Street insiders, who were already sweeping millions from the market, had become greedier still. Now it appeared as if they were stealing billions directly from investors' pockets. As a consequence, the NASDAQ and its member firms were forced to pay out hundreds of millions of dollars.

And just as revelations of fraudulent accounting practices rocked large American companies to the core, the allegations of price-fixing on the NASDAQ sorely hurt the nation's second-largest stock market. In the course of the year, some 91 companies left the NASDAQ for the NYSE. Fast-growing computer-maker Gateway was one of the more high-profile defectors, and maybe the one that hurt the NASDAQ the most. The innovative mail-order computer-maker at the time located in South Dakota, Gateway symbolized what the NASDAQ championed. In contrast to the NYSE, which represented the long-powerful corporate interests of America, the NASDAQ was formed to represent companies that were outsiders, owing to their innovative way of doing business. What must have been even more upsetting to NASDAQ officials, the Gateway defection was followed up by the flight of two comparable high-profile tech firms, Bay Networks and America Online.[18] This caused some to ponder If "the stock market for the next 100 years" couldn't hold onto its brightest stars, what was its future?

It took a major reform effort by the NASD's new chairman, Frank Zarb, to put the NASDAQ back on track. (See chapter 7, for a full description of Zarb's tactics.) In the same way, *Business Week* claims, companies must now mount Herculean efforts to revamp their tarnished images. During the 1990s, *Business Week* noted, the big challenge for managers was to streamline operations in order to compete more effectively. In the years ahead, managers' biggest challenge may be to reshape their organizational cultures in a way that engenders integrity along with "creativity and entrepreneurship."[19]

An Unfortunate Confluence of Events

Just as airline crashes are typically the result of several untoward events that occur simultaneously, companies that go down in flames fall victim to several fatal flaws. The *Fortune* article cited instances where several factors contributed to a company's demise. Enron, for example, fell victim to just about all of the 10 fatal flaws the two reporters identified. According to Charan and Useem, the company was a slave to Wall Street, pushing the envelope of acceptable reporting standards to meet ever-higher earnings expectations. Its past successes prompted management to ignore the potential dangers, and it overdosed on risk. Meanwhile, the company's board of directors failed to exercise sufficient oversight, while employees, fearing repercussions, didn't voice their concerns. The result was what *Fortune* claims was a dangerous culture. Ultimately, the company that was substantially built on intangible assets suffered the steep fall of a dot-com.

Not that companies need so many reasons to secure their doom. Kmart, the *Fortune* article claimed, was guilty on just two counts: Its board failed to exercise proper oversight, while management followed a "strategy du jour," never settling on a strategic course of action long enough for it to succeed.

As will be shown in my list of 10 specific causes of failure, often a single misstep is all that's needed.

4

When Stock Price Dictates Strategy

More than 20 years ago, two Harvard professors, Robert H. Hayes and William J. Abernathy, wrote a landmark article that appeared in the *Harvard Business Review*.[1] Entitled "Managing Our Way to Economic Decline," it charged that American companies were falling behind their foreign competitors precisely because their managers had focused on short-term results. That focus was in an effort to appease Wall Street analysts who wanted a predictable stream of earnings to ensure that the companies' stocks might rise at a predictable rate. However, the focus on quarterly earnings came at a heavy price, the two professors claimed. Principally, it caused companies to avoid investing in research and development and any other long-term programs that risked shrinking their quarterly margins. In addition, regarding products already developed, companies were tempted to skimp on quality or cut back on customer service.

Meanwhile, foreign competitors—mainly in Germany and Japan—were fortunate because their boards allowed them to take a longer view. Often these boards consisted of labor union representatives, in Germany, or creditor banks, in Japan. Because the boards were less beholden to their companies' stock price of the moment, they weren't forced to cut corners in production, as was the case with their American counterparts. Thus, the Germans and the Japanese made products that were superior to those of the United States.

To understand the impact of this article on American managers, we need to think back to that era, in the 1970s, when America suffered from a malaise similar to the prevailing mood today. Communism was making inroads from Afghanistan to Nicaragua, while unstoppable German and Japanese government–backed businesses were stealing market share from America's proudest companies. The economy had soured as a result, the stock market was in a seemingly permanent slump, capital was hard to come by, and many Americans found themselves unemployed. Entire industries, such as electronics and automobiles, seemed imperiled. And companies could only hope to maintain their financial numbers, in an effort to save their stock from being punished further.

Creative Financing

To accomplish that, management decided to focus on the company's finances—its borrowing and equities strategies, for example—rather than on its products. Finance, after all, was an area where American business excelled and one where it was exceedingly creative. And financial management strategies really bolstered the bottom line faster than changes in production methods could ever hope to. Corporate America's critics—those hailing from Japan, in particular—were fond of pointing out that American managers cared more about stock price than about products and risked turning their cash-cow industries into hollow shells. A growing trade deficit suggested that the Japanese had a point.

In fact, the malaise of the '70s had its roots in a boom period of a decade earlier, a time when techniques to propel a company's stock price skyward became a veritable art form. During this boom period—the so-called go-go years of the '60s—entire industries rose up and their stocks with them, only to crash a few years later. The period, like the late '90s, illustrates how a strategy that focuses solely on fast stock market rewards will often destroy companies in the process.

During those years, initial public offerings (IPOs) of small companies proliferated. Much of the information about the IPO process during that time (and much of the information I include here) comes from a massive report called *the Special Study of the Securities Markets,* which was prepared for Congress by the Securities and Exchange Commission in 1963.[2] The report reveals that just as tech stocks and dot-coms propelled the stock market's rise and fall during the '90s, in the '60s investors couldn't get enough of stocks in companies that had even the remotest connection to aerospace and electronics. This was the era when NASA led the Free World's race to the moon.

Even companies whose names suggested they were part of the great space race found eager buyers. In 1962, shares of Welch Scientific Company hit the market at $18. By the end of the day, these had reached $52. The investors who received calls from their brokers may have believed they were buying into a company that would let them share the journey to the moon. In fact, the Skokie, Illinois, firm manufactured laboratory equipment. In addition to its techie-sounding name, though, one reason Welch's price shot up so quickly was that the offering consisted of only 545,000 shares.

Limiting the offering price was just one tactic in the arsenal used by an ad hoc industry that at the time was devoted to bringing new companies public and capturing often-exorbitant profits from an IPO. Evidence suggests that the methods used to locate IPO-worthy companies and to unleash their shares on the public were in some cases even more advanced than they are today. Broker-dealers, for example, maintained networks of scouts, called finders, who located companies that were ripe for a public offering. Finders received a fairly modest salary of $35 per week. Investment banks also competed for companies, this being one of their traditional roles.

With competition fierce to find ripe IPO candidates, due diligence often fell by the wayside. The SEC's *Special Study,* as a result, leveled a charge that may sound familiar: "Many of the companies offering stock to the public through such firms had no history of earnings, no plant, no product, and management with no experience in which the company claimed to be engaged." One company, called Transition Systems, Inc., possessed a product called an All-Purpose Correlator—a highly versatile machine. According to some of the stock's promoters, it could "detect cancer, heart disease, and oil." In fact, no such machine existed.

Once suitable companies were located, the IPO grooming process began in earnest. To be sure, many companies were legitimate. Yet undeniably, many were not. Philandering and abuses were common. Financial firms took advantage of their relationship with the soon-to-be-public companies, loaning them money at high interest rates, overcharging for services, and adding these fees to their already-high commissions on the eventual sale of stock.

Setting the price of that sale, when it occurred, was always a well-thought-out process. As one broker described it: "We believe . . . that you can offer a stock at $20 and it can go to $35. But you could very well offer that same stock at $28 and it would go to $26." As a result, many IPOs were deliberately *underpriced* so that they could produce an initial pop when they debuted. Investors would see this quick rise in the stock's price and falsely believe they were buying a stock with the potential to rise more. The underwriters naturally had a vested interest in seeing the shares rise past their offering price, since many deals gave them options to purchase even larger quantities of shares at the initial offering price or, in some cases, below the offering price.

Sales of new stock were often handled by an ad hoc syndicate, formed by trading firms and retail brokers for the express purpose of trading that one stock. In the months after the issue debuted and sales cooled off, the syndicate might disband. In many instances, the final link in such syndicates consisted of the boiler rooms, where traders, sitting in rows of desks, hyped the stocks to unsuspecting investors over the phone.

The New Wealth Creators

In the face of these outlandish tactics, a crash of mammoth proportions seemed all but inevitable. And a crash is exactly what occurred. The year 1970 greeted the financial markets much as 1930 or 2000 had. There was a dismal recognition that the '60s go-go era had gone for good. The Dow had flirted with the 1,000 mark just two years earlier. In the first months of 1970 it tumbled below 700.[3] So-called story stocks, the over-hyped electronics and aerospace firms that had fueled the '60s boom, fell the hardest, hurt by an oversupply of weak new entrants that swamped the market.

Brokers looked for a final surge of panic selling that would signal capitulation and a market bottom. Instead, the market inexorably stair-stepped downward in a classic bearish pattern of progressively lower lows and lower highs.

Although it took a long time, something good finally did come out of that period. And it's not unreasonable to suggest that the article "Managing Our Way to Economic Decline" was in some small way a catalyst for that positive change. The article suggested that there was a better way for business to operate, by focusing once again on production and on ensuring that products were of the highest quality possible.

A new generation of business leaders heard that message loud and clear and set to work. Instead of floating concepts for quick profits, they built the next generation of industrial behemoths, which were destined to carry the nation into the new century.

In fact, this became one of the strangest generations of American business, led by people like Bill Gates, Steve Jobs, and Larry Ellison. Known to be ruthlessly competitive and wildly eccentric, the new generation re-energized business. Often, they shaped cult-like organizations after their own, at times eccentric, image. Thanks to Gates's enormous holdings of Microsoft stock, his wealth eventually surpassed that of the Brunei sultan. Not bad for a guy who spent his Harvard years playing high-stakes poker and who by some accounts went without bathing for days at a time.

Larry Ellison, the database software tycoon who founded Oracle, reportedly made no bones about his company's out-for-blood culture. "It's not enough that we win," he reportedly once said. "Everyone else must lose."[4]

Luck sometimes played a critical role in this generation's success. Compaq's founders, for example, reportedly sat around a table at House of Pies in Houston, trying to decide what business to get into.[5] Ideas allegedly discussed by the three founders included a Mexican restaurant, a company manufacturing disk drives, and a key chain that would beep on command if it got lost. In the end, they resolved to create a computer manufacturing company—but one with lower overhead and thus better margins than IBM.

And then there's Steve Jobs of Apple, whose now-legendary visit to Xerox's Palo Alto Research Center forever changed the way personal computers are used. During that visit, Jobs was shown a roomful of startling innovations devised by Xerox's brain trust. To date, none had been brought to market. Had they been, it's likely that Xerox, and not Microsoft or Apple, would have grown to dominate the personal computer industry. These inventions eerily foretold products that competitors would develop in the years ahead. Among the most impressive innovations Jobs saw was a first-generation graphical user interface that allowed all programs to share a common control panel. The Xerox interface inspired Jobs to create the Lisa, Apple's business computer. Lisa's high price caused it to bomb, but Jobs and Apple got it right with the less-expensive Macintosh.

The companies founded by these eccentric leaders created a new boom during the '80s. And the fact that their companies remain vibrant today points to the solid foundations their leaders bequeathed them.

As is normally the case with sustained market booms, the first phase takes off on firm footing. Microsoft, for example, went public in March 1986. Unlike the Internet initial public offerings (IPOs) that were rushed to the market 10 years later, Microsoft had already proved itself to the investment community when its stock first went on sale. In an interview, Alfred Berkeley III, currently vice chairman of the NASDAQ, said of Bill Gates: "We didn't grasp his profound understanding of business strategy." Years earlier, while a partner with the investment firm Alex Brown, Berkeley helped to put together Microsoft's IPO. Berkeley was also advising the NASDAQ on ways to utilize new technology at the time, and Gates was invited to take part in these discussions. Microsoft's IPO came 11 years after Gates and Paul Allen had developed Basic, the programming language that ran first-generation microcomputers, and three years after the debut of Windows. The offering raised a relatively modest $61 million with its opening price of $21 per share. In September 1987, Microsoft stock was selling for $114, when the company opted for a two-for-one split. Weeks later, the crash of 1987 lopped roughly 30 percent off its value.[6]

But alas, like the boom 20 years earlier, the good times of the '80s and '90s were destined to end. As the stock market momentum shifted inexorably upward, many astute businesspeople saw little need to create companies for the long haul, when concepts like the earlier space-age firms could possess investors just as well. Thus they invented a veritable assembly line for creating new companies—specifically, Internet companies. And that assembly line had more in common with Hollywood than with Wall Street.

Return of the Fast-Buck Artists

Movie people in Hollywood often complain about the freaky unreality of their business—what with multimillion-dollar deals scribbled on napkins and movies based on concepts instead of on story lines. It's a place where bankable actors and directors are more important than scripts—an entire industry built on fantasy.

But anything put out by Hollywood is small time, compared to the business of Internet IPOs during the 1990s. Centered 300 miles north of L.A. in Silicon Valley, the IPO moguls, like their Hollywood counterparts, attracted world-class talent. Yet instead of writing scripts, these Gen-Xers and Gen-Yers were busy writing business plans. And talk about fantasy! "How can a company that doesn't have any earnings and has William Shatner for a spokesperson and nothing else be worth $15 billion?" asked UCLA finance professor Ivo Welch during an interview. He was referring to Priceline.com, the high-concept "reverse-auction" e-commerce firm that IPOed last March. Priceline's $15 billion market cap roughly equals the total market value of Delta, United, and American airlines combined, Welch explains. "I would love to come up with a reason why this is rational." But, he admits, he's failed so far.

The similarities between Hollywood and the Valley go well beyond that, however. In Hollywood you have high-concept movies. In the Valley you have business models. Package an eBay model with some former executive talent from Amazon. Score some good press. You might just have a blockbuster—which is to say, a stock that shoots up 100, 200, or 300 percent on its first day of trading—more than enough to reap a fast fortune for the relatively small number of people who were lucky to acquire a significant number of shares in the fledgling company.

Just as in the '60s, the Silicon Valley IPO process during the '90s illustrates to the extreme how companies made bolstering their stock price the very fulcrum of their strategy and how many of those companies failed as a result.

What was behind the mania? "During the first five months of 1999, the average first-day return on IPOs was 68 percent," Jay Ritter, finance professor at the University of Florida, said in an interview. "That is an aberration." Typical first-day returns hover around 15 percent. "There are a lot of investors with the perception that it's easy to get rich on getting allocations of hot IPOs," he laments.

The aggregate statistics told a different story, however. Internet analyst firm CommScan looked at 3,477 companies that went public between 1993 and 1998. Afterward, some 55 percent traded at or below their offering price.

And for that reason, from company management to venture capitalists, to underwriters, to the brokers who sold the shares, the IPO process during the '90s became a well-oiled machine—one that learned a thing or two from Hollywood. Everyone knows how movies can lose money on the books but still make their backers millions. Likewise, a typical IPO firm can debut carrying years of red ink, but that doesn't prevent it from making a lot of people rich along the way. The only difference between Hollywood and Silicon Valley is the number of zeros after the dollar sign.

Built on Buzz?

Experts say that in order for a boom to succeed, there must also be an overabundance of capital that is sitting around, waiting to be spent. This was precisely the case during the late 1990s, as venture funds raised enormous amounts of capital, year after year. A record $24 billion in fresh funding flowed from venture capitalists to startups during 1998 alone, according to the National Association of Venture Capitalists. At first, this money could find only a few companies that were ready to take the idea and run with it. This, in turn, prompted investors to snap up the precious few shares that could be had, even as the companies' prices steadily rose. So it was with the Internet during those early years, when a few highly publicized companies went public.

Venture capitalists represented the first formal step in the assembly-line IPO process. You could think of them as deal-makers or packagers, similar to the super agents who emerged in Hollywood during the '80s. The more prestigious the VC firm backing a startup, the better that company's chances of scoring big when it IPOed.

Startups accepted a VC's benign oversight as a precondition to being funded. Besides providing companies with good buzz, VCs furnished wet-behind-the-ears startups with needed management expertise. VCs might, for instance, recruit a key CFO or IT manager to fill out a company's management roster. VCs also establish the company's initial value—a process that can be extremely arbitrary, based on discussions with prospective large-scale buyers, such as fund managers. "If you examine the current process, it leaves a lot to be desired," an investment banker said in in interview. "You have your company valued not by the people who buy your products and services but by large mutual funds that took a one-hour meeting to determine that you're worth X amount."

It's not unusual for a company valued at $6 million to suddenly jump to $10 million, following the sign-up of a key executive. And during the boom period, it was common for VCs to double a company's valuation, then double it again, before investment banks got their hands on it.

Roughly 70 percent of venture capital typically comes from institutional investors, who at the height of the boom period expected something like a 40-percent annualized return. Sometimes the returns can be far greater. For example, eBay handed over $2.3 billion in stock to its VC backers, Benchmark Capital. The money was payback for a $1.5 million loan that Benchmark made in 1997—a 1,500-percent return!

With that kind of money in play, it's no wonder the venture capital business thrived.

The Culling Fields

Often the decisions over which companies to fund are based on what business models are hot at the time. One financial journalist talked about VCs' herd mentality—like Hollywood movie moguls who compete with the same types of films. If one venture capitalist firm has a certain type of e-commerce company in its portfolio, then the others need it, too.

Meanwhile, only 10 percent of the startups that manage to sign with big-name VCs actually wind up being IPOed. The more likely exit strategy is a merger or a plain old buyout, as Microsoft did with Hotmail. From a VC's point of view, buyouts provide fund investors with an assured rate of return, and the money can be quickly put back in play, improving the VC's long-term performance. IPOs may offer the chance at greater rewards—but with greater risk.

Bankable Stars

Firms that go the IPO route typically do so through an investment bank. Here again, there's a definite pecking order. Prestigious banks like Morgan Goldman Sachs compete to bring public the most promising companies. One investment bank acts as lead underwriter, with other names tagged on. The more impressive the roster of investment banks, the more positive buzz the IPO will generate.

And again, who was actually underwriting the shares could ultimately be one of the biggest determinants of their success. "The thing that you get when you buy an IPO from somebody like Merrill Lynch or Goldman Sachs is you know that this is a reasonable company," says UCLA's Ivo Welch. "You know that probably it's going to be a good deal on the first day." Like a good auditor, he says, quality investment banks perform their own due diligence before taking a company public and providing it with a de facto seal of approval.

U.S. investment banks receive a 7-percent commission, or spread, when they take a company public. Meaning, a $100 million offering would net management roughly $93 million after the underwriters take their cut.

"Those spreads are about twice as high as in Australia," notes Jay Ritter at the University of Florida. "The average in Europe is 4.9 percent." Oddly, the 7-percent rate rarely varies with the size of the offering, even though large IPOs come with economies of scale, he says. And despite increasing competition among investment bankers, the percentage rate remains a de facto industry norm. As an unidentified investment banker reportedly told Ritter, "The fact is, we'd be cutting our own throats to compete on price."

Fast-Track Finance and Cooked Books

Seven percent of a major deal can prove a powerful motivator. Indeed, investment bankers have been accused of rushing companies into the public arena. Ernst and Young polled managers at companies whose IPOs bombed. Two-thirds admitted they weren't ready for the added bookkeeping and investor scrutiny that public companies face. Which, of course, can have disastrous consequences for both shareholders and the company itself.

Case in point: A southwestern robotics company appeared to have all the right ingredients for a sexy IPO. It had a cool name and a cool product: laser-based medical devices. The company's IPO debuted in 1995, while its products were still in development. Subsequently, the company incurred a series of losses. Revenues dropped below NASDAQ's minimal levels. Kicked off the exchange, the company's shares were forced to trade in "bulletin-board hell"—that is, the online penny stock exchanges, all but ignored by brokers and investors alike.

To better appeal to investors, many freshly hatched firms try to push the envelope of generally accepted accounting principles. For example, one bookkeeping method popular with startups is called positive accrual. It enables companies to denote expenses as bills are paid, while receivables are used to state earnings. Positive accrual accounting can make it appear as if earnings surpass cash flow.

Earnings misstatements were likewise common among some technology and Internet firms as a positive story here, too, could enhance a company's stock price. Researching the topic, a doctoral degree at New York University reportedly found that the tech sector was responsible for nearly 40 percent of those companies that needed to restate their earnings.

I'll Wash Your Back; You Wash My Back

Valuations become flaky again in the weeks before the actual IPO. The so-called quiet period that extends from the time that investment bankers first meet with management is anything but quiet for insiders, as they set the final offering price. Here again, it's not unusual for companies to restate earnings or adjust valuations in preparation for the big day. What's more, investment banks may price their offerings at a 15-percent premium. Numbers are floated as trial balloons. If interest proves insufficient, the investment bank may cut back on the number of shares offered, rather than risk seeing the price decline. Like movie studios that control a film's initial release, investment banks may also buy back shares in an effort to maintain the price. At the same time, investment banks will prohibit brokers (and, consequently, individual investors) from selling shares within a specified period.

All these tactics, aimed at controlling supply, are ultimately why opening-day IPO shares explode in price, at least during a bullish market environment. Getting them is tough. That alone contributes to their often wild price swings, as one investment banker remarked "You place 80 or 90 percent of the stock institutionally; the stock's up 100 percent, that means there's a high likelihood that the people who own the stock a week into the offering are very different from the people you sold it to. Consequently, supporting the stock in the aftermarket creates more volatility because you don't really know who you're targeting it to."

So, why not sell IPO shares directly to the public? "The traditional retail channels for distributing public offerings are never used because they're dysfunctional," Andy Klein, the man who is credited with inventing the concept of the online IPO, said in an interview. Klein also founded a company that aimed to make IPOs directly available to the public. "It's absolutely too expensive to mobilize human stockbrokers to deliver the information and solicit orders and allocate shares to individual investors."

How shares are actually doled out tends to be political in the extreme. In a sense, what investment banks are doing is they're giving kickbacks to investors, one stock market analyst remarked. And it's especially true with high buzz–generating IPOs like Priceline.com that in the boom period were virtually assured of an explosive opening. Who wouldn't jump at the chance to make 68 percent before the market closed?

Investors who receive coveted shares might include VCs, as an inducement for them to continue bringing lucrative deals to the investment bank. Institutional investors get red-hot offerings as an incentive for them to continue buying or sometimes to make up for a money-losing IPO that they previously bought.

All too often, retail investors—especially those with small accounts—get pushed to the end of the line, says Klein. "Even if you went to Merrill Lynch and said you had a million shares to sell and you let each broker pick his five best customers."

Netscape was the company that brought the Internet to the masses and launched the boom. It has since been absorbed into AOL Time Warner, and its rise and fall were typical of the period. Appropriately enough, Netscape was the era's first parabolic initial public offering (IPO). In August 1995, shares of Netscape priced at $28 immediately jumped to $71 at the market open. Anyone who had been lucky enough to receive shares before the open could have made a fortune. As long as investors snapped up these shares, the boom might be allowed to continue. Investors proved amazingly eager to do just that.

Seeds of Destruction

During the latter phases of a bubble, as famed stock market analyst and author Martin J. Pring describes it in his landmark book, *Investment Psychology Explained,* there is a feeling among investors that they must buy now before the opportunities disappear. This feeling is reinforced even as the boom lasts longer than anyone anticipates—and even as prices rise to ridiculous levels.

Yet for those who cared to look, an entirely different story could be gleaned by taking a longer view. Thomson Financial Securities Data analyzed 20 Internet firms that were IPOed by Merrill Lynch between 1997 and 2001 and found that three-quarters of them were trading for less than their offering price. Two others shut down.[7] Merrill's most spectacular dot-com flameout was probably Pets.com Inc., which earned $66 million from its IPO and then closed down 10 months later. A hugely expensive TV ad campaign gobbled up much of the company's cash. But the company's business plan, which called for customers to order their pet supplies online, leaves one to wonder, "What were they thinking?"

Pets.com joined other spectacular Internet flameouts that sold everything from gardening supplies to groceries online. In fact, when new companies with dubious business plans deluge the market, it's a sure sign that the bubble is about to burst, according to Pring. This happened with electronics and aerospace firms during the late 1960s. The Internet was history repeating itself.

"Greed broke the system," wrote Peter Elstom, of *Business Week*. Faced with the opportunity to earn billions, "many leading U.S. financial firms threw out their business standards and started grabbing the loot."[8]

During the late 1990s, major U.S. commercial banks and financial firms saw a new gold rush in California's Silicon Valley and began acquiring smaller investment banks that were already tapped into the local deal flow. Regarding the dot-com startups these firms brought public, the long-term performance of their portfolios was dismal at best. As of mid-April 2001, according to *Business Week,* the average return on Merrill Lynch's Net IPOs was –82 percent. Robertson Stephens's portfolio did only slightly better. It returned –65 percent to investors, while Credit Suisse First Boston's returns were –41 percent.[9]

To be sure, a crazed psychology drove the NASDAQ market ever higher during the tech boom. And an argument can be made that people who lost money in the crash that followed have only themselves to blame for giving in to greed. But there is a less obvious and perhaps more ominous explanation for why the market mania persisted for so long: The boom was expertly ridden by a loose consortium of venture capitalists and investment banks. Skillful publicity firms and the news media also played a key role, as did scores of online brokerages. Many of the companies launched during the period have become viable producers in our economy, but many others fizzled and died. Yet while they continued to function, those marginal companies formed part of an oversupply that deluged the market at the end of the 1990s. And this oversupply, as much as anything else, led to the crash.

If there's a moral here, it's the obvious one: that companies created for the sole purpose of manufacturing vast and fast wealth for their creators are usually doomed to fail. Boom periods, such as those in the '60s and the '90s, are aberrations. During the long and often lackluster times between them, companies are more liable to succumb to the sin of tweaking their numbers to satisfy stock analysts in a difficult and unforgiving business environment. Those companies, as Harvard professors Hayes and Abernathy charge, also risk their futures.

Another sin related to letting stock price dictate strategy, and one that appears just as likely to induce failure, is somewhat less obvious. And that is the temptation to grow too fast.

5

Growing Too Fast

C ompanies fail by growing too fast in two, perhaps obvious, ways. Either they aggressively build an organization ahead of the market's actual growth, or they hurl too many resources at a product or a service they provide and find themselves overextended. In either instance, the effect is akin to an army that has advanced too rapidly against its enemies, leaving itself vulnerable as a result.

But let's begin with a third, less obvious, way that companies overgrow themselves into ruin. That is by creating too much infrastructure. Such was the fate of countless dot-coms at the turn of the century. Startups all, they seemingly defied logic by flaming out even when their tills were flush with millions in venture capital cash. In fact, some quite literally choked on cash.

CIO Magazine recounts the story of a dot-com dry-cleaning service that had a vision of expanding nationwide and quickly moved into 25 markets.[1] The idea, presumably, was that busy customers in those markets would prefer to order pick-up and delivery of their clothes via the Net. And the online service even permitted those customers to select the times that were most convenient for them.

Efficiencies wrought by the Net would supposedly enable the cleaner to crush the competition in the $7- to $32-billion (estimates vary widely) dry-cleaning industry, especially considering that the competition mainly consisted of small chains or even single-store mom-and-pop operations. Still more efficiencies would be achieved by operating as a virtual company. That is, the actual dry cleaning would be done by large-scale facilities that already handled dry-cleaning in bulk for hotels.

To transform the idea into reality, the dry cleaner received a reported $8 million in venture capital cash. And because the company aimed to conquer the industry in one fell swoop, it used much of that money to create the infrastructure that normally would be needed only to support a far larger operation. Revenues, meanwhile, grew slowly. And as a result, the company simply ran out of money. Some claimed that a better strategy would have been to expand more slowly and stretch out its funding. The company also reportedly learned that it had underestimated the competition. As it turned out, the highly fragmented market, dominated by fast-on-their-feet small business owners, was a lot tougher than expected.

Besides battling a competitive industry, the erstwhile national dry cleaner may also have stumbled by forcing too much change on consumers. Although many in California were comfortable ordering books, flowers, and even travel on the Net, dry cleaning proved to be something else entirely.

Deadly Business

The idea that you could create a profitable organization that focused solely on order handling, while leaving the actual work to others who were steeped in industry experience, seemed enticing. Yet it's a strategy flush with perils. One of the most vivid examples of what can go wrong occurred in an industry with as much of a captive market as anyone could hope for. No matter who we are in life, there's no avoiding that final visit to the funeral home.

As with dry cleaning, there appeared to be huge opportunities to reap efficiencies of scale and to dominate a business that was mostly run by small operators. By some estimates, there are 23,000 funeral homes in the United States alone.[2] A typical funeral home performs just two funerals each week, and small companies account for somewhere between 75 and 80 percent of the entire industry. So, it was no surprise that during the cash-plentiful '90s, several funeral home companies tried to become sector leaders. According to *Forbes* magazine, "The industry spent $6.2 billion in acquisitions from 1995 to 1998." But in the end, some firms found themselves one step from the morgue. The second biggest publicly traded funeral firm, the Canada-based Loewen Group, for example, racked up $2.3 billion in debt, *Forbes* claims, before filing for bankruptcy protection in 1999 (the company now operates under a new name). A similar fate was experienced by other companies in the industry. And, indeed, many a grandiose growth plan was delayed for years thereafter, as companies worked feverishly to reduce the mountain of debt their acquisition strategies had produced.

The story of the Loewen Group makes for a classic turnaround case, as recounted in the book *Creating Value Through Corporate Restructuring*.[3] For a time, the company was growing revenues at an average of 30 percent annually. Total revenues topped $1 billion. Moreover, the company could boast of owning 1,100 funeral homes and 400 cemeteries. But on the liabilities side, the company at one point had $2.3 million in debt and losses of nearly $600 million.

The book *Creating Value* notes that the Loewen Group and the other large public so-called death-care companies devised a business model that was quite different than the one relied upon by their family-owned competitors. Because the typical small funeral home conducted an average of just two funerals each week, the book said, many of its assets, from visitation rooms to hearses, were unused much of the time. Moreover, staff members, such as receptionists, needed to be paid a weekly salary, regardless of their workload. Also effectively capping earnings was the industry's slow growth outlook. Statisticians could pretty much determine how many people were liable to die in a given year, and that number normally grew by a small percentage annually as the nation's population climbed. Although having a dependable and never-ending client base gave unprecedented stability to the industry, the growth rate was anything but breathtaking. Given those facts, the only ways to push margins in an otherwise moribund industry was to either get bigger—or else streamline. And the latter course could only go so far with a small operation.

Seeing both the challenges and the opportunities, many in the death-benefit business who were bent on expansion deduced that if they could purchase several funeral homes within a relatively small geographic area, they could make better use of any redundant assets—which is to say, the hearse that drove a customer from Funeral Home A to the cemetery on Monday could be used to drive a customer from Funeral Home B to the same final resting place on Tuesday. Yet this strategy, too, had its potential faults, according to the book. Funeral directors saw themselves as skilled professionals. Many were loathe to report to the MBAs assigned to manage them, since they didn't take—shall we say—a hands-on approach to the business.

For that reason, Loewen followed a slightly different expansion strategy. Instead of organizing homes into clusters, the company often reportedly bought a stake in the funeral homes it wished to add to the company roster, according to the book. Then it hoped to bring in enough funding to make needed improvements, while incentivizing the original owners to run the business efficiently. The strategy preserved the integrity of local homes, in a business where customers naturally must place a good deal of trust in the company they pick.

But Loewen's plan also had a downside. Namely, it required huge amounts of cash, some of which came from stock sales, while additional amounts were financed by debt. Yet by building an ever-larger organization, the stock rose to $30 and higher. And the company even received takeover offers of $45 per share. As debts mounted, however, and the company filed for Chapter 11, those shares eventually became worthless, according to *Forbes*.

Like a Drug

Fortune magazine commentator Herb Greenberg notes that the strategy of growing by acquisitions has become quite common, especially in business areas that are so ubiquitous and mundane as to be overlooked by glory-seeking investors and managers.[4] Funeral homes provide a great example. But there's also the car dealership AutoNation, which bought up scores of car dealerships. And a company called Iron Mountain expanded into the hardly known but necessary off-site record storage business by acquiring its competitors.

A company known as Quanta Services set its sights on the equally mundane repair of electric, telephone, and gas lines. As revenues climbed, Greenberg notes, the strategy appeared "brilliant." But then the telecom industry went bust, and the company's stock fell from a high of $63 to a late February 2003 price of roughly $3 per share.

Ironically, giving a company's stock price a steroidal injection is a chief appeal of the growth-by-acquisition strategy. With each new acquisition, revenues experience an automatic jump, while margins presumably stay within acceptable ranges, especially if the deal is accomplished through stock swaps. The growing company buys not just market share but expertise. And as long as the numbers are in agreement, Wall Street analysts stand ready to applaud each new purchase.

However, therein lies the fundamental flaw with the growth-by-acquisition strategy, the *Fortune* columnist notes.

> As with any addiction, the growth-by-bulk acquisition approach necessitates increasing doses of the drug to preserve the high. The only way to keep revenues growing fast enough for Wall Street is to buy ever more companies.

Halt the growth curve and the stock instantly gets punished. And that is many times enough to start a vicious downward spiral.

As capitalization decreases, the company loses its leveraging ability, and pressures grow to rein in costs, something that can quickly alienate customers in a highly competitive business. Debt may get downgraded, causing the company to pay higher interest rates. The company that looked like a winner just months earlier can quickly find itself struggling to survive.

Clothes and Credit

This is why some firms take an apparently safer route to achieving accelerated earnings growth, and that is to aggressively grow a product or a service. But this strategy has dangers as well. The clothing catalog company J. Peterman offers a good example. It enjoyed 25 percent name recognition among American consumers, thanks in large part to the hit TV show *Seinfeld,* which portrayed a humorous fictionalized version of the company on many episodes. The company also planned an ambitious expansion strategy. According to a separate *Fortune* article, the company hoped "in five years they'd go from one full-priced store to 50, from three outlet stores to 20 and launch two new catalogs."[5] And at the end of this explosive growth phase, there might be a lucrative initial public offering. But in the end, soft catalog sales were blamed for the company seeking a buyer instead.

The faddish clothing business is apt to have its share of fast winners and losers. But when large, more staid companies embark on a turbocharged expansion strategy, they also risk getting into trouble. That's what happened to mighty Sears, as it expanded into the competitive and sometimes dangerous business of consumer credit.

Over time, the retailing giant got more involved in the financial end of its business—that is, among other things, in financing purchases made by its customers. In fact, by 2002 Sears reportedly was making 70 percent of its income from its financial divisions.[6] That strategy must have been tempting, indeed, given the high-volume, high-competition, and low-margin nature of the other products it peddled. While revenues from retailing during the first quarter of 2002 were said to have fallen by 1.4 percent, finance revenues rose 26 percent. Wall Street rewarded the company's stock with a 60 percent rise. With 22 million MasterCard accounts, Sears grew to be the 13th-largest issuer. The risk was that rather than holding billions of dollars in accounts receivable from its credit card holders, Sears might find itself sitting on a growing pile of bad debts.

In fact, that's what occurred with Sears during the 1990 boom years. Even as the nation's consumers embarked on an unprecedented spending spree, their savings rate declined. Meanwhile, personal bankruptcies increased. And, as *CFO Magazine* reported, Sears found itself in a class action lawsuit that centered on its collection methods that ultimately cost a reported several hundred million dollars.[7]

Drug and Media Giants

If there is a moral to the Sears case and to the more serious failures that occurred to other companies that got hooked on fast growth, it is that size matters—but not always in a good way. A report by the research firm Bain & Company notes that over a 10-year period, the five largest drug makers have "grown fivefold to $16.8 billion dollars. Yet their operating margins rose a mere one percent."[8] One chief area holding back profits was a reported poor return on research and development efforts. Despite the fact that R&D spending by the industry increased four-fold, the number of drugs receiving approval from the Food and Drug Administration during the same period remained the same.

To boost revenues while lacking an ample pipeline of new drugs, the industry has looked to mergers. But as with a bundled growth strategy, this eventually created a dilemma. Larger drug firms needed to launch three or more new drugs per year just to achieve a modest 10-percent annual growth in sales. The pharmaceutical companies compounded their problems by pursuing a

product-development strategy similar to that of the music industry. That is, they pegged their success on hits. As a result, all the
large drug companies came to resemble one another, as they each
pursued an undifferentiated product-development strategy aimed
at nurturing big money-producing blockbusters. The downfall of
this strategy was that when a promising new drug failed in its
much-publicized trials, Wall Street was quick to punish the company responsible. One possible solution in lieu of growing ever
larger, Bain & Company notes, would have been to organize business units based on their therapeutic function.

Media companies faced similar problems of scale. For a time,
the prevailing wisdom was that to succeed in an industry where
product-development costs were growing ever higher, a company
must become large, too. Sony Corporation, with its forays into
music and films, was one of the first companies to act on that idea.
The French firm Vivendi Universal, the German company Bertels-
mann, and, of course, the U.S. media giant AOL Time Warner followed a similar course. The theory was that a product could be
developed, then marketed through a wide range of in-house channels, from compact disks and DVDs, to Web sites and theme
parks. Yet the best ideas on paper don't always translate seamlessly to real life. Looking at the conglomeritization of media companies, the *Wall Street Journal* noted that "The result is a
sprawling mix of businesses that each have their own set of problems—many of which are now coming to a head at once."

To illustrate, during the first part of 2003, many of these companies were busy scouring their upper management ranks, according to the article, with the hope, perhaps, that some as yet
undiscovered talent might devise a way to lead the disparate organizations. But this would likely prove difficult, because the skill
set needed to run, say, a movie studio was quite different from that
required to manage a theme park, and very few people have the
talent for both. The newspaper noted that "it may turn out that
these companies have grown too large and complicated for anyone
to manage."[9]

Fast on Their Feet and Level-Headed

By some accounts, small-scale entrepreneurs stand a better chance of succeeding in their growth strategies than do large corporations. For one thing, they tend to be more conservative, for the simple reason that their own livelihood is at stake. Moreover, the successful business they've already launched in all probability represents their life's work, their proudest achievement. That said, when small business entrepreneurs do expand, they're apt to be more patient than their large-company colleagues are. No one from Wall Street is looking over their shoulders. And although they pay attention to numbers and want a profit, they're usually more willing to nurture their startups than a larger corporation is apt to be.

The ear-to-the-ground attitude of small business operators may also help them avoid another problem that leads even the largest companies to fail—ignoring paradigm shifts.

CHAPTER
6

Ignoring
Paradigm Shifts

Just think of certain things you do now that were unknown 10, 20, or 30 years ago, and you'll understand how common paradigm shifts are in our culture: instant messaging a colleague via your cell phone, renting a DVD, downloading an MP3 file, or laying in a supply of Cipro as a precaution against an anthrax attack. Paradigm shifts are an inevitable consequence of technological society. In ages past, humankind needed to adapt only to changes in the seasons. The natural world around our ancestors remained a dependable constant—albeit a dangerous and often uncomfortable one. Humankind learned to use technology to shield itself from this environment. All too well, as it turns out. Someone once observed that unforeseen consequences have sprung from this successful cultural adaptation. While obviating the need to adapt to a natural environment, mankind ensured the necessity of continually adapting to the artificial and ever-changing technological environment that humans themselves created. Ironic, isn't it? It leads one to speculate: Perhaps this learned ability to continually adapt to new circumstances is the real secret to our species' success.

Notwithstanding, paradigm shifts paralyze modern-day civilization as effectively as a flood or earthquake disrupted mankind's activities in times before these natural phenomenon were clearly understood. Perhaps nothing better illustrates the devastating power of a paradigm shift more than the crash of 1987, a day of infamy, better known as Black Monday. Thanks to little understood yet profound change in the way the world's cash and equity resources were being leveraged, the global economic system took a tumble from which some believe only luck and some quick thinking saved us. And many companies found themselves at the crossroads of survival and ruin.

The Long Road to Black Monday

During the 1980s, the average American profited indirectly from the rising stock market through mutual funds or pension funds. While ownership of individual stocks was hardly pervasive, mutual funds came into their own during the 1980s, growing from some $95 billion at the start of the decade to over $1 trillion by 1990.[1]

But the real profits in this era were won by professional traders—the high-flying leveraged buyout specialists as well as global financiers like George Soros, who could rock markets with huge bets. Soros and a short list of his peers led a cadre of megatraders who understood the frightening leverage provided by derivatives, such as options and futures. As financial author Gregory J. Millman revealed in his book *The Vandal's Crown: How Rebel Currency Traders Overthrew the World's Central Banks,* in the hands of the right person, derivatives were to the financial markets what nuclear weapons were to warfare. And during the 1980s, derivatives began trading in increasing amounts in exchanges in Europe, Asia, and the United States.

The megatraders of the period were joined by yet another new breed of trader, the so-called quants (quantitative analysts). Quants were also known as rocket scientists. Financial geniuses all—at least in the ethereal realms of financial theory—rocket scientists tended to be shy, brooding, academic types, notably lacking in the killer instincts that many professional traders possess.

Nevertheless, brokerages desperately sought out leading rocket scientists from the nation's top universities, knowing that the survival of their business might depend on having their talents on board. That is because rocket scientists, like megatraders, understood well what few of the officers or traders at these houses did, namely, the absurdly complex relationship between stock or currency prices and the prices of their respective derivative products. More important, the rocket scientists knew how to program computers to exploit these relationships, a practice that became known as programmed trading.

The new breed of traders were further empowered by the fact that world markets were becoming increasingly intertwined, even as the systems linking them together were new, somewhat fragile, and largely untested—all the more reason that those systems could be exploited by those smart enough to understand how they worked.

The result in several instances was havoc on a grandiose scale. The 1980s was characterized by a series of dangerous financial shocks that reverberated around the world and with frightening speed. They included the Mexico debt crisis, the Continental Illinois Bank crisis, the Ohio savings-and-loan crisis, and the stock market crash of 1987. Each debacle came about in an environment where the old rigid checks that had once reined in the world's financial systems were fast giving way to something far less predictable and controllable.

Things Become Unhinged

The old financial systems first began unwinding in 1971. That was the year that President Nixon led the industrialized nations in abandoning the Bretton Woods Agreement, which had maintained order in the financial system since World War II. The United States would no longer make dollars convertible into gold at a fixed exchange rate. Thus, other world currencies linked to the dollar would no longer have a predictable, agreed-on value. Instead, they would be allowed to float up and down in relation to one another. Their value would be based largely on the perceived fortunes of each country at a particular moment. In an era dominated by the Cold War and frequent Mideast crises, a nation's fortunes could change rapidly in the eyes of the market.

Yet by March 1973, all the world's major currencies had adopted floating exchange rates, which introduced yet another variable into the world's already volatile equities markets. Since a company's assets were denominated in its home currency, the value of those assets as reflected in the stock price would move somewhat in tandem with the denominating currency.

Unfortunately, this major sea change to the financial system came at a time when rising oil prices as well as severe price rises in other commodities and real estate led to a protracted period of higher inflation that reached double-digit levels in 1979. Inflation only amplified the destabilizing effects of delinking currencies to gold. Under Chairman Paul Volker, the Federal Reserve mounted an aggressive anti-inflation campaign from 1979 to 1982 that eventually succeeded in reining in inflation. The savings-and-loan crisis was collateral damage.

Stocks also declined as money flowed from equity markets into debt instruments. Little wonder that while stocks churned, money markets yielded a virtually riskless 18 percent annual return. Companies strapped with draconian interest payments saw their earnings wither. The result was that during 1981–82, the United States experienced its worst economic slowdown since the 1930s.

Pennies from Heaven

But as often happens in the equities markets, out of the depths of decline comes a new beginning. And the cause can often be one or more catalysts that had previously been ignored. One of those catalysts was the personal computer revolution brought about in large part by fledgling young computer tech companies. These companies promised to radically change the face of business: The paperless office would allow companies to operate faster, cheaper, and better. Companies hoping to remain competitive would have no choice but to plant a personal computer on every worker's desk.

Meanwhile, the stock market, blue chips especially, was in the throes of a rebound. The impetus was big money, specifically overseas money that mostly sought out powerhouse U.S. firms. Roughly $198 billion in overseas money circulated in the U.S. capital markets in 1980. By decade's end, that amount was nearly $4.2 trillion.[2] Much of it came from Japan, where an economic bubble of near biblical proportions was in progress. Real estate values in Tokyo reached such preposterous levels that the few acres of land within the royal palace for a time exceeded the value of every building on every street in Manhattan, and the total value of real estate in Tokyo exceeded the value of all the property in the United States. The U.S. stock markets offered a relatively safe way for the Japanese to leverage that value.

Big Board stocks got another boost from the takeover barons who put companies on Dickensian regimens in order to squeeze more value out of their share prices. Speculators like Ivan Boesky bought shares of companies that seemed ripe for a corporate raid, boosting their share prices, while a tangent industry led by Michael Milken dreamed up imaginative ways to finance those raids.

The result was a speculative buying frenzy based on very little that was substantive. The money flowing into U.S. markets from overseas did bolster stock prices. But it did not make companies necessarily more productive. Likewise, the share price boost reaped from a hostile takeover often had more to do with increased speculative demand for those shares than with any improvement the raiders hoped to make in the company they had snatched. Nevertheless, overseas investors and the raiders at home succeeded in pumping up the volume on the exchanges. Trading on the NASDAQ at the time was near 150 million shares per day, for example, less than one-tenth of its present level, but within striking distance of the 189 million shares then traded daily on the Big Board.[3] Share prices in the United States rose to post–World War II highs between 1983 and 1987.

Something had to snap. The signs were clear. Volatility increased, as it always does during the crazed weeks before a crash. On Black Monday, the Dow dropped more than 500 points, hastily dispatching almost $1 trillion in aggregate market capitalization to "money heaven." The NASDAQ, meanwhile, lost roughly 100 points.

And panic reigned. People waited on the phone for hours to get through to their brokers. A popular joke following the crash asked how to get a broker down from a tree. The answer: Cut the rope.

Markets and Metamarkets

So, beyond the fact that markets were being pumped higher by speculators and overseas investors, why did stocks fall so suddenly? Some said that investors feared a renewed rise in interest rates. Others blamed the huge Reagan budget deficits as well as America's growing trade deficit with Japan. Still others cited rumblings in Congress to limit future takeovers, thus putting an end to the rallies they had sparked.

If those were the root causes, a spark of some kind was still needed. That spark, according to many, was provided by the enormous, nearly-out-of-control derivatives markets. As *Time* magazine correspondent John Greenwald described it, a hidden universe of futures and options investments by the market's big players had emerged. Valued at a breathtaking $14 trillion, it amounted to more than three times the aggregate value of NYSE stocks traded in an entire month. "Much of the smart money is really riding on computer-generated hypersophisticated financial instruments that use the public's massive bet on securities to create a parallel universe of side bets and speculative mutations," Greenwald wrote.[4]

By the 1980s, this parallel universe of derivative investments had become global in scale, and it closely linked currencies with the world's stock and debt markets. Corporations were among the heaviest users of derivatives—since futures and options allowed a company to hedge the cost of raw materials, their own stock price, as well as the non-dollar-denominated value of their assets worldwide. Institutional investors, hedge funds, and securities firms also turned to the derivatives market for both hedging and speculating, drawing the linkages between markets into an ever-tightening knot. There are "interlocking commitments of trillions of dollars," famed investment banker Felix Rohatyn was quoted by *Time*. The world economy would likely remain safe from catastrophe so long as the markets and the relationships they encompassed functioned smoothly.

But expect the world financial system to go into arrhythmia if these commitments ever broke down, he mused.[5] Tightening the knot even further were the new light-speed trading networks and globe-spanning exchange-linkages. What happened in the U.S. markets seamlessly carried over to trading in Tokyo and then to Europe the instant those exchanges opened for business. In addition, changes in stock values were reflected instantly in the prices of their derivative products—at least that was how it was supposed to happen. At times, minute differences existed between the value of derivatives and stocks. On Black Monday, those differences widened into chasms.

Countdown to Meltdown

On October 15, 1987, the House Ways and Means Committee approved a bill that would have disallowed interest deductions on debt used to pay for a corporate takeover.[6] That may well have provided the initial spark. Whatever the case, when markets opened the following Monday, the computer programs that had been devised by the rocket scientists triggered sell orders. Momentum grew as mutual fund shareholders called their brokers to cash out. This meant that the mutual fund managers needed to liquidate shares in order to pay defecting shareholders in cash. The problem was that by this time, the cascade of orders was deluging both the NYSE and the NASDAQ.

Indeed, some market makers on the NASDAQ reportedly refused to answer the phone. Lacking buyers other than the market makers themselves, some stocks ceased trading altogether. Trading in option contracts of the affected stocks at the Chicago Board Options Exchange (CBOE) was likewise halted. The result, in the minds of many analysts who have looked at the 1987 crash, was a dangerous disconnect between the derivatives markets and the equities markets. In other words, the prices of equities were no longer predictive of the prices of derivatives and vice versa. Stock index futures began selling at a large discount and even ceased trading for a time. In the back offices of the financial powerhouses, there was real reason to panic. Rumors circulated that banks were refusing to extend loans to brokers to bail them out. The system appeared on the brink of collapse.

Some claimed that luck was the only reason the world financial system avoided disaster. But prompt action by the government also played a role. No one was about to repeat President Herbert Hoover's mistake during the crash of 1929 and keep silent. Thus, both the White House and the Treasury Department made coordinated announcements aimed at calming public fears. Hasty phone meetings took place between officials at the U.S. Treasury and their counterparts in London, Tokyo, and elsewhere. All agreed to pump liquidity into the markets. Still, by noon on October 20, the market continued to drop. Rumors and misinformation continued to spread up and down the Street, including one rumor that several major market participants, among them a major clearinghouse, were about to fail. Meanwhile, brokerage firms, swamped with customer orders, pressured the NYSE and the National Association of Securities Dealers (NASD) to close their markets down. The markets might well have closed. But in the darkest hour, the first tentative signs of a turnaround emerged. A faint all-clear signal came from the derivatives markets that had sparked the downfall in the first place. Stock index futures contracts began ticking upward. By Friday, calm had been mostly restored. As a General Accounting Office study of the crash later put it dryly, "The market break was extraordinary in terms of the speed and extent of falling prices and skyrocketing trading volume. This crisis showed that the size and potential impact of increased linkages between the equities markets and futures markets could change the character of a financial crisis."[7]

Space: The Ultimate Money Pit

If paradigm shifts in the ethereal realm of high finance have the power to plunge the world's financial system into chaos and without warning, individual companies would seem to have as much chance of surviving as flotsam in a tidal wave. And history shows that many have not fared well. From the time the Pony Express was replaced by the telegraph, to the pre-Internet bulletin boards that couldn't compete with the World Wide Web, to the small-town shops that couldn't compete with the new regional shopping mall, to the malls themselves that faced serious new threats from so-called big-box retailers, examples of failure to adapt form a vast organizational graveyard over the landscape of business.

Much of the remainder of this chapter will look at one of the most notable and large-scale failures on the part of an entire industry. Specifically, these multiple failures resulted from paradigm shifts that occurred in the satellite broadband industry. This industry is devoted to bringing high-speed Internet access directly to people's homes via a satellite dish, in the same way that direct TV delivers cable stations to a rooftop dish instead of by coaxial cable. The failures in this business are especially remarkable, because many intelligent people bet many millions of dollars on a technology that, in hindsight, seems to have been doomed from the outset.

Yet there's a good reason for this. As it turns out, delivering broadband Internet services from space has always appeared seductively simple. All you need to do, it seems, is launch a single satellite into geostationary earth orbit (GEO) at a cost of roughly

$300 million, and you can theoretically link together hundreds of thousands of users back on earth, instantly, and for a lot less money than it would cost cable or DSL providers to connect to each of those subscribers individually via hardwire. Yet the satellite industry has never managed to fully capitalize on this business model. Instead, it has succeeded only in offering service that is typically more expensive and less reliable than its competitors. As a result, satellite broadband has ranked a distant third behind cable and DSL, in terms of the number of subscribers.

A few years ago, however, major companies in the industry began to bet millions that they could leapfrog the competition by using promising new paradigm-shifting technologies developed by NASA in the '90s. Those technologies included ultra-thin spot beams and advanced onboard routing. As you'll see, some also hoped to win over consumers by bundling broadband with direct-to-home TV, including local stations. In Europe, Asia, and North America, several new GEO satellite broadband services planned to come online during 2003 and beyond. Their efforts played out while the economy was still struggling. And many in the tech press wondered whether these new-generation satellite ISPs would be able to attract users in meaningful numbers.

Hard ACTS to Follow

The answer to that question largely determined the course of the satellite broadband industry for years to come, not to mention the survival of multibillion-dollar organizations. To understand how the industry arrived at this critical juncture, however, let's look at NASA's role in developing these proposed new-generation satellites and how satellite broadband service had the potential to improve dramatically as a result.

Shift back to the pre-Internet era. During the late '70s, information traffic over satellites continued to increase. Much of it consisted of bandwidth-hogging analog phone conversations and TV transmissions. A NASA study at the time concluded that existing capacity in the C and Ku bands—the principal regions of the spectrum used by satellites then—would be wiped out by the early '90s. So planners set their sights on higher frequencies to meet the world's expanding future needs. In particular, they focused on the 20–30 GHz Ka band. To exploit that as-yet-untapped slice of the spectrum, the agency launched what it would eventually call the Advanced Communications Technology Satellite program (ACTS) in 1980. The program's goal: to develop a proof-of-concept Ka-band GEO satellite that would serve as a model for future civilian and military platforms.

As ACTS program veterans Richard T. Gedney, Ronald Schertler, and Frank Gargione describe in their book *The Advanced Communications Technology Satellite* (SciTech), spot beams quickly became a key element of the design. The term *spot beam* refers to the coverage area or footprint of the satellite, the area within which both upstream and downstream communications can be sent. Up to that point, satellites had typically transmitted their entire allotted spectrum onto a single continent-spanning footprint. Which is to say, the signal that TV viewers in New York saw emanated from the same antenna as the signal that viewers received in Los Angeles.

A large footprint works fine if you're broadcasting the *U.S. Open* to a nationwide audience. But it's an inefficient approach to the kind of interactive communications that form the basis of the Internet. That's where NASA's ACTS program brought satellite communications to a new level. The experimental satellite that began operations in 1993 demonstrated that instead of a single beam, satellites could cast down multiple beams, creating footprints as narrow as 120 miles in diameter.

Using both fixed and moving antenna, the prototype ACTS satellite also created beams that could "hop" from one location to the next. One possible use of the hopping beams might be to provide a reserve communications link in the event of an outage. In a time of war, hopping beams might also relay critical communications from a number of battlefields to headquarters.

But multiple spot beams had another important use. Theoretically, an ACTS-inspired satellite containing many smaller antennae could project a grid of spot beams to thoroughly cover, say, North America. To do this, the satellite would divide up its allotted spectrum. Contiguous beams could operate at different frequencies (within the allotted spectral range), to prevent interference. The result would be a kind of black and white mosaic of alternating frequency deployment, projected across a huge portion of the globe. By reusing its allotted frequency in this way, a spot beam satellite could handle roughly 10 times the traffic as a satellite casting a single wide beam.

Advanced Onboard Routing

In addition to spot beams, NASA's ACTS prototype incorporated a far more sophisticated method of onboard routing of signals than had ever been attempted before. Routing refers to how signals are directed from one source to another. Earlier communications satellites simply received and then retransmitted signals used for telephone conversations, TV programs, and data transmissions. The aerospace term for this is *bent pipe architecture*, which simply means that data streamed skyward is "bent" by the satellite, enabling it to shower back down to earth.

However, recall that the ACTS satellite was designed to transmit multiple spot beams simultaneously. This required that each of the spot beams have a separate transponder, which is the transmitting and, in some cases, the incorporated receiving device. It also meant that the transponders—if they were to handle Internet traffic—needed to be linked together on board the satellite so that an e-mail sender in, say, Cleveland, could reach a recipient in San Francisco.

Carrying aboard all this processing capability has its pros and cons. "Geostationary satellites are not going to be serviced," joked one engineering professor involved in ACTS-related research. "You really want to make the spacecraft as simple and as reliable as possible and also provide the maximum amount of flexibility on the ground." To boost reliability, designers typically build in a 25-percent redundancy in transponders.

But that added investment can pay off, because more sophisticated onboard processing allows more varied, less-expensive ground-station designs. The latter is vital to keeping the costs of satellite dishes low. Remember, the success of satellite systems being launched would be based on their ability to attract consumers who would otherwise opt for cable. This meant that the receiving equipment had to be cheap enough that consumers would be willing to buy it at their local Wal-Mart.

Combating Signal Latency

As it turns out, handling the processing aboard the satellite—as opposed to doing it on the ground—had one other important benefit. It helped compensate for signal latency. Particularly with the point-to-point applications typical of Internet protocol (IP), the routing aboard a satellite is often faster than would occur with terrestrial networks, where data packets may navigate through 30 or more routers. In fact, the signal propagation delay due to the satellite's orbital position was responsible for only half of the signal latency.

High Hopes

Capitalizing on the spot beam and advanced onboard routing techniques pioneered by ACTS, several major satellite industry firms announced plans to launch new GEO satellite broadband services. All planned to operate in the Ka band. A Thailand-based group called iPSTAR hoped to begin broadband service in Asia late in 2003. Also among the entrants is a European consortium made up of telecom giant Alcatel, along with veteran satellite firms Gilat Satellite Networks and SES Global, which announced plans for broadband service on the Continent and in the United States, perhaps in 2004.

In North America, the biggest player likely would have been a new company formed via the proposed merger of EchoStar and Hughes-owned DirecTV. Both companies already delivered direct-to-home TV and broadband Internet services via their existing GEO satellites. The planned merger would enable the new company to consolidate channels and thus offer more bandwidth to Internet subscribers. In addition, the merged satellite provider hoped to offer local TV stations in over 200 markets, together with the usual national cable channels. Subscribers would receive both TV and broadband via a single dish. Such bundling, discussed in more detail further on, was seen as key to winning over subscribers. The merger—hotly contested by competitors—eventually received a thumbs-down from the FCC, however. And at press time speculation continues over whether one or both of these companies will seek another partner.

Down to Earth

Backers of each proposed new service saw a substantial existing customer base, what EchoStar chairman Charles W. Ergen once called "the digital 'have nots' in the U.S., the 40 million households with no access to DSL or cable modem service." Those customers could be connected by satellite for infinitely less than it would take to hook them up via upgraded cable or DSL, much less fiber optic cable.

But if the services were to succeed, they needed to overcome at least two major hurdles, the first being a not-so-starry economy. The second was satellite broadband's short, but thus far spotty, performance record and the industry's seeming inability to adjust to paradigm-shifting changes.

In the case of the former, the new launches were back-dropped by a still-dismal telecom sector—where gargantuan debt, coupled with a massive terrestrial bandwidth glut, have rocked giant companies like Global Crossing, Worldcom, and Qwest. The planned launches would also follow fledgling efforts by Iridium, Teledesic, and GlobalStar, which were set up to deliver voice and data to customers' portable devices using clusters of networked low-earth-orbit satellites. Both the original Iridium and GlobalStar filed Chapter 11, leaving investors wary of backing any new satellite ventures.

Then there was GEO satellite broadband's image problem. Early versions were cumbersome, letting Internet surfers receive signals only via their 1-meter dishes. The "uplink" was created through a standard dial-up connection and then routed to a centralized satellite transmitter. Even so, maximum downstream speeds were limited to 400 kbs—one-third the bandwidth that some cable modem subscribers receive. The satellites used were based on pre-ACTS designs. So users shared a network within the satellite's wide footprint. For this reason, connection speeds often dropped precipitously during heavy traffic periods.

As a result, in the words of one industry analyst, such services had not proved "competitive with cable or DSL." Prices for satellite broadband can reach $75 per month, versus $50 for cable or DSL. Bandwidth is more constrained. Moreover, the performance simply isn't there, both because of bandwidth constraints and the aforementioned signal latency. For that reason, satellite broadband had a tradition of being largely restricted to rural areas that were not adequately served by its cable or DSL competitors.

Compounding the consumer acceptance problem, cable and phone service subscribers might view cable broadband or DSL as a simple upgrade. Whereas, satellite requires consumers to mount seemingly cumbersome antennae on their rooftops.

Co-Location, Co-Location, Co-Location

Satellite broadband had one secret weapon: DTH TV. By co-locating two or more satellites in the same orbital neighborhood, both broadband and TV services can be accessed from the same rooftop dish. Europe's SES GLOBAL has been especially successful at co-location, explains a former ACTS project manager. Seven of SES GLOBAL's satellites reside at the 19.2-degree East orbital slot, for example. Indeed, SES reportedly has a wide assignment of spectrum, which meant that any single satellite might utilize only a small portion of the company's total allotment. Co-location could be a boom to nonindustrialized nations, allowing them to upgrade Internet, TV, and telephone services at relatively little cost.

Co-location also appeared to be part of the business plans of at least two companies hoping to launch new GEO satellite broadband services in industrial nations. Here in the United States for example, EchoStar and DirecTV, hoping to win public support for their doomed merger, ran full-page newspaper ads describing their plan to bundle broadband and TV services through a combined fleet of 16 satellites, 5 of which would be spot-beam enabled. "The merger will eliminate the need for each company to transmit more than 500 channels of duplicative programming," DirecTV chairman Eddy W. Hartenstein told a Senate committee in March.

SES AMERICOM, a branch of the aforementioned European firm with expertise at co-locating satellites, likewise hoped to bundle broadband with TV. In late April, SES petitioned the FCC to locate a DTH satellite at the 105.5-degree West slot. The company also holds a Ka-band license for the same location. Although the company would not confirm this, the Ka-band slot would likely be used for broadband. Dean Olmstead, president and CEO of SES AMERICOM, said as much when he addressed the Satellite Entertainment conference held in late April 2002 in Monterey. "TV and broadband will be available to U.S. consumers who purchase a single, small satellite dish and related equipment, into which the latest two-way digital technologies have been incorporated." Service could begin in 2004.

Such bundled packages might well prove to be satellite broadband's killer application. Companies like EchoStar and SES AMERICOM might also stealthily add IP in the form of interactive TV and e-commerce, leapfrogging the clunky offerings currently available via digital cable. Only time would tell if such services would finally place GEO satellite broadband on par with cable and DSL, or, alternately, if satellite broadband would remain that third choice, used largely by those who can't be reached via terrestrial links.

LEO Satellites, Robot Blimps, and Flying Wings

Yet time was running out. Even as these GEO services were putting the finishing touches on their business and financial plans, others were devising paradigm-shifting alternate ways to deliver broadband services to areas ranging in size from individual communities to the entire world. In some cases, these new delivery platforms would likely prove cheaper than a GEO satellite. In other cases, they would prove outlandishly more expensive. Yet all had one thing in common.

As it happened, higher wasn't necessarily better when it came to sky-based Internet services. At least, some major companies and their backers believed that to be the case. The reason, they said, is that the lower the platform, the less power it would take to transmit a signal, while the signal latency problems that plague GEO satellites would disappear.

But, as proponents have discovered, good technology doesn't always translate into a viable business model. What's more, newer technologies can quickly render obsolete even the best of schemes.

Witness Iridium. Originally backed by a Motorola-led group, it lofted a network of low-earth-orbit (LEO) satellites to create a global mobile phone service. Customers failed to sign on, however, despite an ambitious branding campaign. By some accounts, the company's backers, which lost a bundle from its demise, greatly overestimated the size of the market and also the rate at which consumers would adapt to the new service. Most people, as it turned out, did not need a seamless communications link wherever in the world they happened to be. In fact, the people who traveled en masse most, that is business travelers, were more likely to stay within cities where Iridium phones' signals could be blocked by buildings. Cheaper and equally reliable communications media also tended to be plentiful in cities. The market for global communications was thus limited to companies such as oil and mining concerns with operations in remote parts of the globe along with far-roaming journalists and yachtsmen. Emerging from bankruptcy, Iridium has successfully resumed operations under new ownership. (See chapter 10, for more about Iridium.)

More ambitious still were Teledesic's original plans to create a $37 billion LEO broadband service in the sky. Backed by multi-billionaires Bill Gates, Craig McCaw, and others, Teledesic sought to launch 405 satellites. Collectively, they would serve up bandwidth at an astounding 3 terabits per second, an amount roughly akin to 2 million T1 lines. Scaled back dramatically, plans later called for an initial fleet of 12 satellites, later growing to 30.

Meanwhile, as this book went to press GlobalStar, with a network of 72 satellites already in place, was emerging from a Chapter 11 filing. The company continues to provide worldwide phone service and data services.

Analysts say that backers of Iridium, Teledesic, and GlobalStar failed to factor in the growth of competing mobile networks. Thanks to new mobile phone designs, for example, travelers can call virtually anywhere from virtually anywhere else, using the same phone, and will pay less than LEO satellite services charge. That fact limited LEO satellite services to customers who are still beyond the reach of ever-expanding land-based networks. Worse, faced with a diminishing base of potential customers, the LEO satellite services are nevertheless weighed down by the huge costs of lofting and maintaining a network of satellites.

Big Balloons and Planes

Which is why three other groups set their sights even lower than low-earth orbit, unveiling plans to loft suborbital platforms over major population areas. Specifically, they planned to use blimps or powered aircraft, the latter either piloted or remote controlled.

Former secretary of state and United Technologies chieftain Alexander M. Haig, Jr., was behind one venture, called Sky Station International Inc. Sky Station proposed to employ solar-powered, remotely operated blimps, flying at a lofty 21 km. The blimps would furnish third generation (3G) wireless services to an area about 1,000 miles in diameter. Using onboard switching systems, the giant lighter-than-air "routers" would project down as many as 1,000 spot beams per platform, enabling data feeds of up to 2 Mbs for mobile users. Later, using the 47 GHz spectrum, Sky Station planners hope to achieve downlink speeds of up to 10 Mbs. Sky Station wants to build a fleet of 250 blimps worldwide—each with a five-year lifespan. If a blimp goes awry, backers say that it could be brought down remotely or, in a worst-case scenario, piloted out to sea.

NASA helped to fund another broadband-in-the-sky venture called SkyTower. The venture's ethereal-looking, robot-piloted flying wing, powered by solar cells, was tested to a record 23 km. It was based in Monrovia, California, and like Sky Station's blimps, it too would receive and send signals presumably from fixed and mobile users.

Finally, yet another California company, called Angel Technologies, hoped to launch fleets of piloted aircraft that resemble the military's AWAC planes for the same purpose.

A network of blimps or oddly shaped drone planes hardly seems an elegant solution to last-mile bandwidth connections. However, all three business plans take pains to point out the advantages of suborbital ISPs. It's far cheaper to launch a plane or a blimp than a satellite. Plus, the technology is highly scalable. A single plane or a blimp can theoretically bring everything from mobile video conferencing to IP telephony to millions of customers.

Still, some people aren't sure that these systems won't be supplanted by other paradigm-shifting technologies. Long before suborbital routers reach the skies, usage of these paradigm-shifting technologies could grow in the millions in the years ahead.

Pie-in-the-sky ideas include inexpensive repeaters that might occupy the tops of telephone poles or street lamps, providing ubiquitous broadband communication to fixed and mobile users.

Hybrid Networks

The multibillion-dollar question arising from the previous case is a simple one: How could satellite broadband's proponents have avoided leaping into their grandiose schemes? The perhaps too-obvious answer is that satellites' backers championed a high-orbit solution to delivering broadband, whereas the financial interests funding them had no such bias. It was the latter's role as cash supplier to look at far-flung solutions to delivering the same connection. And in doing that, they undoubtedly saw the handwriting on the wall.

In the end, neither satellite broadband nor any of the schemes involving blimps or endlessly circling aircraft seems likely to depose the cable system. Instead, the real threat appears to be from wireless, as urban office buildings and suburban neighborhoods quickly got wired up with far-less-expensive Wi-Fi connections. Yet as technology moves forever forward, this case study of nearly constant paradigm shifts is far from over. A newer and even cheaper technology could one day replace Wi-Fi: What some see as an endless mosaic of peer-to-peer relays, in which everyone's cell phone, PDA, or wireless laptop becomes part of a cooperative network that transmits signals from one device to another.

Yet satellite-borne communications will always have a place. Ironically, while some major satellite industry firms prepared platforms to deliver broadband directly to consumers' rooftop dish receivers, others saw a better use for ISPs in the sky—and that is to use satellites in combination with terrestrial networks. The end result, called a hybrid network, draws on the strength of both to catapult over many of the Web's traditional bottlenecks. Hybrid networks may prove especially useful in the delivery of live content.

Here's how: Suppose you want to view a CEO speech or a sports event online. Normally, your request competes with that of everyone else who accesses the same Web site—a major source of delays. Then, on its way to your computer, that request may go through 30 or more routers, any of which could cause further delays. Although this isn't a significant problem if you're watching a downloaded movie trailer, a backlog will cause annoying glitches if you're viewing a live Web cast.

So-called server farms, which store popular content and distribute them to ISPs, eliminate some of the hops. And as a result, they can speed up delivery of bandwidth-hogging content like music files. But server farms are ill suited to simulcast live events.

Enter satellites, with their acknowledged strength as a broadcast medium. Under some networking schemes satellites can transmit content to numerous ISPs simultaneously. In this instance, latency hardly matters, because everyone receives the event at a nearly identical time.

Of course, it's not that simple. One vexing issue with hybrid networks is finding an optimal transmission rate that will minimize packet loss when you're dealing with many different kinds of receivers. Leading the research efforts to overcome such problems is the NASA-sponsored Center for Satellite and Hybrid Communication Networks at the University of Maryland (www.isr.umd .edu/CSHCN/).

New Technologies, New Challenges

Direct broadcast satellites aptly demonstrate how paradigm shifts can occur even over a span of months and can cost companies billions as a result. In the future, rapid and fundamental shifts could well become even more the norm. A recent issue of a technology magazine[8] amply illustrated that fact, detailing four earth-shattering new technological shifts that may come to pass over the next 10 or 20 years. Alone, each is the likely equivalent of the shift from coal to oil power or the invention of the computer. That is, if they succeed. The far-sighted companies involved in developing these technologies stand to be on the forefront of self-created technological revolutions. Or, just as likely, they could end up spending untold millions, with little to show. Worse, they might well have bet wrong, and while the elusive technology they pursue fails to fulfill its promise, some other company working toward a quite different paradigm shift will find itself at the forefront instead.

Cars That Create Water

Perhaps no major company has made a larger bet on the future of its fundamental product than General Motors. Knowing, as we all do, that the world's oil supplies are destined to run out at some point, GM has reportedly invested "hundreds of millions" of dollars on developing cars able to run on petroleum's replacement—namely, hydrogen. In doing so, the company needed to begin from scratch and create an alternative to the enormous infrastructure that exists to build, fuel, and repair gasoline-powered cars. Moreover, in the process, GM has fundamentally redesigned the car of the future, as well as how it will be paid for, will be driven, and will contribute to society.

For starters, GM's car redesign will be powered by hydrogen-consuming fuel cells, a technology that's far more complicated and therefore expensive than the highly evolved piston engine. Because of that cost factor, GM engineers opted for a kind of modular approach to their car of the future. Families might own just one fuel cell for decades. To make it affordable, car payments will be restructured to resemble home mortgages.

The fuel cell that customers purchase will be linked to a chassis. Four electric motors, one connected to each wheel, will supply the power. As for the car body, people will continue to want the latest styles, thus old, outmoded bodies will be removed and recycled every so many years, to be replaced by all-new ones that more or less snap into place like a child's toy.

GM planners devised another ingenious way to offset the cost of the car. Most autos, it turns out, sit idle during the bulk of the day—a waste of resources, when you think about it. GM planners believe that the company's hydrogen cars, when not in use, can be plugged into a power grid to supply electricity to a home or even be connected to the national power grid.

And what about the fuel itself, hydrogen? Indeed, there are many ways to store it: as a gas, as a frigid liquid, or—the most promising, perhaps—as a solid. Researchers are looking at ways to cram hydrogen molecules into tiny holes created in carbon material, called nanotubes. It's possible that instead of visiting a gas station to refuel our hydrogen cars, we may visit an auto shop to have a fresh slab of hydrogen-saturated carbon bolted into the car's trunk every six months—yet another paradigm shift that should be of concern to the filling station industry.

Quantum Leaps

And what are some other new technologies destined to profoundly change the way we live and work? One of the most bizarre and earth-shattering is so-called quantum computing. This technology offers an exponential and perhaps unfathomable increase in storage and computational power. All computers today are based on digital logic. The tiny transistors—millions of them—at the heart of today's devices perform by signaling whether they are in one of two strictly defined states: on or off, which can be taken to mean yes or no or the numbers 0 and 1. In the quirky and difficult-to-understand subatomic world of quantum mechanics, particles are able to manifest themselves in more than one state simultaneously. Because of this, they are theoretically capable of performing, in mere seconds, calculations that it would take all the computers on earth all the time remaining in the life of the universe to perform. Such astounding power will no doubt lead to true artificial intelligence and, beyond that, to paradigm-shifting changes that we can barely imagine.

One of the companies most involved in quantum computer research is Microsoft. At first glance, this would seem a departure for a company that is almost entirely devoted to software and its relatively near-term applications. But as those involved with Microsoft's research maintain, an understanding of quantum computers is essential if Microsoft is to write the software that drives them.

Changing History

If there's a lesson to learn from GM and its hydrogen car and Microsoft and its quantum computer, it's an obvious one: that companies attempting to effect paradigm-shifting changes must have at their disposal gargantuan resources. Other, more limited, examples are also available. The first businesses that located in the newly freed nations of Eastern Europe and the Soviet Union found that their mere presence constituted a paradigm shift from the way business had been conducted under communism for decades. There was little or no infrastructure in place, of the type they were familiar with. No wholesalers were waiting in the wings to bid on the business of Moscow's newest McDonald's restaurant, and no trucking firms were at the ready to transport the buns and ketchup envelopes to the chain's expanding franchises. McDonald's and other companies that relocated in the newly freed Eastern Bloc had to create that infrastructure themselves—at a huge cost, no doubt. But the benefits, serving a large percentage of the world's population, were also huge. Again, those companies entering the Eastern Bloc often succeeded, based on the fact that they possessed the resources to persevere. Countless other less-well-funded ventures undoubtedly succumbed to the vagaries of postcommunist capitalism.

The same failures are also prone to occur in societies such as ours, with a well-developed capitalist infrastructure. How often have new products brought down companies because they were too far ahead of the curve? You have only to think of the many doomed Internet ventures for examples. Companies that asked us to buy our groceries, music, and pet supplies online were among the casualties of the dot-com bomb. As for the companies that succeeded, think of eBay and Yahoo. Both worked to develop online communities, as much as to produce revenues. Their focus was strictly customer-centric. And as you'll see in the next chapter, any company that deviates from that focus greatly increases the odds of its own destruction.

CHAPTER

7

Ignoring Customers

Way back in the 1920s, Montgomery Ward found itself engaged in a fierce battle with rival Sears Roebuck. Together, both companies dominated the national retailing scene. And, in fact, both were examples of how a business could efficiently expand from the isolated local markets that were the norm in that era to serve an entire region and then become a force throughout a nation—even one as geographically diverse as the United States. To reach their customers from Arizona to Maine, both Montgomery Ward and Sears had turned mail-order merchandising into a business art form.

Yet as Montgomery Ward struggled, year after year, with its larger and more powerful rival, Robert Wood, the second in command at the company, saw a way to break out. He argued for a revolutionary change for the company. Why not set up a national network of brick-and-mortar department stores as an adjunct to the company's famous catalog? Instead of waiting weeks to receive their merchandise, customers throughout the country could purchase the same items in a store and take them home that very day. Wouldn't customers be better served this way? The time was ripe for just such a move. The automobile was radically changing life in America. People could travel further with relative ease. Stores in cities could attract customers from the surrounding areas. Rural customers no longer solely depended on catalogs and traveling salesmen for items they needed. Nor were they content with just the essentials in life. Times were prosperous.

As it turned out, Wood's boss, CEO Theodore Merseles, had led Montgomery Ward to within striking distance of Sears's own catalog sales. And perhaps for that reason, he disagreed with his subordinate's idea. The result: Sears, correctly sensing that its future lay in brick-and-mortar retailing, succeeded in luring Wood away. With that simple move, the nation's largest department store chain was born.

In his book *When Giants Stumble,* author and business history professor Robert Sobel notes that Montgomery Ward made several crucial missteps over the decades that forever placed it behind Sears. One mistake was not being quick enough in opening department stores to augment its catalog business. Eventually, Montgomery Ward's failed strategies brought about its demise.

By being overly cautious, it hadn't stayed abreast of its customers' desires. As a result, those customers shopped elsewhere. Indeed, Montgomery Ward's caution apparently persisted, which turned customers away in ever-greater numbers. Decades later, when shopping malls gave way to boutique malls, urban festival-marketplaces, and so-called big-box retailers like Sports Mart, Montgomery Ward stuck to the old model. And, as author Sobel notes:

> [Its] stores seemed dowdy as though out of another era. In the mid-1980s the company tried to redesign itself as a collection of specialty shops, "The Seven Worlds of Ward," which included the likes of Rooms & More, Homes Ideas, Gold 'N' Gems, Auto Express, and Electric Avenue.[1]

In the end, however, the Seven Worlds makeover was too little too late. Although it succeeded in reviving sales for a time, according to Sobel, a few years later the company left the business scene. Lesson: By under-innovating, Montgomery Ward had ignored its

The Big Deal Over Odd-Eighth Quotes

What became known as the NASDAQ market-maker scandal began obscurely enough. Two professors, William Christie of Vanderbilt University and Paul Schultz of Ohio State University, announced that they'd studied a sampling of 100 of the most actively traded NASDAQ stocks during 1991. In particular, they wanted to learn how market makers quoted the prices of those stocks to investors.[4]

Market makers are the middlemen sanctioned by the stock market to buy and sell shares from those wishing to trade. The theory is that by trading through a market maker instead of directly with another investor, you are always assured that a buyer or a seller is there waiting, when you wish to enter the market. This has the effect of stabilizing prices. If market makers were not present, so the theory goes, it would be similar to attending an auction where no one wished to buy. The auctioneer would have no choice but to continually lower the price until someone was prompted to make a bid.

But back to Christie and Schultz. The two professors discovered that market makers appeared to consistently avoid quoting bid or ask prices in odd eighths.[5] To illustrate, suppose a market maker were quoting shares of *xyz* stock at 30¼ bid. Wishing to increase his inventory, for whatever reason, he might raise the price he was willing to pay. But rather than raising it to 30⅜, he would jump it to 30½, thus avoiding the odd-eighth quote. Market makers do more than post prices at which they're willing to buy shares. They post sell prices as well. And Christie and Schultz observed that when market makers posted sell or "ask" prices, they likewise avoided odd-eighth quotes.

On the surface, it appears as if the market maker is actually cheating himself out of one-eighth point per share. That is, he is paying one-eighth more by posting a bid at 30½ than he would at 30⅜. True enough. But the Christie-Schultz research implied that by avoiding odd-eighth quotes, the market makers were creating

customers, an unpardonable sin in the hotly competitive world of retailing, where consumers were offered more and more choices.

Not an Airline

Ironically, companies can also send away customers in droves by over-innovating. That happened with famed long-haul bus line Greyhound. During the '90s, it, too, was being passed by, thanks to low-priced airfares and a dramatically expanding system of regional and commuter airlines that reached from the cities deep into rural America. As a consequence, Greyhound became the transportation service that served low-income customers or those who lived beyond the reach of even the smallest airports.

Yet, as it turned out, competition from the airlines wasn't the company's biggest problem. The reason Greyhound endured humiliating losses of passengers, not to mention strikes and highly publicized bankruptcy proceedings stemmed from its decision to emulate the airlines. In 1993, the company created the same hub-and-spoke system that airlines use. So, for instance, if you wanted to travel by bus from Cleveland to Miami, you might need to connect at a regional bus terminal in Philadelphia. Adopting the hub-and-spoke system seemed like a brilliant idea, superficially. The bus company could reap the same efficiencies that airlines enjoyed, things like fast turnaround and concentrating resources in a few key locations. A bus company might save even more money than an airline by using the hub-and-spoke system, because its fixed costs from items such as buses and terminal space were but a small fraction of what airlines were forced to carry.

There was one problem, however: Customers reportedly hated the hub-and-spoke system, according to an article in *Fortune*.[2] The hub-and-spoke system is aimed more at cost savings than at customer convenience, as anyone who flies frequently can understand.

Critics charge that the system is anything but customer-friendly—namely, because it forces people to change from one connection to another or else wait in a terminal for hours. For bus travelers, the hub-and-spoke system was even worse than for air travelers. Whereas airports are at least mildly pleasant places in which to spend time, bus terminals in some locations are anything but.

However, aside from that, Greyhound's clientele posed special problems. According to *Fortune,* during the company's darkest days, 80 percent of Greyhound riders failed to show up for their reserved seats. Moreover, Greyhound was powerless to get them "to pay for [those seats] because many Greyhound customers lack credit cards."

The company's turnaround CEO Craig Lentzsch attacked this and other problems head on. His first step was to pinpoint why customers had become dissatisfied with Greyhound. As it turned out, this was easy. "You just have to go down to the terminals and ask people. They'll tell you it's a real pain to change buses three times when you go from New York to Miami," he's quoted as saying in *Fortune.* It's even more of a customer turn-off when airlines (also in the death grip of competing with each other) enable people to reach their destinations in one day for little more than bus lines charge and over distances that buses might take 48 hours or more to travel.

Realizing that some people still prefer the bus to the plane, Lentzsch focused his company's growth strategy on precisely these markets. Instead of banking on long-haul fares to keep the company going, he began bus services to casinos and airports, as well as routes to Mexico. In essence, he pulled Greyhound back from the brink by redesigning the company around its customers' needs.

"The Market of Markets"

Greyhound nearly floundered by alienating its lower-income client base. But organizations that deal with some of America's wealthiest individuals—that is, private and institutional investors—can get themselves into trouble just as easily. In the wake of the 2000

market crash, some brokerages and their erstwhile respecte lyst departments are paying a hefty price for the way the ducted business during the '90s boom. Yet what is little outside of investment circles is that in the earliest days boom, the very market that would launch hundreds o growth technology and Internet companies—the NASDAC found itself in trouble.

To the casual observer and even to seasoned regulator seemed to be wrong with how America's second-larges market conducted its business. Indeed, business was ve for all concerned. Between 1990 and early 1999, the NA composite rose seven-fold, from 500 to over 3,500 soundly outperforming the NYSE composite, which fa even double during the same period. On Wall Street, the of the market swell, those employed by the financial i raked in fortunes faster than economic analysts could tall And these newly minted millionaires were transformir York in the process. Young couples in restaurants wer heard discussing their British nannies and online investin drinking Cote Rotie at $150 per bottle. *Fortune* magazin ing the market's excesses, asked the question on its cove This Market Gone to the Pigs?"[3]

History would show that the magazine was definitel something. During the mid-'90s, the National Associatio curities Dealers (NASDAQ's quasi-public parent organizati forced to launch its damage-control efforts, following a investigations by the SEC and the Justice Department ove price fixing and other abuses by NASD member firms. T vestigations and the resulting charges and lawsuits led to foul play in the business press. Here was a sure sign th Street insiders, who had already swept millions from the had become greedier still, taking money that might other into the pockets of individual investors. As a conseque NASDAQ and its member firms were forced to pay out h of millions of dollars. But let's start at the beginning.

artificially wide spreads—the spread being the difference between the bid and ask price that each market maker quotes.

The truth is that market makers make their money from a stock's spread and not from the actual price at which they buy and sell the stock. They buy at one price and sell at a slightly higher price, just like any other middleman. And because, over the course of the trading day, prices of individual stocks routinely fluctuate, the spread follows these fluctuations. If you were to buy a stock and then immediately sell it back, you would lose an amount equivalent to the spread—perhaps 25 cents per share.

The money would be pocketed by the market maker. Under normal circumstances, this would be deemed fair payment for holding the stock in inventory and assuming the risk of ownership. Nevertheless, for market makers, wider spreads meant bigger profits. And studies showed that spreads on NASDAQ were an average of 15 to 18 cents wider than similar-sized NYSE-traded stocks.[6] This negated the potential argument that NASDAQ spreads were wider than average because of the large number of small-cap lightly traded issues listed there and the relatively higher risks of trading those stocks. If the Christie and Schultz findings were true, it meant that investors were being cheated out of billions.

Flak Attacks

Christie and Schultz planned to publish their results in the December issue of the *Journal of Finance*. However, word of their research reached the press in late May. The result, predictably, was a public relations nightmare—one that the NASD and its members badly mishandled at first. A panicked meeting was held at the office of Bear Sterns headquarters on Tuesday, May 24. The NASD's leaders in attendance addressed a group of more than 100 market makers, representing all the NASD member firms. NASD officials reportedly told the gathered market makers to narrow spreads so that they'd be in line with those of other exchanges.[7]

If they didn't narrow these quickly, officials allegedly stressed, the result would be heavy-handed regulation by the NASD. More ominously, it would permit the SEC to meddle in NASD's own turf.[8]

The message at the meeting was received perhaps too well. By the end of the week, the spreads on stocks such as Amgen, Cisco, and Microsoft miraculously narrowed by 50 percent. And market makers began quoting prices in these stocks in odd eighths. By then, the *Wall Street Journal,* the *Los Angeles Times,* and other newspapers had picked up the story.[9]

NASDAQ submitted a study of its own, rebutting the Christie-Schultz results to the *Journal of Finance.* But this tactic also backfired. The NASDAQ rebuttal was soundly rejected by the *Journal's* peer review committee. When NASDAQ appealed to the editors, they, too, rejected it. Later, lawyers suing NASDAQ market makers pointed to the rejection as further evidence of NASDAQ wrongdoing. "A lame industry rebuttal has been rejected twice by the *Journal of Finance,*" they wrote in one of their briefs.[10]

Alas, the NASD's problems were just beginning. By July, civil lawsuits alleging collusion had been filed against 33 major dealers. The Justice Department began looking into possible antitrust violations in October.[11] Meanwhile, the NASD's critics charged that the practice of quoting in odd eighths had been common knowledge within the financial industry for years. Worse, the NASD not only knew about it, NASD officials were accused of covering up any attempts to make it known. By doing so, the NASD had shirked its responsibilities as a self-regulatory organization. In November 1994 the SEC launched an investigation.[12]

Just for starters, the SEC accused NASDAQ market makers of systematically indoctrinating new colleagues on how they were expected to quote shares to each other. The resulting damage was horrendous. The NASDAQ spent an enormous sum placating the SEC and other critics. And after a great deal of stumbling, it underwent massive restructuring.

Who's the Boss?

The market-maker scandal, as we learned years later, was symptomatic of a larger problem. NASDAQ, like many organizations, served a variety of different customers. As an organization, it was often at odds with itself over which group should have precedence over the others. Among the customers the NASDAQ served were the aforementioned market makers, who enabled the stock market to run efficiently. Along with them were the brokerages that traded shares through the NASDAQ and the large institutional investors that traded on behalf of America's great pension funds and mutual funds. Add to that group the individual investors who owned relatively small amounts of stocks or mutual funds.

Finally, there were companies that chose to have their shares traded on the NASDAQ. Many companies questioned whether the NASDAQ was where they wanted to be, especially since they had to answer to their own customer constituencies: shareholders who might wonder if the market-maker scandal had adversely affected the way their stock was traded over the years.

During one year of the scandal period, some 91 companies left the NASDAQ for the NYSE. Fast-growing computer-maker Gateway was perhaps the most prominent defector, and the most painful. A high-tech firm, headquartered on the plains of South Dakota, Gateway epitomized what the NASDAQ was supposed to be all about: a market for spry, upstart technology firms. More painful still, the Gateway defection followed the flight of two comparable high-profile tech firms, Bay Networks and America Online.[13] Some in the business press openly wondered: If "the stock market for the next 100 years" couldn't hold onto its brightest stars, what was its future?

Again, the question was which customer groups' needs should take precedence, because all were vital to the market functioning smoothly. It's hardly a unique problem. In a similar fashion, any public company must serve its investors and its customers. Some analysts would also add to those constituencies the company's employees and the community in which it operates.

A slightly more complicated model exists with a television network, in that it has even more customers to serve: The advertisers pay for the programming. Affiliates air the programs, and viewers watch them. A network that puts viewers ahead of advertisers risks losing revenue. If it chooses to favor advertisers over viewers, it might appear too pandering and could lose viewers. And finally, if it alienates its affiliates, they might well switch to another network, resulting in fewer viewers and, accordingly, less advertisers.

If the NASDAQ was going to rescue itself, it needed to correctly balance the interests of all its stakeholders. And therein lay the reason why the SEC demanded that it restructure.

The Turnaround

Part of that restructuring entailed hiring Frank Zarb to serve as the NASD's turnaround chairman. Among other things, Zarb had served as energy czar under Gerald Ford at a time when gas lines at the pump were the norm and the nation's production, distribution, and consumption of energy sorely needed a makeover—which in a sense made Zarb the ultimate turnaround manager. Zarb had also previously served as chairman and CEO of the brokerage firm Smith Barney, which was then a division of The Travelers Inc. Here, Zarb had proved himself adept in this role. Smith Barney had recorded a $100 million pre-tax loss when Zarb took the helm. Much of that loss stemmed from failed risk-arbitrage trades in the aftermath of Black Monday in October 1987. To quell the losses, Zarb cut costs and focused the firm on retail trading.[14] By 1993, when Zarb left Smith Barney to take on broader responsibilities with The Travelers Inc., the brokerage reported an after-tax profit of $200 million.[15]

Zarb's strategy for healing the NASD reveals what managers may be forced to do to rescue many of the fallen, scandal-plagued companies that made headlines in the early part of this century.

Some saw Zarb's new role as chairman as similar to that of a court-appointed trustee at a company that had filed for bankruptcy. The SEC and the business press would be watching his every move. Zarb, however, says he saw it differently. Well off and in his early sixties now, Zarb made it known that he wasn't taking the job to build up his resume. By some accounts Zarb considered the appointment to be the culmination of his career. Moreover, Zarb considered the NASD the "soul of the industry." He had no illusions about the difficulties ahead. At the NASD helm, he'd be charged with pushing through reforms that might be to the industry's long-term benefit. Sometimes, though, the "industry doesn't appreciate having integrity driven into its soul."

The key for Zarb was to paint a positive vision of the future for everyone involved, something all managers of broken firms must do, to some extent. In coming up with that vision, Zarb at first recognized that powerful and fundamental forces were at work. Just as automobiles and affluence were transforming America when Montgomery Ward and Sears laid the groundwork for their respective futures, the Internet and a new generation of affluent corporate workers were bringing in a new era.

"It was clear," Zarb said in an interview, "that the world was moving toward a more democratized model of equity ownership." As evidence of that, he pointed to the growing popularity of company profit-sharing plans. In the 1990s profit sharing often meant stock options in fast-growing tech firms. The result was thousands of freshly minted millionaires.

> We had an enlightened generation of boomers who were computer-literate and had a keen interest in sharing in some of the wealth that they helped to design. And we had companies that saw participation as a way of keeping key employees. Microsoft, Intel, and Starbucks were companies of the people. The pipeline was beginning to look fuller.

To Zarb and his new colleagues at the NASD, it became increasingly clear that NASDAQ had a critical role to play in this new economy, where the prospect of wealth through stock options was luring the best and the brightest throughout the world. If workplaces were becoming more democratized through profit sharing and stock options, the market where those options ended up must likewise be democratized. "It was no question that democratizing the market was a key objective," Zarb said.

But in order for that to happen, people needed to have confidence in the market—just as they now need to regain their confidence in the ethics of business after the more recent era of corporate scandals. "Confidence only comes with a sense of integrity," Zarb said. The public needed to know that the NASDAQ was being adequately policed.

Then, as now, the key to building this trust was to create an unimpeachable audit trail, so that people would be able to trace back and document questionable stock trades and other practices. Likewise, for the first time, all NASDAQ member firms were required to execute trades on the same time clock. This would allow orders to be tracked each step of the way, when necessary. This reform was intended to prevent market makers from rigging trades by shifting stocks back and forth among themselves. The clock would build a bulletproof paper trail.

Also, to ensure that NASD's internal decision making didn't reflect only the objectives of member firms, NASD had already acted to open its important governing boards to "at least 50 percent independent public and non-industry membership."[16]

While juggling the interests of member firms and regulators, Zarb also faced problems with his own staff that were typical of an organization under duress. Low morale reportedly plagued the association's 570 employees. Many left for other jobs.[17] One of Zarb's first orders of business was reassuring staffers who remained that the bad times would pass. "All institutions have difficult times," he said. When the NASDAQ reformed, it would become a far stronger institution.

In order to enact his reforms, Zarb first needed to streamline the association's Byzantine decision-making process. Too many board members on too many committees had contributed to lax enforcement in the past. Thus, in June, just months after he took office, Zarb proposed a major restructuring. "We're part of an industry that moves with great speed," he explained. The NASD must be reorganized so it could keep up. A total of 48 board members had previously looked over the shoulders of NASD regulators and the NASDAQ stock market. Meetings of subsidiary boards might be held one month, yet the decisions they reached weren't acted upon by the parent board until weeks later. Zarb cut the number of board members to 27 and slashed the amount of meetings by more than half, coordinating the schedules of subsidiary board meetings with the parent board. Now, recommended actions could receive prompt attention.[18]

Perhaps looking toward the day when the NASDAQ might spin off as a separate company, Zarb proposed especially deep cuts in its board membership, from 16 to between five and eight members. That board would have broad authority to make rules for the market.

Zarb's restructuring proposals were no doubt designed to take the NASD away from the overweighted rule-making model used by associations and universities and to substitute a corporate model that could react faster. Fewer board members meant fewer minds to win over.

But the critical question that NASDAQ still needed to address was how to balance the needs of its various customer constituencies. Alfred Berkeley, president of the NASDAQ, was charged with doing just that. As he recalled during an interview:

> When I first got here, I hired McKinsey to find out who was our customer. And it turned out not to be an easy question. And the reason is that we receive money from our companies and from market makers and from data vendors. But our real customer is the investor from whom we receive nothing directly. A market business needs to understand that even though it receives no money from its investors, it needs to put its investors first. What if we put it some

other way, if we put companies first, or market makers first? If the issuers aren't happy, traders have nothing to trade. And if we have nothing to trade, then we have no data to sell.

The result of these moves was that Zarb positioned the NASDAQ for a day when it could function as a private company. Many executives in Europe and Latin America charged with running moribund state-owned businesses had tried this before him, but with a spotted success record. Zarb, by contrast had taken a quasi-private institution and turned it into a streamlined for-profit enterprise. The feat was particularly significant, coming at a time when the financial world was changing radically. Ultra-small, ultra-efficient private trading networks, known as electronic communications or ECNs, were threatening to become full-fledged stock exchanges. The public, faced with years of declining markets, had turned a cold shoulder to investing, while initial public offerings (IPOs), which are the life-blood of any stock market, had slowed to a trickle. But the NASDAQ instead focused on the long term and attempted, with varying degrees of success, to open up cloned versions of itself in Europe and Asia.

Putting Customers Second

Not all companies must face the epiphany of ruin before refocusing their attention on the customers who ultimately are responsible for their being in business. Southwest Airlines is one company that is legendary for its innovative customer service. Not so well known is the fact that the company *does not* put its customers on top of the organization chart. Ironically, it caters to customers not via costly perks but through the lack of them. While other airlines were offering in-flight meals—and becoming the butt of jokes about airline food quality—Southwest gave customers "a beverage and a bag of peanuts. Lest anyone forget what the modest meal represents, the bag is labeled 'Frills,'" wrote Fred Wiersema, in his book *Customer Service*.[19] The result? As fierce price competition forced other airlines to cut back on service, customers reacted harshly to the ever-diminishing value of their tickets. Southwest Airlines, meanwhile, was able to continue as before. It focused on two things that customers value most from an airline, other than safety: price and timeliness. What Southwest added to this mix, Wiersema explained, was notably courteous service, which in the end costs nothing but is often what customers remember most about a flight.

How the airline makes a specialty of customer service is somewhat ingenious: First, its employees are taught that "intangibles are more important than tangibles." For example, a simple friendly hello can mean more than a well-prepared meal. To operate under that edict, the airline puts its employees ahead of customers, the very opposite of what most companies say in their mission statements. Presumably, happy employees will be *motivated* employees. And on their own, they'll envision and innovate often cost-free ways to keep customers happy. Again, Southwest Airlines, like the NASDAQ, looked closely at its stakeholders and made a studied evaluation of how their varying interests should be prioritized.

Rules to Follow

In addition to Southwest, Wiersema looked at other companies noted for their customer service, such as Lands' End and Charles Schwab. At Lands' End, he found that customer loyalty was successfully courted by its ironclad return policy. At Charles Schwab, customers took solace from the fact that its brokers were not motivated by commissions when they recommended a stock. All companies have unique programs that have been proven to work for them; however, Wiersema found that companies legendary for their customer service have several things in common.

Point one: Wiersema discovered that excellent customer service is a key component of the company's "value proposition." That is, the underlying customer service sells the product as much as does any other attribute. This is a seemingly innocuous but important decision. We choose auto dealerships that readily stand behind a car's guarantee, just as we choose insurers that handle claims in a no-hassle fashion. We pay more in some retail stores than in others because we are comfortable with their return policy.

Yet another attribute is common to all businesses that excel at customer service, the author says: The company follows well-developed operating models. This is especially critical and difficult in the area of customer service, which has increasingly become a one-to-one endeavor. Employees must be well trained to deal with customers in a spirited, helpful, and prompt manner, in the unique situations that inevitably arise during human interactions. Think of the company that decrees that all customer phone calls be returned within hours of receiving them, or the retail store chain that empowers cashiers to quickly resolve pricing disputes in the customer's favor—without enraging everyone else in the checkout line by the delay that results from calling over the manager.

Still another virtue of customer-service-committed firms: They implement the latest technology wherever it's of benefit. NASDAQ president Al Berkeley described his own management style in just this way. "Embrace the technology," he said. "Use the technology to move the organization ahead. Change the business model to take advantage of what the technology can do. Specifically, to reach out to develop relationships with our customers and suppliers."

Wiersema also found that customer service tends to be the defining attribute of a company's culture. Think of Wal-Mart and its pep rally–style morning meetings or Saturn dealerships where the entire staff comes out on the floor to welcome a new purchaser to the fold.

Getting Personal

Successful companies also tend to create personal relationships with their customers. We know about the high-end hotels that take copious notes about their frequent guests' preferences, from the specific rooms they desire to the items stocked in the mini-bar. Successful online companies like Amazon have used technology to create the same sort of personalized relationships. When you visit the Amazon Web site, you're greeted by name, reminded of what you did there during your last visit, and presented with new recommendations that your profile suggests you might be interested in.

That same ability to make service personal and friendly is found at the Web site for Ameritrade, one of the few online brokers to weather the stock-trading downturn. Ameritrade's oft-touted slogan is "Believe in yourself." As you explore this online broker's cleanly designed site, you get the feeling that they're really on the side of the online investor. For starters, Omaha, Nebraska–based Ameritrade makes a big deal out of its customer service reps being available 24/7 by toll-free phone. If you click on a section of the company Web site detailing its history, you'll feel like you're joining a family, not an online brokerage. You'll learn, for example, that Ameritrade's clearing broker was established in 1983, about the time Sally Ride became the first American female astronaut.

When customers visit Ameritrade's "education center," they can peruse the easy-to-understand articles and an interactive financial encyclopedia. Ameritrade wisely makes its educational content available to accountholders and non–account holders alike. Unlike competitors that offer many of these same benefits, though, Ameritrade charges rock-bottom commissions and allows customers to place orders online, through a broker via touch-tone phone, or, most recently, by using a Sprint PCS phone.

Furthermore, Ameritrade's order entry system has a touchy-feely design that's in keeping with the broker's user-friendly personality. Specifically, the order entry form contains definitions that tell you the difference between a limit order and a market order—a simple, yet helpful, idea.

Ameritrade smartly positioned itself to become a survivor in the cutthroat world of online brokers. In a business that's notably antiseptic and devoted to the rapid processing of transactions, Ameritrade added a distinctive human element. Customers can order an Ameritade T-shirt or a coffee mug at the broker's online store. And finally, there was the company's acquisition of Datek, a brokerage devoted to more active traders.

One-to-one marketing is really not that new. For years, some food vendors have known the secret of giving people a choice in how they create a product. Ordering take-out pizza or a submarine sandwich is far different from buying other fast food, for example, because you are allowed to mix and match ingredients. Doing this, while arguing with family members over pizza toppings, is integral to the buying experience.

The Amazon Web site is perhaps the ultimate example of mass customization. Another high-tech product that enjoys a cult following is Tivo. It steadfastly wades through endless lists of cable programs and selects shows that your past viewing habits suggest you'll want to watch.

Likewise, personal computers have increasingly become more personalized, even though the workhorse word-processing and Web-browsing programs we use are necessarily standardized. Years ago, Microsoft Windows users could choose from a variety of color, background, and layout schemes. Increasingly sophisticated users download even more options from free sites on the Internet. And they customize their computers with macro programs, sounds, and other options that are reminiscent of previous generations customizing cars with bright paint and add-on engine enhancements.

Evidence suggests that the future of computing will be built around mass customization, and necessarily so—because no single company, including Microsoft, can possibly exploit all of the machine's possibilities. A prime example here is the Linux operating system, which is built around the idea that individuals or groups will add workable enhancements within the operating system's open-source requirements. Knowing that such enhancements are sure to come from a variety of sources is a key reason why company information technology officers opt for Linux over Windows.

The One-to-One World of Computer Gaming

An even more apropos example can be found in the $10-billion-per-year computer gaming industry. It's worth digressing for a moment to discuss how that industry differs dramatically from the previous century's art and business model it may be destined to replace: movies.

Movies, though created by large teams, essentially employ a singular vision, that of the director, producer, or studio. The essence of movies as a mass medium is to impart the same experience to everyone watching. Moreover, the movie industry has steadfastly fought any and all after-market attempts to alter that vision, even from subsequent owners of the product. Communications pioneer Ted Turner encountered stiff resistance when he wanted to colorize his company's massive black-and-white film library. Another company wishing to remove explicit language and scenes from popular movies, to adapt them to a family audience, likewise faced a barrage of criticism.

Like movies, computer games are also produced by teams of people with highly diverse skills, from the sports figures and actors who model the game's characters, to the computer-rendering artists, to the "authors" who map out the game's storylines. But unlike movies, some of the most highly successful computer games welcome customization by their viewers. The theory being, the more users "hack" the games and introduce their own characters and situations, the more they develop a vested interest in the games.[20] And the more likely that they will buy the game developer's enhancements.

The result of intimate customer involvement is that as computer games migrate online, they will become the elusive medium of interactive television. The situation is analogous to early versions of the Internet (see chapter 10). These failed because a single company sought to control the medium's content. The Internet succeeded, by contrast, because individuals (customers, if you will) used the medium as a means to disseminate their own information. Various attempts at interactive television have also been tried, but the interactive elements have been limited to marketing ploys of one type or another. Watching a popular sitcom, for example, the viewer could mouse-click on an item of clothing and receive it in his size via a mail-order catalog shipper.

In contrast, the newest online games, like *The Sims* online or There.com, are entire worlds, in which users (that is, customers) can enact their own dramas. Likewise, they can choose their style of dress, the virtual house they live in, and so on. They can even buy and sell from one another using a virtual currency system.

The Deadly Game of Business

What better way to build customer loyalty than to have customers create an entire life around your product—whether virtual or real? Unfortunately, many companies fail to achieve this extreme differentiation from their competitors' products. In fact, they move in quite the opposite direction, turning their product into a commodity. All too often, the result is that they become locked in a competitive battle to the death. In such an environment, innovation is often stifled because it is either too costly, as margins become razor thin, or too risky, because a wrong bet will surely sink the company. And yet, such a strategy of differentiation may be one key way to win a war of attrition.

8

Fighting Wars of Attrition

Computer-maker Michael Dell is said to play the hardest game of hardball in a very tough league. His hypercompetitive approach to product pricing likely led to Hewlett Packard's acquisition of Compaq Computer. Likewise, Dell was the reason that IBM, inventor of the modern PC, quit selling its desktop models via retail outlets. As Big Blue chairman Lou Gerstner is reported to have said: "Price wars in a commodity business are really dumb." And yet a commodity business is the very environment Dell Computer appears to thrive in. As a recent *Wired* article, the "Dell Curve," pointed out, Dell is emphatic about letting customer needs dictate strategy. If a product doesn't sell, it is mercilessly cut from the roster, with no subsidies while waiting for the market to develop. And no tears. The philosophy goes hand in hand with Dell's Darwinistic business model, which, unlike other online models that flourished before the dot-com crash, has survived with flying colors. In fact, in the current recession environment Dell has proved to be more powerful and resilient than ever. Its market share increased in a decidedly down economy and an even more miserable market for PCs.

So, what's the magic behind the Dell model? It is to create a connection as seamlessly as possible between supplier and customer, according to *Wired*. Theoretically, when you go online to order a Dell PC with a turbocharged graphics processor and a recordable DVD, the components leave the suppliers' shelves for the factory just moments after you check these options with a few mouse clicks.

Other computer makers have good reason to fear this hyper-efficient model, since no other supply chain is nearly as seamless. And Dell has worked to expand it to include such things as peripherals and servers, which will surely spread even more fear throughout the sector. But, asks *Wired* magazine, if the Dell model is truly as formidable as it appears, why hasn't it been duplicated by others? Why can't car makers, for instance, allow customers to order the Chevy or Honda of their choice, down to the color and shape of the ash trays, via the convenience of their home PCs, for delivery to their door just days later—and why can't automakers knock thousands off a car's purchase price in the process?

Wired says the answer to that question is easy. Dell's take-no-prisoners business model demands total commitment. Either you structure your strategy to be totally online or the numbers just don't work out. Dell built itself around the all-or-nothing online model. But other companies have too many vested interests—like the dealerships that automakers sell through—which means their commitment can't be total.

And if there's a lesson in all of this, it's that a company structured from top to bottom around being a ruthless low-cost producer can indeed vanquish all comers in a war of attrition—a price war, if you will. But other companies not totally adapted to the model enter the fray at their peril.[1]

Telecom Titanics

The most vivid, not to mention most expensive, illustration of the dangers inherent in a war of attrition can be found in the telecom sector, according to *Fortune* magazine writer Ken Belson.[2] Prior to the 2000 crash, Belson says, giant telecom providers smelled a gold mine in fast-developing Asian markets, for example. There was, company executives believed, a huge unmet demand for broadband services among Asians. And based on that belief, companies borrowed heavily and turned the ocean floor into a fishnet of expensive fiber cables. In effect, Belson says, they were following a Field-of-Dreams strategy: If you build it, they—the customers—will obediently come.

But it didn't happen that way. Instead, as hindsight reveals, an overabundance of fiber caused, by some estimates, 90 percent of the cables to remain unused. The drama then playing out in the telecom sector in Asia and the rest of the world as a result is that, desperate to repay their debt following the crash, the companies were drawn inexorably into a vicious price-cutting war of attrition, the corporate equivalent of a full-blown superpower nuclear exchange. As a result, the amount of cable now being laid each year amounts to one-tenth what companies gleefully unwound before the bust. And some experts predict that the bandwidth glut and hard times could continue into 2007, according to *Fortune*.

Examining the reasons for the telecom failure, an earlier *Fortune* magazine article[3] noted that a vicious chain reaction cascaded through long-distance providers in the United States as well. The top providers collectively lost $145 billion in market value within months of the stock market meltdown, while the largest equipment makers, Lucent, Nortel, and Cisco, dropped an estimated $275 billion. And that, incredible as it sounds, was only the beginning. Stock prices continued to tumble amid the nervousness that followed September 11. Once again, a major reason for the decline is that companies were understandably duped by the logarithmically expanding data market. Indeed, the volume of data traffic was said to be doubling every quarter. Like the transnational broadband carriers, the domestic companies embarked on a major build-out campaign, only to find that their slow-growing voice traffic still accounted for most of their revenues. Seeing that the companies' data lines were being underutilized and that price cutting of data traffic was all but killing margins, Wall Street analysts punished the companies. As a result, the lowered stock price greatly diminished the companies' leverage, because borrowing terms are often predicated on capitalization.

This left the telecoms with little choice but to channel voice traffic through their data lines and engage in yet another price war with each other for that market. Very quickly, the sad state of the wide-pipe providers began to affect the equipment providers whom *Fortune* said had previously functioned like fattened arms merchants during the ascendant phase of the telecom battle. Now desperate for cash, the providers all but stopped making new purchases, which rapidly ground the industry to a near halt.

What kind of lesson can be derived from this titanic struggle? It is an old story, and it has to do with the fact that market share and the size of the market don't necessarily translate into success. The carriers were readily able to handle the huge data traffic increases wrought by the Internet, but they weren't able to figure out how to make money doing it. *Fortune* suggests that the reason is quite simple. The providers carried the data but didn't add any value. In other words, all of them reliably transported data bits from point A to point B, which commoditized their products as surely as PCs had become commodities. In order to make money, the companies needed to do things like prioritize routing for such services as TV. True, the companies did look long and hard for services that might add value. But these proved elusive. In particular, they were elusive when it came to reaching everyday consumers. The ultra-thick broadband pipes ended a tantalizing mile or so from the homes of most users. Until that last mile was bridged, the services and hence the profits would have to wait. Meanwhile, in a kind of chicken-and-egg problem, consumers for the most part saw little reason to pay extra for incrementally better broadband connections such as DSL because very few services as yet available made good use of the added speed.

Caught in the resulting quagmire, an industry that spent years and more than $1 trillion in an effort to consolidate now found itself frantically disposing of units in order to raise cash, according to *Fortune*.

Corporate Commoditization

Perhaps the ultimate war of attrition is the one that is waged every day on Wall Street. According to Michael T. Jacobs in his book *Short-Term America*,[4] business ownership has itself been commoditized, right along with many of the products companies make. To explain, he says that a share of stock at one time actually represented an ownership stake in a particular company—ownership in the truest sense of the word. For the company, it was a means of raising capital, whereas for individual investors it was a gesture of support for the firm that they hoped would bring some future reward. The situation is analogous to how partners or angel investors feel toward the enterprises they put their money into.

Several trends acted to distance the concept of company ownership from the ownership of stock. For starters, professional managers may strive as best they can to rebuff interference by shareholders—that is, with respect to corporate strategy. You hear often enough about a high-stakes investor buying up millions of shares of stock, in the hopes of gaining a board seat and thus influencing the company's policies. More often than not, the move is fiercely fought by management. Management is even more likely to resist the actions of shareholder activists. Depicting these activists as annoyances at annual board meetings, management may enlist the help of other shareholders to fend them off. Only the fund managers and analysts are given some heed. Management's autonomy, when it comes to day-to-day strategy, grows more pronounced as shares become more widely held. Although management certainly feels accountable for the stock's price, it may remain aloof from suggestions on how to influence that price.

Another, perhaps more significant, reason behind the commoditization of shares is the ease with which those shares can be traded. A partial ownership in a restaurant or an apartment building might take months to sell. But a share of stock can be dumped with a few clicks of a mouse, via a home computer and an online broker. The ultimate form of this phenomenon is the day trader, who in the course of a day might buy and sell tens of thousands of shares, holding them for only minutes at a time.

Trading Wars of Attrition

The consequence of this is that managers must emphasize short-term results at the expense of long-term growth. The alternative is to have their share price decimated as short-term investors dump the stock. Armed with information that used to be the province of fund managers, individual investors who engage in active trading have little patience with anything but superior short-term results, as better opportunities always await in the market. Those opportunities can be easily discovered. Moreover, they can be entered into by paying a mere $15 commission. By some estimates, the volume generated by these active traders accounts for as many as half of all the shares bought and sold, and ironically it has pitted brokerages in a fierce war of attrition.

Years ago, trading commissions were much higher. It was the gradual erosion of commissions, Jacobs says, that furthered the commoditization of corporate ownership. "No one but the owner makes money when an investor holds stocks." So legions of brokers, whose livelihood depended on getting their clients to buy and sell, manned the phones daily to generate some excitement. Their efforts to drum up business had minimal effect back in the days when commissions on a typical sale earned brokers hundreds of dollars; this made investors reluctant to sell without careful thought. But when the SEC allowed brokers to charge whatever commissions they cared to, a predictable phenomenon occurred. Brokers found themselves in the beginning of a price war.

The industry relies on good advice, good information, and, to an extent, a good traffic record by its brokers. So, at first, even the lower commissions didn't accelerate the price war, because firms were able to differentiate themselves. Technology—or the lack of it—also kept competition to a minimum. Brokerage back offices were automated, but the front offices, where the orders were taken to buy and sell stocks, were not. And this acted to set a floor on the amount firms could charge their customers and still make money.

It was the advent of the Internet that accelerated the commission price war beyond anyone's imagination and, not coincidentally, sent stock prices reeling skyward—something that inevitably happens as trading volume increases. And increase, it did. Suddenly, average investors were told that they no longer needed the services of a flesh-and-blood broker. After all, brokers often have been accused of being more interested in generating commissions than in generating wealth for their clients. Thanks to the Internet, the average investor could plug in a home computer and access many of the same resources that brokers used to hold, like a hand of cards, close to their chests—that is, SEC statements, analyst reports, and mathematical tools with which to analyze and chart a stock's every move. Because trades could be handled seamlessly from the customer's mouse click, to the brokerage office, to the trading floor of exchanges, a new type of brokerage emerged—one that offered an Internet presence and sometimes little more, all in exchange for rock-bottom commissions. Commissions quickly dropped from $40 one way, offered by the online branches of certain prestige brokerages, to as low as $1, offered by the upstart online trading firms. The software to create this online presence was readily available from a plethora of providers, meaning that the cost of entry for brokerages plummeted. Within the space of months, a dizzying array of new online brokers emerged. As competition increased, margins predictably became razor thin.

Not that the brokerages didn't wisely try to differentiate their products in terms of more than price. Some heaped on analytical tools to add value; others emphasized the speed to the market that would enable seasoned traders to take profits ahead of their peers. Still others emphasized handholding or training. The online brokerage industry appeared to be one Internet business model that worked. Unlike some of their wired peers, many Internet broker-ages did generate profits. All went well, as long as the public's attention remained captivated by the markets. As the price of stocks increased, newcomers added their life savings to the ever-expanding pot, driving prices higher still.

When the bottom fell out, as hindsight shows it must, many upstart brokerages found that customers had lost their appetite for trading. Some firms quickly went out of business as a result. Others, such as Datek, were bought out, or else they geared their services toward professional traders. And still others, such as E*Trade, had enough resources on hand to branch out into bank-ing and other services. But this was the exception. Because com-petition had made margins impossibly thin, many brokerages were already existing on borrowed time and cash. A price war had once again devastated an industry.

The Right Price of Victory

There are ways to avoid a price war. Principally, they involve fight-ing off any attempts to have your product commoditized. And ex-amples of how to do this can be found among both large and small companies. An independent children's clothing store in a New York suburb, for example, stood little chance of competing with national chains like Gap Kids. But the manager shrewdly differentiated her store from the giants by adding service. She sent personal shoppers to the homes of busy and wealthy potential customers, complete with a supply of clothes those customers could browse through. Similarly, a high-end beverage maker added bone-strengthening cal-cium to his drinks. The calcium reportedly costs $4,000 per pound. But customers concerned about osteoporosis are willing to pay the extra price and then some, and they choose the calcium-fortified drinks over better-known national brands.[5]

As you'll see, price, too, can be a potent weapon in a war of at-trition. But this approach demands a certain amount of creativity.

End-Around Strategies

In their book *Power Pricing* authors Robert J. Dolan and Hermann Simon offer an array of tactics designed to give companies needed maneuvering room in a war of attrition.[6] One such strategy involves something called segmenting a brand. The undisputed leader in this field is Starbucks. A generation before the ubiquitous coffee-house chain arrived, coffee was a generic drink for the most part. And the closest most of us got to a coffee house was a brightly lit establishment that sold donuts. But just as those early coffee houses offered myriad varieties of donuts, Starbucks took a simple cup of coffee and created an infinite menu of varieties. Moreover, customers could take the segmented product and further customize it to their liking.

Yet another tactic is customization, examples of which can be found everywhere in business. If you purchased a glass of wine at a restaurant you would expect to pay more than if you bought that wine in a grocery store. And that's because the wine served at a restaurant was in a sense customized. It was packaged together with the establishment's décor, and the attitudes of the serving staff, not to mention the food. Similarly, convenience stores offer a kind of customization in relation to supermarkets, longer hours and the opportunity to rapidly acquire the products you want. Timely delivery is the value added or customization that courier services provide over routine delivery. Similarly, movies are customized in a variety of ways. The most expensive way to see a first-run film is at a theater when it first debuts. Months later, the DVD becomes available for considerably less, while at the same time the film likely appears on pay-per-view cable. Later still, the movie might debut on pay cable channels. And finally you'll be able to watch it for free on regular TV.

Other businesses succeed by putting a time value on their products. The newest cars to hit auto showrooms are seldom discounted, and their quantities may even be deliberately limited to enhance their long-term value. The same business might offer heavy discounts later in the year to clear inventory in preparation for yet newer models. In this example and others time serves as a fundamental negotiating tactic. Without a deadline from either or both sides, there's little incentive to do anything but talk forever. Sales employ this basic strategy by offering lower prices for a set time period. But a more clever application of the time principal is to apply it to individual negotiations. A realtor, for example, might say that the owners' offer on the house is only good for 24 hours.

A strategy called bundling in a sense customizes products by combining them. When you shop for a car, you're offered packages of options, the sport package for example, or the luxury package. Similarly, computers come bundled with software or perhaps components like monitors, printers, and Internet service. Bundling exists in the vacation industry with all-inclusive resorts, the best known of which is Club Med. These resorts provide lodging, food, activities and other amenities as part of a package price. Similarly, some cruise lines bundle airfare with a week on the ocean.

The Ongoing Battle

Just as surely as companies fight to differentiate themselves and thus avoid a war of attrition, their competitors may blindly move to draw them into a price-based conflict. This can happen even when a price war will bring about the ruin of all involved. One manager remarked that he would much rather compete in an industry dominated by smart companies than in one where competitors flew blind. The reason is simple. Smart companies compete against themselves by using the bottom line as the ultimate measure of performance. Like you, they will work to differentiate their products and avoid being drawn into a profit-decimating price war. In the end, such strategies on the part of all competitors within a sector would tend to greatly increase the amount of innovation. Inevitably, that innovation will spawn improved products, perhaps even blockbuster products.

Fortunately, it is relatively easy for smart competitors to recognize the first volleys in a price war. And strategies for edging out of the conflict are equally well defined. The same, unfortunately, is not true of another danger that can cause companies to fail. By its very nature, this danger often strikes with stealth and in a way that can quickly overwhelm a company. As discussed in the next chapter, the danger is ignored or there are unforeseen liabilities. And as you'll see, it has ruined vast industries in the past and could cripple other sectors like medicine, aviation, and fast food in the years ahead.

CHAPTER 9

Ignoring Liabilities, Threats, and Crises

No industry is more plagued by liability issues than the medical profession. Thanks to generous jury awards that run into seven, eight, and nine figures, doctors in some states have seen their malpractice insurance rates climb 40 percent or more in the space of a year, and that on top of a long series of annual double-digit increases. Combine rising malpractice rates with limited reimbursements from insurance companies, Medicare, and Medicaid, and the very practice of medicine can quickly become a bankrupting proposition. Many doctors, faced with paying a third or more of their income in liability insurance premiums, have as a result opted to shut down their practices and either retire or move to states with friendlier liability laws.

As a result, in some states, West Virginia being one, the situation is said to have grown so grave that some rural areas completely lack such vital specialists as obstetricians and neurosurgeons. As might be expected, this has spawned a dangerous health crisis for the people of those regions. Consider, for example, what happens when the closest neurosurgeon resides hours away. Medical experts call the first hour following a severe injury "the golden hour." During that time, if treatment is administered effectively, the chances of the patient avoiding lifelong paralysis are much improved. It's easy to understand the tragic consequences for someone who is forced to wait longer than that golden hour for treatment.

Grave injuries occur with even more frequency in urban areas. And in Nevada, another state plagued by high malpractice rates, doctors felt compelled to shut down a Level I trauma facility in Las Vegas because they claimed they couldn't afford the skyrocketing increases in malpractice insurance. A Level I trauma facility is like a dedicated emergency room that caters to, among other things, dire injuries like gunshot wounds and auto accidents. The Las Vegas Trauma Center was the only one in the city before it was shut down. The closing meant that seriously hurt patients were forced to go to often-crowded hospital emergency rooms. Thankfully, negotiations finally prompted the reopening of the Las Vegas facility. And months afterward, the state legislature passed a law that capped certain damage awards in malpractice cases.

But the sad truth is that even sweeping tort reform can take years to bring about lower malpractice rates. Only after legal challenges to the law have worked their way through the courts can insurers get a true sense of the malpractice risk posed by the area. Like Nevada, the Mississippi legislature, for instance, also recently passed a cap on malpractice awards. But physicians still migrate to neighboring Louisiana, despite liability insurance rates there being higher than Mississippi's, in some cases. The reason is that a similar cap passed by the Louisiana legislature some years ago has been thoroughly tested by the courts.

The health-care crisis brought about by runaway jury awards begs for a solution. And because the industry is already highly regulated and highly fragmented, it's likely that no single solution will suffice. And that's despite efforts on the state and federal level to impose caps on non-economic damages in malpractice litigation that were ongoing when this book went to press. In the long run, a series of piecemeal efforts, like contract provisions requiring patients to settle disputes through mediation, will continue to allow the system to muddle through, and the bottom line is that until the American public finally notices that a slow-burning crisis exists, hospitals will continue to cut back on the vital operations they per-form. Some have shut down entire units, because of a shortage of doctors willing to pay the escalating liability insurance rates. Simi-larly, community medical centers, vital to the well-being of low-income areas, have been forced to cut back on services, as well as hours, because malpractice rates continue to drain their scant op-erating funds. The poor, who can least afford the cost of health care, are among those hardest hit by the liability crisis in health care. But this is a crisis that is bound to affect everyone. And that's because everywhere, physicians have likewise limited their services. No doubt, many will continue to be forced out of business. And many more will voluntarily decide not to practice medicine. Some surveys show that by 2010, the nation will need 200,000 more doc-tors than it has. Perhaps sometime between now and then, when the public realizes that its own health and safety are at risk and that people have been paying for the outrageous jury awards themselves in the form of higher health insurance premiums, coupled with di-minished service, then and only then will true reform take place.

Ever-Present Risks

The health-care industry—which contributes something like $1 tril-lion annually to the U.S. economy—is a frightening example of what liability issues can do to an organization such as a hospital or a medical practice and also how an entire industry can be crippled, with severe repercussions to public welfare. The vulnerability of the medical industry is made all the more poignant by the fact that it is a vital industry, one that people have no choice but to access.

And, no surprise, liability issues and related risks are present in every sector of the economy. And so it's easy to imagine what the effects of a liability crisis might be in an industry that depends on the discretionary decisions of its customers in order to survive. The effects in that case can be even more disastrous. Whatever your feelings about smoking, for example, it is impossible to deny that lawsuits by individuals and governments have hobbled the

American tobacco industry more than years of anti-smoking campaigns could. Now, some business leaders fear, the tactics that worked successfully against big tobacco may be applied to the fast food industry.

Meanwhile, terrorism has created a whole new paradigm of liability issues. And one area where this is most evident is in the food industry. However, companies have ways to successfully defend themselves—by taking preemptive action, for example; by acting decisively when a liability issue arises; or, finally, by creating a workable mediation strategy that will resolve issues before they get out of control.

The Vulnerable Food Supply

To get a sense of what an agroterrorism attack might look like, think back to the spring of 2001—a time when black smoke billowed up from the placid English countryside. The source of the smoke was thousands of cattle carcasses being burned in an attempt to contain hoof and mouth and BSE or mad cow disease.

The outbreak devastated the British beef industry, affecting everyone from farmers, to exporters and their shippers, to the entire British tourism industry. Who wants to visit a nation whose countryside is pockmarked with burning carcasses?

Agricultural officials here in the United States could only ponder the horrific consequences if hoof and mouth or another serious bovine/human disease, namely mad cow or BSE were to cross the Atlantic. The U.S. beef industry is far bigger than Britain's. And it is far more decentralized. What would happen if terrorists laid siege on the $54 billion U.S. beef industry? asked a USDA analyst at a conference on homeland defense, organized by the Rand Corporation. "If we were to lose that $54 billion commodity from the marketplace overnight, I think the results would be catastrophic," he said.

Also, because BSE is eventually fatal to the humans and livestock that eat contaminated meat, the liability issues would quickly mushroom out of control. Everyone within the supply chain could be held liable, from the ranchers to the restaurateur. The liability issues might well turn out to be just as grim if—God forbid—the food industry were ever subjected to terrorist attack. In fact, liability issues would be worse. A single incident, if it were proved to be the work of terrorists, would likely raise liability rates across the board in the industry. Food prices might skyrocket as a result, further straining an already wounded economy.

For that reason alone, food industry officials had good reason to study well the BSE outbreak in Britain. And, indeed, they were able to find some reasons for optimism from the British experience. First, thanks largely to hard work by regulators and businesses, BSE did not spread to our shores. Second, following the scare, U.S. consumers continue to purchase meat products, confident of their safety.

Business leaders of every stripe can glean many valuable lessons from the recent mad cow disease epidemic, as well as from similar threats such as the e-coli and Tylenol scares. The most important lesson, perhaps, is that companies must plan ways to protect themselves from a possible threat. Equally important, they need to rehearse how they'll communicate with their customers if they fall victim to an agroterrorism attack.

"Food is a zero-tolerance issue," claimed a PR industry executive who is a specialist at helping companies respond to crises. By zero tolerance, he means that people buy food products expecting them to be 100 percent safe. Thus, if companies fail to take reasonable steps to protect their products, the public will have little sympathy if a problem arises—even if the problem is clearly not management's fault. "Food companies can't afford to have a bioterrorism attack and say we didn't do anything to prepare for it," he explains.

Little surprise, following the September 11 attacks, that America's food companies rushed to create preparedness plans. "We're taking a number of steps in that area," advises Larry Cunningham, senior vice president of corporate affairs at Archer Daniels Midland. Cunningham cited coordinated efforts with trade associations and government agencies. But like other food industry executives in these uncertain times, he was understandably reluctant to discuss specific measures.

Connecting with Customers Now

Some companies, meanwhile, devised ways to go on the offensive against agroterrorism threats. One example: Fort Dodge Animal Health. The Overland Park, Kansas, maker of animal medicines enlisted its own customers in an effort to increase vigilance. In early November, Fort Dodge, which is a subsidiary of American Home Products, released a booklet on bioterrorism to the firm's 50,000 veterinarian customers. A goal of the booklet was to use those vets as a first line of defense against potential threats.

Veterinarians, after all, through their long years of service to a community would already know the normal disease patterns prevalent there. Which would put them on the front lines of defense against a bioterror attack aimed at the nation's livestock, since they would be the first to notice any deviations. Using a simple chart, the clinic's guide summarizes the symptoms of potential bioterrorist diseases like foot and mouth that are harmless to humans but might nevertheless devastate livestock populations. It also describes more serious threats such as plague and hemorrhagic fevers that can spread from animals to humans. Part of the guide's purpose in the tense post–September 11 era, its creators say, is to help vets recognize when something is *not* a threat. In a hair-trigger, fear-ridden environment of constantly heightened and lowered threat levels, overreacting can divert crucial resources and potentially prove as dangerous as underreacting. Using the vet clinic's method, it's easy to think of ways that tech workers, physicians, and others on the front lines of possible terrorist attack might devise similar strategies.

Discovering a Company's Vulnerabilities

Knowing when and how to react in the face of a potential threat depends on understanding precisely where a company is most vulnerable, experts say. To that end, consultants that assist clients in bioterrorism preparedness efforts may instruct clients to study their entire operation. It's an exercise that's similar to the risk assessment outlined in chapter 14. But it differs because it singles out one potential threat: terrorism. And the analysis of operations is focused solely on mitigating that threat. The goal: Identify vulnerabilities and devise ways to nullify them. Following such a review, a company might decide to improve its packaging, for example, or conduct more aggressive employee background checks.

Sometimes threats can arise that have nothing to do with the company's own products. A PR executive recounts that a recent client asked for advice after it learned that its mail-order catalogs were processed at a postal facility later found to contain anthrax. In the end, the executive and the company sought advice from the health department, which assured them that the catalogs were safe.

Knowing whom to call—from the health department to law enforcement—for such expert advice is crucial to any preparedness plan. But with overlapping agencies regulating the food industry, that's not always easy. If a company believes its meat products have been tainted, the local USDA should be consulted. But if the problem arises from contaminated feed, then it may be an FDA problem. Failing to contact the responsible agency can waste precious hours in a time of crisis.

Disaster Drills

Besides consulting the right agencies for help, during crises it's important to have the right people supporting you when you speak to the media, advises media consultant Eileen Wixted. Much of the work of her Des Moines–based firm Wixted Pope Nora Thompson & Associates involves helping companies communicate effectively in dire times. Her client list includes major airlines, food producers, and nuclear power plants nationwide. Wixted's advice: "Always coordinate your communications efforts with the proper agencies." Relevant trade associations, law enforcement officials, regulatory agencies, and local health authorities should all speak from the same podium during news conferences, for example. "People feel more reassured when they know many organizations are working together."

Like other companies specializing in crisis management, Wixted's firm has seen a pick-up in business since September 11. During the months immediately following the World Trade Center attacks, she observed that "90 percent of the work we're doing right now is fire drills." Such drills can take several days and involve people from all levels of the company. The goal is to realistically simulate an actual crisis.

Knowing what audiences to reach and when it's appropriate to speak to them is especially critical. Company employees, for example, are often the first group in need of information, Wixted says. One reason for that is employees want to know steps are being taken to protect their safety. Another reason: In a crisis, rumors inevitably spread within an organization and can quickly reach the public. "The tendency is to circle the wagons during a crisis, when in fact the opposite is necessary," she says. "Because, in the absence of communication, people think the worst."

During the fire drills Wixted's firm organizes, executives also learn the art of grace under pressure. To train them, reporters badger executives with hard questions in mock TV interviews, while newspaper reporters demand minute details, facts, and figures for their lengthier stories.

Wixted says that FBI and other law enforcement officials may take part in these drills, working with management to devise a consistent response. Company lawyers may participate, too, approving drafts of media releases, along with the company's management team.

The Truth Helps

Industry consultants say it's vital to get just that sort of "buy-in" from all levels of management. Likewise, it's important that the public receives the right information. During an agroterrorism crisis, one executive observed, people will want to know three crucial pieces of information from a company: "What did you know; when did you know it; and what did you do about it?"

Unfortunately, companies—governments, too—often stumble badly when they face the press. During the height of the BSE crisis, for example, a prominent U.K. official fed his child a hamburger on TV. His intent was to show that the meat was safe. But the action outraged viewers. Similarly, some believe health officials in the United States made mistakes communicating details about the anthrax attacks during the early going. Some openly speculated that the disease's first victim might have caught it while hunting, for example.

To keep communications efforts focused and helpful, companies are often advised not to speculate as to the cause of the disaster. Rather they should provide a detailed account of what's being done to counter the threat. Equally important, company spokespersons should recommend specific steps people can take to protect themselves.

One of the worst things a company can do is offer false reassurances that can come back to haunt you. Case in point: The Japanese government at first assured its people that BSE would not spread to Japan, when in fact such assurances were impossible to make. When BSE did show up in Japan, the government was forced to recant. The lesson: Companies should never proclaim that their products are immune from a bioterrorist attack. Because in today's uncertain environment, it is simply impossible to make such assurances.

The postal service gives us a positive example of how a large organization can assist its customers who may in some way be endangered by the firm's products or services. Instead of claiming the mail was 100 percent safe from anthrax, it stressed the relatively low risk of becoming infected. Then, to assist its customers, the Post Office sent a card to every U.S. mail recipient. The card clearly explained how to detect possibly tainted mail and how to handle it if found.

Faced with a possible agroterrorism threat, companies would do well to emulate that approach. For example, if one item on the grocery produce department were somehow contaminated, it would be a mistake for other produce firms to claim that their products were safe. Rather, they should inform consumers that security measures were in place and encourage people to decide whether buying the product was worth the risk.

Positive Lessons from the Tylenol Scare

Terrorist attacks aimed at the food supply or anything else we may ingest are particularly frightening because even the smallest incident can cause rampant fear—and can devastate an entire industry. The effects can also linger for years to come. And unknown to most Americans, terrorists have attacked the food industry in the past. In 1984, for example, members of an Oregon religious cult allegedly contaminated restaurant salad bars with salmonella, resulting in 751 illnesses, none of them serious. The incident has since been forgotten.

An earlier terrorist incident generated far more concern across America, but smart action by the affected company's management minimized the long-term damage. In 1982, seven people—three of them from the same family—were killed in the Chicago area after taking Tylenol capsules filled with cyanide.

In the face of this threat, the approach pioneered by Johnson & Johnson, in close cooperation with law enforcement and health authorities, is considered a classic on how to take positive steps to inform and aid the public, while preserving a valuable brand and company goodwill at the same time. Thanks to Johnson & Johnson's quick handling of the Tylenol crisis, millions now take the over-the-counter pain relievers each day without giving a thought to the deaths that occurred years ago.

Of course, that did not seem possible in the early 1980s. When police identified the contaminated Tylenol as the cause, no efforts were spared to warn the public. Warnings poured from TV and radio stations. Patrol cars with loudspeakers hit the streets. Meanwhile, executives at Tylenol's parent, Johnson & Johnson, struggled to save their company's most profitable brand. Tylenol accounted for 37 percent of the over-the-counter pain-reliever market. But its survival remained very much in doubt. "I don't think they can ever sell another product under that name," popular ad guru Jerry Della Femina reportedly told the *NY Times*.

Undaunted, J&J executives ordered $100 million worth of Tylenol products pulled from stores. People who had already purchased Tylenol capsules were offered tablets in exchange. Product ads were likewise pulled, and J&J sent warnings to health officials. The company also actively assisted investigations by Chicago law enforcement, the FBI, and the FDA, offering—among other things—a $100,000 reward for the suspect's capture.

Next, company officials planned a comeback phase for their product. They created triple-sealed packaging and offered $2.50-off coupons in newspapers. Incentives to retailers helped regain lost shelf space. And J&J executives made presentations to doctors about their upgraded safety standards. "What Johnson & Johnson executives have done is communicate the message that the company is candid, contrite, and compassionate, committed to solving the murders and protecting the public," the *Washington Post* wrote.

Tragically, the suspect was never caught, and Tylenol products were again tampered with in 1986. Yet as a result of J&J's efforts, Tylenol remains one of the world's most powerful global brands. Recently, in fact, Johnson & Johnson ranked first in a *Wall Street Journal* survey of America's most trusted corporations.

Creating a Risk-Fighting Culture

Under normal circumstances, the success of any business depends on a close cooperative relationship between all parties involved with it. But in a time of crisis, the cooperative relationship must be seamless—that is, if a vigilant campaign such as that mounted by Johnson & Johnson has any hope of succeeding. When a crisis develops, long-hidden rivalries and mistrusts can surface, both within the company and between the company and its stakeholders. And for some who oppose the company for one reason or another, the crisis makes the company an "I-told-you-so" target of opportunity. And indeed, the entire industry can become a target. If there's a chemical spill, for example, the environmentalists' stances that might have been viewed by the public as extreme, now gain more credence. "Maybe antiquated plants should be shut down immediately," the public is liable to think. "Maybe far more restrictive regulations are the remedy."

Companies can also become targets when they plan expansions or introduce new products. A planned facility, for example, is bound to bring out opposition community groups. And those groups measure their effectiveness by how long they can succeed in delaying the project. For the company, of course, such delays can prove costly and even, perhaps, lead to failure. While there is no sure way to counteract obstructionist actions, companies can successfully head them off. What this entails is developing ongoing relations with stakeholders in a project. And even in the planning stages of that project, it's important to reassure all stakeholders that their views will be taken into account and that fair methods will be employed to resolve them.

Little wonder that companies and other large organizations have devoted their energies to refining their mediation tactics to minimize their vulnerability and subsequent liability to mishaps. And with some success.

Here is one simple example. Back in the late-1990s, the Army Corps of Engineers (CoE) was charged with removing dozens of aging 50,000-gallon underground fuel tanks from a former Air Force base. Complicating matters, the base was now the site of the Salina, Kansas, airport. Work needed to be done quickly and safely—and without delay-causing disputes.

So the CoE turned to an alternative dispute resolution (ADR) technique called partnering. Long before they broke ground, CoE project planners brought together all concerned parties—from the private construction firms and their workers, to engineers, airport officials, and regulators. The ad hoc group's goal sounded simple: to brainstorm, then implement objectives everyone could buy into. But the partnering approach was a far cry from traditional dispute-resolution techniques, where people argue on behalf of their own agendas before finally compromising.

The CoE credits partnering with shaving more than $6 million from the airport project's $14 million budget. "When it works, it really works," one of the participants later said. "Ideas flow and people come up with good solutions that everyone buys into."

Similar positive results from partnering brought about a major sea change at the Corps. According to one study by a Corps member, called "Partnering Lessons Learned in the U.S. Army Corps of Engineers," during "the late 1980s, Corps construction projects were extremely adversarial." Litigated settlements became routine, while costs skyrocketed.

By contrast, the study claimed, "On partnered projects, cost increases, schedule growth, change order costs, and claims costs are all reduced. Overall, the CoE claims, partnering has helped save taxpayers more than $400 million annually in project-related litigation costs.

Partnering in Five Easy Steps

Partnering, by far the most common alternative dispute-resolution technique, can bring together even the most diverse interests in a dispute. In the early '90s, for example, the technique was used to unite farmers, loggers, environmentalists, and citizens of a five-county south-central Kansas region. All participants somehow depended on the 543,000-acre North Fork Ninnescah Watershed that became threatened by pollution-caused algae problems. Knowing that their region's future depended on a clean water supply, the group members agreed on two goals right at the outset:

reduce algae-causing pollutants to acceptable levels and increase the reservoir's useful life by an additional hundred years. The actual methods used, as well as the tools to monitor compliance, were also reached via consensus. And the objectives, thanks to the partnering approach, were met within four years.

Regardless of where it is applied, partnering recognizes that while different parties in a project have diverse goals, those goals themselves are legitimate. Construction firms legitimately want to make a fair profit on their work, for instance. Likewise, community members want the work done without damage to quality of life. The challenge is finding the overriding goals—rallying points, if you will—that everyone can buy into. In its "Partnering Guide for Civil Missions" the Army Corps of Engineers provides these five guidelines, each crucial if partnering is to succeed.

1. Participants must be actual stakeholders.

2. Participants must commit to the team approach.

3. Participants must commit the time and resources for the entire period the group remains active.

4. Participants must be representatives of organized groups that are capable of implementing agreed-upon solutions.

5. Participants must enjoy the support of the respective groups they represent.

Bag Full of Tricks

In fact, partnering is just one of a grab bag full of tactics that managers can use to help manage disputes. Charged with running hundreds of projects simultaneously, the U.S. Army Corps of Engineers, for example, relies heavily on an escalating series of alternative dispute-resolution tactics outlined briefly as follows. If one tactic fails, another can quickly take its place.

Informed Discussion.   Tensions are kept low via this technique because the parties discuss a matter without an obligation to devise a solution. Often, simple information sharing alleviates tensions.

Cooperative Decision Making.   Here the parties agree on ground rules for any future discussions, preventing shouting matches.

Conciliation.   Parties continue their discussions, but a neutral mediator stands ready to assist in fact finding or resolving procedural issues.

Facilitation.   A third party actively structures the discussions and acts as moderator, ensuring equal time to all parties, for example.

Mediation.   Third-party mediators—unlike facilitators—can huddle with stakeholders and walk disputes from meeting room to meeting room. For mediation to be successful, all stakeholders must share a desire to reach consensus.

Mini-Trial.   A third party acting as judge hears each side's case and presents his or her findings. The nonbinding judgment gives stakeholders a chance to amend their positions.

Third-Party Decision-Making.   Unlike facilitators or mediators, third-party decision making uses arbitrators to impose a decision on stakeholders. This is also known as arbitration.

All these tactics come with powerful advantages. First, they're designed to identify and resolve problems early on and in a tension-free atmosphere. Moreover, the range of solutions they provide goes well beyond what costly, time-consuming court proceedings would likely bring. Courts base their decisions on whatever the applicable laws happen to be. ADR solutions are limited only by the creativity of their participants—who are sometimes aided by outside facilitators.

Causes for Gripes

Despite the benefits, many experts believe that ADR isn't used nearly enough. Worse, even as many within companies fail to give dispute management its due, the potential causes of disputes continue to rise.

In the future, experts say, companies will need to manage armies of freelance tech workers and temporary workers who are often brought together to work on time-critical projects. Pressed to their limits, forced out of the information loop by managers, any one of these groups could spark a conflict. Some call this group the Information Age version of blue-collar workers. If that's true, unlike their hard-laboring predecessors, today's information and tech workers aren't unionized, a fact that's significant, according to some experts, because while unionized blue-collar workers are well versed in working through gripes—usually through arbitration—this new and still largely nonunion group of workers lacks formal channels for its grievances.

The all-too-frequent result: Problems fester, and productivity declines. The solution may often be to analyze a project plan while it's still on the drawing boards, identify potential problems—between two work teams with conflicting goals, for example—and then look for solutions. Perhaps a facilitator can jockey between teams, listening to gripes, and then propose solutions to streamline everyone's work.

In the future, more and more conflicts will likely arise from teams located in different nations. Just as manufacturers have long done, IT firms now routinely outsource programming tasks to cheap labor centers in India and Russia. If they are to remain competitive, companies must find ways to bring together such workers who are widely dispersed, both geographically and culturally. Yet in far too many projects, managers lack understanding of team-member cultures, how they differ and how they may conflict with one another.

When and How to Step In

It doesn't have to be that way. Some organizations outline dispute-resolution routes before work on a project even commences—often through a series of steps. When disputes first arise, for example, outside experts might appraise the situation and make recommendations. Then, if need be, mediators enter the picture to work out a voluntary compromise. Failing that, arbitration—where solutions are imposed—is the next required step, followed as a last resort by litigation.

Timing is critical with each step, say experts. Introduce a mediator too soon into the process, for instance, and some may feel they themselves aren't being paid attention to sufficiently, and for that reason they'll lack any sustained commitment to an agreement. Conversely, if a mediator comes on board too late, growing hard feelings may prevent stakeholders from compromising voluntarily.

Mapping a route for disputes isn't limited to defense projects. Building roads in sparsely populated Western Australia, for example, managers employed by the public works department wanted to move from "an 'inspection' culture towards a 'teamwork' approach." So when a contracting firm was chosen, it sent representatives to partnering workshops, where participants hammered out work methods and ways to manage disputes. Frequent site visits by public works officials reinforced the ties that developed at these meetings.

Similarly, when the U.S. Air Force worked with private contractors to build housing on its Lackland base near San Antonio, Texas, it used partnering, together with facilitators. The latter met with construction firms every two to three months.

The Future: E-Mediation and Trust Management

Sometimes, experts say, facilitators act preemptively, playing the role of fly on the wall by watching how work groups interact and maybe interviewing workers and managers to see if conflicts might be brewing. The results of such detective work may find their way into a report, which might in turn lead to, say, team-building sessions as a remedy.

Not everyone is entirely sold on ADR tactics, of course. Citing a lack of empirical research, a World Bank brief (www1.worldbank.org/publicsector/legal/adr.htm) stated, "Many questions remain regarding their actual success in increasing efficiency." The report focused largely on ADR tactics applied to developing nations and noted that their main drawback was lack of enforceability. "One theory holds that potential litigants who may well know they are in the wrong have no interest in a speedy resolution," the brief stated.

It is hoped that such cases are the exception. Because in the future, fast, efficient dispute-management tactics—call them ADR, or whatever—will become more crucial than ever to project success. One of the newest techniques being considered is online ADR, according to a March 2000 article in the *Michigan Telecommunications and Technology Law Review.* Using messaging or videoconferencing, online arbitration works best when distances and costs bar participants from meeting directly for lengthy periods. Other good uses include quick follow-on meetings. Online ADR can also filter out bad feelings during hostile disputes.

In the end, online ADR shares the goal of all other dispute-management techniques. And that is to build team trust by communicating and by demonstrating responsiveness to others' concerns.

International Threats

The companies most in need of workable dispute resolution tactics are those with broad-spanning international operations. Not only must they be able to forge effective relationships with their own workforces, whose worldview and customs are liable to be quite different from those of management. But they must also win over

local governments, businesses, and interest groups, where the differences in goals and outlook are liable to be wider still. Finally,
they must do all of this while keeping a sharp eye out for potential
political risks and with the knowledge that they may be the target
of enemies of the United States. Sounds like a tall order. And yet
America's best companies manage to do this every day. Their secret is to include dispute resolution with a grab bag full of risk-
mitigating techniques. Those techniques might include insurance
as well as hedging.

Preparation Is Key

Whether relying on careful contract negotiations, alternative dispute-resolution tactics, or finely honed communication skills, in
the end, combating liabilities and related risks perhaps comes
down to realistically assessing them and being prepared with a
contingency strategy when and if the risks present themselves. And
finally, it entails acting with measured prudence. Unfortunately in
a fast-changing business environment, it is not always possible to
avoid risk or even to adopt a conservative strategy. But by gearing
themselves to seize opportunities when these occur, companies
place themselves ahead of the curve.

Ironically, as a result they may find themselves floundering just
as surely as if they'd played it safe.

10

Innovating Too Much and Too Little

Lots of people try to build better mousetraps. But Joe Z. Tsien wanted to create a better mouse. And thanks to genetic engineering, he did. The Princeton University professor bred a strain of "genius" mice with turbo-charged neurons. Compared to their peers, Tsien's mice are whizzes at memory games, and they can navigate mazes like reality TV–show contestants. Someday, genius mice may help us treat diseases like Alzheimer's, or—ominously, perhaps—allow parents to raise brainier kids. And yet, at the dawn of the biotech era, they offer a mere peep at what's to come.

Cloned farm animals, plants that fight off insects, drugs that target viruses with cruise-missile accuracy, tiny chips that perform hundreds of medical tests in an instant: Right now all that's off-the-shelf technology. Wait a couple of years. Researchers have already grown living rat teeth in molds. Human teeth are sure to follow, and at some point kidneys, hearts, and other organs may also be grown in a test tube. Then there's the whole arena of gene therapy that will be able to target maladies that are genetically programmed into us and render them harmless. Recently researchers devised a way to deliver gene therapies via what are called micro-bubbles, tiny enough to circulate through to the smallest inner reaches of our systems. When ultrasound is applied to the body, the bubbles burst, creating tiny perforations in the lining of cells as a means of delivering the therapies. Thanks to discoveries like this, a family history of Alzheimer's, breast cancer, high blood pressure, or schizophrenia will no longer be cause for concern, as scientists discover the genes responsible for manifesting them and devise repairs.

With an unlimited frontier ahead, the lure of biotechnology transcends mere money. As a venture capitalist, where would you rather bet your money: on a company with a possible cancer cure, or some ecommerce wannabe that lets you order pizza online?

If truth be told, many VCs aren't sure. That's because few industries are as "out there" as biotech. It's an industry where over-innovating is a prerequisite. But it's also an industry where over-innovating can quickly lead to ruin—or undreamed-of success. Who could put a price tag on a cure for cancer? But by the same token who can estimate the cost of developing such a cure, or deduce how long it will take? In the biotech future, many companies will live and die based on their ability to correctly make such estimates.

Take Nektar Therapeutics. The San Carlos, California–based company is developing inhalers that administer drugs that must now be given via a shot. It's a technology that would be a godsend to the millions of diabetics around the world who must now inject themselves daily. And that's just one possible market. And yet, the company experienced a net loss of over $100 million in 2002.

The treatment of cancer profoundly illustrates how biotechs will radically change medicine. Right now, chemotherapy is often the treatment of choice. Chemo drugs work because they're designed to target and destroy the body's fast-growing cancerous cells. Problem is, your body's other fast-growing cells absorb the drugs, too. That's why chemo patients usually experience hair loss. Like chemo-drugs, bioengineered cancer treatments are also designed to be absorbed by diseased cells. But instead of destroying them, bioengineered treatments will go to work on select proteins within cancerous cells—in effect healing them from within. The result: Patients can be cured without the fatigue and other uncomfortable side effects of chemotherapy.

"It's Alive; It's Alive!"

Years of research are needed to create wonder drugs like these. Make that years of research with little idea of when the eventual payoff will arrive. Which is why Wall Street avoided biotech like the plague for almost a decade. Back around 1985–1990, you'll recall, biotech start-ups like Genentech were all the rage on Wall Street. But the bubble burst by 1991, as investors took a closer look at the time horizons to profitability. The prognosis appeared terrible. Between preclinical research, clinical studies, and a final review by the FDA, the approval process could take 13 or more years, while costs often topped $200 million. Burn rates like that scared away venture capitalists. Brokerage analysts quit covering biotech issues. The entire sector languished. Along came the Internet and its frenzy of sizzling new issues. The rest—as we all know—is history.

Or maybe not. Throughout the 1990s, surviving biotech firms doggedly pursued their work in relative obscurity. Improved computers and other information-age tools vastly speeded their efforts. Gradually, more biotech treatments traversed through the arduous FDA approval pipeline, even as FDA officials vowed to streamline that process. And a fledgling few companies started recording profits.

For the savvy company, these are not total negatives. The high development costs and lengthy treatment approval process creates enormous barriers to entry, which keeps competitors locked out. What's more, biotech drugs are patent protected. And that can effectively block competition for years. All of this can translate into hefty margins for companies that succeed in getting drugs to market.

But most exciting to biotech proponents is this simple fact. The industry is still in its embryonic stages, so to speak. In the pre-crash late '90s, if you added up the market cap of biotech's top-100 companies, if would total out to just over $200 billion, according to Cynthia Robbins-Roth, founding partner of BioVenture Consultants, indicating just how much room for growth exists. By contrast, Pfizer, one of the largest mainline drug companies (biotechies call such companies Big Pharma) has a market cap of $182 billion. GE's market cap stands at roughly $238 billion. And while that company undeniably "brings good things to life," you've got to wonder: How would investors value a company that could extend our own lives by 25 or more years?

On the Other Hand

Detractors are quick to point out just how much of a crapshoot developing biotech products can be. Start-ups may sift through 5,000 compounds in their search for promising drugs. Only five of these "finalists" ever make it to clinical trials. And only one of those five will get FDA approval. Meanwhile, the cost of developing that drug could reach $1 billion, according to some sources. Little wonder some analysts estimate that a frighteningly large proportion of companies only have months worth of cash left, and that in a sour economy.

Forced to operate in that extreme Darwinian environment, biotechs, like the life forms they work with, have no choice but to adapt or die. One way companies attempt the former is to maintain plenty of products in the pipeline. That way, if one fails, the successes can offset the loss. Obviously, it's not that simple. An optimal pipeline would include new cures to treat maladies where previous remedies have failed. Healthy biotech companies may also focus on a specific disease. And their long-term strategy would allow them to leverage their knowledge by developing a series of products. Still other biotechs may choose to focus on a single technology, such as drug delivery systems, and then develop a series of applications based on this technology. Protein Design Labs, for example, develops monoclonal antibodies used to treat or even prevent diseases, a once-hot area in medicine research that's recently gotten renewed attention. A horizontal technology like that can be sold to the many other firms hoping to develop a vaccine.

Size Matters in the Food Chain

BioVenture Consultants founder Robbins Roth says biotech companies' prospects for success can be ranked depending on their market cap. She's come up with three tiers. So-called tier 1 companies are on top of the food chain. These companies have a successful track record of shepherding drugs through the approval treadmill. Plus, they have multiple products in development. Most even have profits—even as they pour billions into research.

Tier 2 companies may or may not have revenues. And many depend on alliances with larger partners for support. Tier 2s make for riskier investments. But the rewards can come quickly following a significant drug approval. Often that's all it takes to propel the company into the first tier.

Tier 3 companies are the most speculative investments of all. And many have yet to win approval for a single product. These companies have bet the farm on a single innovation.

The future of tier 3 companies might not be decided for years as they grapple to master an area of research and then grapple some more to develop salable applications of their work, all the while watching their burn rate as if it were sand running through the hourglass destined to determine their fate.

By contrast, the Internet companies would seem to be an ideal environment for growth. Low fixed cost, minimal regulatory oversight, a fast-growing customer base. And still only a fraction of the Net's potential has been developed. And yet many a company has crashed and burned by over-innovating here as well.

Why No One's Heard of Viewdata

Years before George Gilder grew popular championing a bandwidth-rich networked society, British information technology consultant

James Martin predicted something close to, but not exactly like, the World Wide Web. In his book the *Telematic Society,* first published in 1978, Martin envisioned the kind of city he said would become a reality by the late '80s or late '90s. In that city, he said, there would be cables deep beneath the street that would be used to relay new versions of both radio and TV. More presciently he predicted that people would access the programming on these cables with as yet undeveloped radios or TV sets which would be used in conjunction with small keyboards. The wired and wireless connections would deliver a plethora of communication services. People could bank and shop from home, said Martin, in a chapter presciently titled "New Highways." In Martin's world, telecommunicating was also encouraged. And it would be facilitated "by the workscreens and videophones that transmit pictures and documents as well as speech."[1]

A quarter century later, the United States and other industrialized nations are fast-realizing something approaching the wired utopia that Martin and others foresaw. But the path to achieving that dream has been littered with companies that rushed in ahead of the curve. In fact, a multitude of information-delivery start-ups descended into oblivion years before the Internet even entered the world's lexicon. Among the first species of firms to become information superhighway roadkill were the so-called viewdata companies. As Martin described it: "The owner of a television set with the viewdata addition can gain access to computer systems that store information and programs."[2] In addition to text files, Martin believed that viewdata users might also access software programs stored by the service provider. Such programs might help them when completing "tax returns, selecting or analyzing stocks, or . . . playing games."

Several cable TV providers experimented with viewdata services. Some wired entire prototype communities, only to abandon them because of lack of consumer interest. One part of the problem, no doubt, was that the low-cost, high-powered microprocessors needed to make such online services feasible were still more than a decade away. But an even larger problem may have been the pricing schemes that early viewdata providers devised. Consumers, in some cases, were charged by the number of pages or documents they downloaded. Most people saw no point in paying for the sports scores and weather reports that already came to them free over TV and radio.

Another defect in these early business plans was that the providers—as often happens with a new medium—were vertically integrated. That is, they were the cable providers who controlled not only the content's creation but also its distribution. The two businesses require very different skill sets.

In contrast, the World Wide Web, by its very design, facilitated the launch of thousands and eventually millions of small, highly independent content-creation entities. This in turn created a vast sea of new information—most of it totally free and readily accessible to anyone. Little wonder that the online revolution spread so quickly.

Lessons Never Learned

Years after the demise of early viewdata experiments, wireless communications provider Metricom also found itself on the bleeding edge of the information highway learning curve. Its Ricochet service was designed to provide laptop users with up to a 128 kbs link to the Internet. The company received a reported $600 million in funding, some of it from WorldCom, as well as from Paul Allen's Vulcan Ventures. The money would be needed to create a cellular-like network throughout the nation. But jumping into wireless too fast hurt Ricochet. The modems that transformed laptops into untethered network devices cost as much as $300. Meanwhile, the company partnered with Internet service provider Earthlink, in addition to WorldCom and Go America, which were reportedly selling subscriptions for up to $80 per month.

Years later, the cost of wireless modems would drop to roughly $50, while newer Wi-Fi wireless bands offering speeds of 11 mbs and higher began sprouting up in airports, hotels, and other so-called hot spots where businesspeople congregated. Faced with debts of up to $1 billion, Metricom declared Chapter 11 in the summer of 2001.[3] Like the early viewdata providers, the company had sought to accelerate change by creating an entire infrastructure to support the effort. It would take a new company months later to purchase the rights to Richocet's equipment and work to restart service in a number of U.S. cities.

Pay Phone in the Sky

Satellite phone provider Iridium gives us yet another example of a company that invested heavily in infrastructure before the revenue spigot ever got turned on. Indeed, Iridium, which had to loft 66 satellites at a cost of $5 billion deserves special attention, because here was an undeniably sexy product that could seemingly achieve profitability with a relatively small number of gadget-loving, trend-conscious users. And that was especially true, given that its theoretical customer base was global in scope. While the company was destined to crumble in the wake of its huge expenditures, the exact reasons for its demise in the end had nothing to do with finance.

One of the original Iridium's principal sins (the company is now back in business under new ownership) is that, like the early viewdata providers, it failed to pay enough attention to marketing, according to Leonard M. Lodish at Wharton School. Except for foreign correspondents, yachtsmen, and a few intrepid world explorers, not many people needed the ability to make phone calls from any location on the planet. Or, at least, they weren't willing to pay the relatively high prices the company charged. Common sense would dictate that most travelers, particularly those traveling on business, spend the bulk of their time in cities, where Iridium's satellite phones worked poorly. (Tall buildings blocked a clear view to the skies.) Meanwhile, as cell phones evolved, frequent business travelers were able to use the same phone in Europe as in the United States and Japan and from just about anywhere within those areas.

Who's Going to Use This?

Lodish says that 60 percent of business failures hark back to poor marketing decisions. Problems acquiring the necessary finances or developing the technology are a distant second. Again, Iridium proves his point. The company enjoyed the backing of U.S. telecommunications giant Motorola. It was able to secure the billions necessary to build out its satellite network. And the phones generally worked as promised.

Ironically, Lodish says that the biggest mistake entrepreneurs make "is not exposing their product or service to the people they expect to buy it." And he points to surveys showing that only 21 percent of smaller company entrepreneurs employ any kind of concept testing prior to a product's launch. But big companies can leap into seemingly innovative new technologies just as blindly. Already plagued by debt, phone companies spent billions creating the supporting infrastructure for the so-called third generation (3G) wireless network that would give cell phones a broadband link to the Internet. A single phone company might expect to spend $16 billion on 3G infrastructure in Britain alone. Thanks to this massive worldwide build-out, "one-sixth of the globe will be equipped for the mobile Net, whether they're interested or not," notes *Business Week* European correspondent Stephen Baker.[4]

Undercharging and Undermarketing

Echoing the view that even the best new products need an eager customer base in order to succeed, one entrepreneur who nearly lost his Web development firm, observes, "They say if you build a better mousetrap, the world will beat its way to your door." But that presupposes that inventors understand exactly what kind of mousetraps they've devised.

Launched in a college dorm room in 1994, the company focused on developing corporate Web sites. But the reported trouble was that most companies didn't understand the Web during that period, much less why they needed a Web site themselves. As a result, the company's growth stalled. It wasn't until a new CEO arrived with a radically different marketing-oriented business plan for the company that sales began to take off once again. The new CEO, a software industry veteran, said the company had stagnated because management saw itself as a package firm when it was really in the business of providing solutions. That is, instead of providing the nuts and bolts needed to create a Web site, the company should furnish ongoing consulting. Just as important, the company needed to *raise* its prices. Thanks to this new vision, the company was able to reap far greater revenues from individual customers—from the $7,000 it charged for a software package to roughly $100,000 for consultation. The firm soon grew from 28 to 100 employees.[5]

Indeed, pricing is another reason that new products fail. While Iridium's price tag was too high for the company to achieve sufficient appeal, many entrepreneurs actually underprice their innovations, causing suspicious consumers to pass them by. And still another mistake: overadvertising, which raises customer-acquisition costs to absurd levels. Lodish points to online music retailer CD Now, which had customer acquisition costs of roughly $70 each. The company received only about $1 for each CD it sold, meaning that each of CD Now's customers theoretically would need to purchase 70 CDs before the company even began to make a profit.[6]

Destruction by Disruption

So how can companies avoid the traps that were the bane of highly innovative and heavily bankrolled firms like Iridium and CD Now? In his book *The Innovator's Dilemma: When New Technologies Cause Great Firms to Fail,* Harvard Business School professor Clayton Christensen says that one way is to recognize whether the innovation is sustaining or disruptive in nature. And that rule applies whether the company is developing the innovation itself or is reacting to an innovation developed by a competitor.

"What all sustaining technologies have in common is that they improve the performance of established products," Christensen says. By contrast, "disruptive technologies underperform established products in mainstream markets. But they have other features that a few fringe (and generally new) customers value." That is, as you'll see, they change certain fundamentals of a market.

Companies that develop disruptive technologies can themselves fail in the process, namely by over-innovating. But disruptive technologies are often most dangerous to the health of their competitors who are still focused on sustaining technologies, since those competitors may not recognize the importance of the new product.[7] The term, it seems, is hardly pejorative. Examples of disruptive technologies that Christensen cites include everything from transistors to off-road motorcycles to health-maintenance organizations. By their nature, such innovations challenged the status quo. Transistors put the makers of tube-TVs and radios out of business. For a time, off-road bikes threatened to do to street bikes what SUVs are doing to cars—steal customers—because they provide their owners with many more options for places to travel.

Although they present their makers with serious attendant risks along the way, disruptive technologies eventually do achieve widespread use. And for that reason, firms must devise a methodology for dealing with them.

Nowhere do disruptive technologies create more, well, disruption than in the technology sector. Christensen compares the efforts of companies to stay ahead of the innovation curve to trying to surmount a hill that's in the throes of a mudslide.

The Drive to Make Smaller Disk Drives

This is precisely the dilemma that disk-drive makers found themselves in during the pre–personal computer revolution era of the

1960s and '70s. Much of the innovation in disk drives was sustained in nature, Christensen says. Meaning, companies managed to tweak increased performance from their current product lines through a never-ending series of incremental improvements. These innovations were largely confined to 14-inch drives, which had become the standard for the highly expensive mainframe computers popular at the time. Disruptive technologies involved the use of smaller and smaller drives. At first, 8-inch drives were incorporated into minicomputers. The precursors to the desktop PCs, minicomputers were designed to serve the needs of smaller companies. Soon, however, 5.5-inch drives began appearing, then 3.5-inch drives. And these found a home within desktop PCs that were growing in popularity. Later, 2.5-inch and smaller drives began appearing in laptops.

In each instance, the older entrants found themselves shut out of growing markets and some failed as a result. The reason, notes Christensen, is that they were victims of their past success. That is, by providing exemplary products with sustained improvements to existing customers, they saw little reason to upset the apple cart. The makers of 14-inch drives knew that their mainframe-using customers would have no use for the smaller drives—that is, until those customers replaced their mainframes with minicomputers or PCs. Thus, any innovations that may have been introduced within the company were likely rejected. The better course for these larger companies would have been to foster the development of radically different products via a protected group within the firm. Yet, as you'll see, even this strategy has its risks.

Innovating in Sync

While innovators within larger organizations need space to develop their ideas unhindered, companies must maintain a delicate balance to ensure that their entrepreneurs are proceeding along a path that parallels the larger company's overall goals, according to a group of consultants writing in the *McKinsey Quarterly*.[8]

On the one hand, they say that separation and protection are vital, not just because the creative talent needed to develop innovative products works best outside a regimented setting. But still they say, the innovative team should maintain ties with the parent. There are some sound political reasons why this is so. For example, members of the legacy business are apt to distrust and may even sabotage efforts by the innovative team—and for a variety of reasons. Many in the established business fear that the new product division being nurtured will eventually render the legacy business obsolete. The work methods, customer focus, and spending of development teams may also go against the grain of the company's dominant culture.

As Christensen notes, legacy businesses that have become successful have done so by continuing to supply incremental improvements in service to their existing customers. What the innovation team is engaged in is an effort to reach out to new customers. But in doing so, the innovation team's spending by the innovation team can't be justified in the bottom line–bolstering way that it must within the legacy business. Which is yet another reason the legacy business should be granted a window into the innovation team's efforts in order to allay mistrust.

A Customer-Focused Approach

Christensen has some advice for larger companies that want to out-innovate their smaller, more entrepreneurial competitors. For starters, he says, responsibility for developing so-called disruptive technologies should go to areas of companies whose customers already have a need for them—on the theory that those areas of the company are already attuned to their customers' needs and they have a working rapport with the innovation's ultimate end-users.

Common sense will tell you that this strategy is eons beyond the more typical crapshoot approach of placing a few creative thinkers in an ivory tower. But Christensen gets a bit more technical in his analysis of why his customer-focused approach works.

According to something called the theory of resource dependence, "companies' freedom of action is limited to satisfying the needs of those entities outside the firm (customers and investors, primarily) that give it the resources it needs to survive."[9]

The theory implies that companies couldn't change that focus even if they wanted to. But this isn't necessarily so. IBM built its success by supplying its customers with mainframes and the expert guidance to use them. But it was able to provide that same level of expertise as it taught its customers how to build networks of desktop PCs.

Indeed, companies that go with the flow and devise customer-centric innovations harness a powerful force within their organizations. Ideas for new products typically pass up the chain of command before being fully funded. If all managers along the way cull through the list of possibilities, based on their interpretation of the company's current customer needs, then the highest level will truly receive the best of the best from among myriad ideas.

Trapped in the Past

The theory of resource dependence does explain why companies with established successful product lines often fail to mimic disruptive technologies when they appear—even when those products are simpler than ones the companies currently make.

Case in point, Christensen says, is IBM and Digital Equipment (DEC). Both companies enjoyed success with minicomputers. But while IBM set the standard for the PC—a disruptive technology that doomed minicomputers—DEC failed to create a micro popular with buyers. The reason had everything to do with how the two approached developing their respective PCs. DEC, perhaps underestimating the task at hand, launched its version within the mainstream organization. What happened as a result was that managers within the company were skeptical of the idea from the very beginning, fearing that it would steal sales from their higher-margin minicomputers. Four times the company tried to introduce profitable models, and four times it subsequently retreated.

IBM, meanwhile, can be credited for realizing the importance of the personal computer. While many makes and models were available, like early railroads that ran on tracks of different widths, early PCs used incompatible operating systems. The future of the industry depended on a common standard, and IBM, the acknowledged dean of data processing, was only too happy to provide one.

Acquiring DOS from the as-yet-unknown Microsoft Corporation, IBM set out doing what it believed it could do best: focus on the hardware. It created a standardized computer architecture that the industry would be compelled to emulate. And to do that, it created a separate division in Boca Raton, vertically integrated within itself to create its own supply chains and forge its own customer relationships. Years later, GM would use the same approach with its Saturn franchise, when it sought to create compact cars that could compete with the Japanese in price, quality, and feel.

Christensen provides one other piece of advice that, on reflection, makes common sense: Companies wishing to develop and market disruptive products should do so through divisions that match the "size of the market."[10] That is, while larger organizations may be well suited to serving established markets through incremental improvements, small organizations are needed to be readily in touch with the necessarily small markets their new products will serve.

Gorillas in Our Midst

Authors Geoffrey A. Moore, Paul Johnson, and Tom Kippola discuss companies that are most successful at innovating in their book *Gorilla Game: Picking Winners in High Technology*. Although seemingly dated, because of the dot-com stock market bomb, the essential precepts remain valid and are still followed by many investors and analysts.

The book starts off with the premise that certain companies are destined to become gorillas within their industries. They begin their ascension to the jungle throne by getting a lock on some new technology, preferably a technology the world desperately needs—whether people know it or not. As a next step, gorilla companies entice early adaptors to embrace the new technology. These companies garner so much market clout, they can literally force their new technology on the world. At that point, this new technology changes the very way we live and work. Think of what xerography did for office work and then for the stock of Xerox.

Eventually, this new technology creates its own satellite economy of suppliers and channel marketers. Again, think of the firms supplying the factories churning out Intel Pentium chips, and the computer companies that implant those chips in their latest PCs.

Want another example? VCRs using the VHS standard fit the gorilla definition almost perfectly. They've enabled millions of us to time-shift our lives, recording our favorite soaps during the day while we're at work, for example, and then watching them that night. Likewise, VCRs have allowed us to capture and immediately display important moments in our lives, while at the same time they spawned a multibillion-dollar videocassette rental industry. Only recently, after reigning supreme for well over a decade, is VCR technology in danger of being supplanted by digital cameras and recordable optical disks.

If you guessed that Microsoft was the ultimate gorilla company, you would be exactly right. Without question, the company rules the personal computing industry with its Windows operating system. With the exception of niche markets in graphics software and server technology, users who want to take advantage of the latest software have no choice but to build their platforms around Windows.

Adopting a similarly aggressive and high-margin business model, Microsoft also grew to dominate the markets for office suite software and Web browsers. It is only now, as the computer industry undergoes dramatic changes, that Microsoft's unrelenting hegemony is beginning to crack. The company has been unable to gain a firm foothold in businesses such as ultra-lightweight operating systems used by pagers, personal digital assistants, and cell phones. Many people believe that the future of information lies with these devices and not with desktop PCs. Nor has Microsoft secured a lock on software that would control the greatest software application of all: interactive TVs. These highly visible failures have occurred at a time when its core operating system is facing a stiff challenge from Linux. Some say that in the future, the operating systems on desktop PCs will become irrelevant, as software applications and storage move increasingly to the Web.

Likewise, some might say that Microsoft's failures have occurred in part because of its incredible successes. Customers, both large and small, have grown wary of a single corporation controlling so many aspects of their lives. And they've deliberately embraced alternatives. The clear lesson: Even the most fearsome gorillas eventually fall.

One example of a gorilla company that has garnered much attention is a San Mateo, California, software firm called Siebel Systems. The company has a secure niche within the fast-growing application service provider (ASP) industry. ASPs are companies that deliver software to clients either over the Internet or via some sort of private network. Housing the software in a centralized location saves the client company considerable headaches—principally, its own IT people needn't load programs individually onto thousands of company PCs. As for the ASP firm, it benefits by receiving a steady stream of revenue from clients who rent its software. Indeed, the monthly rents represent a predictable income flow. Moreover, client companies tend to stick with an ASP once they sign on, since the costs of a changeover would be prohibitive. For these reasons, many analysts saw Siebel as a classic gorilla company in the making. It has the high margins typical of a software provider, and it has a lock on its customers.

Gorilla Game authors also like to point to Cisco Systems, a company that was able to grow in tandem with the incredible upsurge in computer networking and the Internet. The company began by making simple routers; that is, devices that direct data traffic within networks. But over the years it proved uncannily able to evolve and continued to innovate right along with the rapidly growing industry, even in the face of stiff competition from nimble, well-funded, out-of-the-box-thinking start-ups. It subsequently grew to dominate the market for intelligent hubs, LAN switches, and remote access devices, according to the authors. As a result, they say, from 1992 to 1997, the company, founded by five Stanford University computer techs, went from "accounting for 15 percent of the industry's profits to nearly 50 percent."[11]

Exactly how they achieved that growth makes for a classic story. Back in the 1980s, two of the company founders, Sandra Lerner and Len Bosack, who both worked for Stanford, became frustrated that they couldn't communicate by electronic mail because they were using different and incompatible computer systems. Never mind that both systems reportedly came from the same manufacturer. Such a dilemma was commonplace during the pre-Internet '80s. As a result, Stanford's engineering school created a computer system that linked the university's various computer networks. From this effort, the term *router* emerged. The router would have likely found a small, though profitable, niche for itself, linking the many networks within companies, government agencies, and departments with one another, were it not for the birth of the Internet as a mass medium. Suddenly, instead of just two or three incompatible systems, there were now dozens, if not hundreds, that all needed to talk with one another. Embracing the router, Cisco managed to grow in tandem with the Internet. And at one point it was the largest corporation in the world—measured by market cap.

Yet even this kind of phenomenal success can come to an end, if a company's management does not have in place a plan to nurture the talent it will need in the future. Failure to produce a successor has brought down many a kingdom over the ages. And in modern times it has caused the demise of many a company. In no instance is this more true than in the case of family businesses.

11

Family Businesses and Poor Succession Planning

Even to a psychologist, the intricate web of interrelationships and hidden conflicts that can exist within a family business might seem more like the stuff of Shakespeare than of management consulting. But to Dr. Bernard Liebowitz, who is both a psychologist and a management consultant, it's all in a day's work. Here are just a few of the dilemmas that he says can exist within family companies.

Suppose, for example, that the son takes over the family business. But the father chooses to stay around. What sort of influence might the father have? It could be good or bad, says Liebowitz. The father might make it appear as if the son were running the business. At the same time, however, the father will be busy pulling the strings in the background—perhaps without the son even knowing it. Indeed, only through subtle clues would the son come to realize that he wasn't really in charge. For example, the son might hear "people saying things like 'But the old man said to me,'" the psychologist/consultant explains.

In some cases, the father might even watch his son take the business to a whole new level but never acknowledge that the son is responsible for its success. That attitude is bound to breed resentment over the years. And all too often, the pent-up feelings eventually boil over.

Bad as they appear, problems like that get exacerbated when the father and his son or daughter have very different views on how the business should be run. Things can get messier still if the father has managers who have grown up with the company and who remain loyal to the father even after he retires. When taking up the company's reins, the son or daughter confronts dad's old cronies. As Liebowitz describes the quandary:

> These "old cronies" may be a threat in some instances but also in many cases they may represent a hindrance to the growth of the company. Their loyalty to the father may also be reflected in their wanting to keep things intact, i.e., "how your father did it." But, also, any change might and frequently does represent a threat to them, that is, they may be unprepared to learn new ways of doing things.

So often, in the course of the transition, new lawyers, new accountants, and perhaps a fresh crop of managers come into the company. "It's a way of closing the door on the father's reign," Liebowitz explains. Nevertheless, it can disrupt operations and alienate employees and customers—sometimes for months on end.

The Generalissimo Franco Dilemma

A great number of family businesses also get into trouble because the patriarch refuses to budge from power, despite the fact that his heirs may be champing at the bit to take over. When this happens, the business can fall behind in a number of respects. Much-needed new technology will not be brought in. Necessary new people will not be hired. The result? As the company falls further and further behind, the heir is set up to fail when that individual eventually takes over. In fact, when the transition does finally take place, often the business is already in trouble. Yet responsibility for the failure falls on the heir's shoulders and not—conveniently enough—on the founder. Indeed, the father can say that he knew all along what would happen to the company.

Sibling Rivalry

Such problems, of course, arise from the convoluted emotions, histories, and relationships that can only be found within families. Ironically, these family conflicts that threaten to ruin the business may have nothing to do with the company itself. Rather, they stem from deep-rooted problems festering between family members—conflicts that may have endured for years.

Suppose, for example, that the patriarch has died. And in due course, the son takes over the business—even though he's incompetent. But there, waiting in the wings, is another brother or brother-in-law who definitely has what it takes to run the company. The challenge for a counselor is to ease out the incompetent son and bring in the person who can help the company thrive. A similar situation can arise when a widow assumes control of the company but doesn't have the proper background to manage it. The delicate task again becomes easing out the old generation in favor of the new.

And the stickiest family business issue of all? Perhaps it is when the father wishes to remarry, but the children strongly object. In their minds they believe they were the ones who labored to help the business and the family succeed. Now they see their interests sorely threatened.

The World's Greatest Economy Is Built on Family Businesses

Finding the right strategies to assist a family business facing problems like these is especially critical. That's because of the vital role that family companies play in the U.S. economy. According to family business expert Shel Horowitz, "Eighty-five percent of North American companies are family owned."[1] Thirty-five percent of the Fortune 500 firms could be categorized as family owned. And what's more, family companies employ half of all workers and create 65 percent of all new jobs in the United States, Horowitz writes.

But if the family is the strongest engine of economic growth in our nation, it is also perhaps the most fragile: "Less than one third of family businesses survive the transition from the first to second generation ownership," according to Nancy Bowman-Upton, who directs the Institute for Family Business at Baylor University in Waco, Texas. "Of those that do [keep their doors open]," she says, "about half do not survive the transition from second to third generation."[2]

Why Family Companies Fail

Bowman-Upton points to four chief reasons why family businesses are unsuccessful at transferring ownership to the next generation. Topping the list, the company simply may not be run properly, which is to say it may no longer be viable. In other instances, the current owner may have no desire to go through the complicated process of transferring ownership. Likewise, the younger generation may not want any part of their parents' company. Solving any of the previous three problems will prove tough going. But that's not true for the fourth major reason why business transfers fail to take place: "lack of planning."

Succession planning, it seems, is something many family business owners are loath to undertake. Many family business experts believe there are key reasons why this is so, all of them delicate, complex, and dicey: On the founder's part, the reluctance could include a fear of death, a hesitancy to relinquish power or control, a fear of a loss of personal identity, and even jealousy and a sense of rivalry toward the successor. Founders may see that their peers continue to work and may feel that the company's customers depend on their staying.[3]

The founders may also feel—justifiably or not—that their heirs don't want to participate in the business. Or they may resist making agonizing choices over which child is best qualified for the top spot, knowing the repercussions of whatever decision they make. While the heirs—perhaps because of deep-rooted family issues—

may feel reluctant to jump into a position of responsibility within the company because they know that in so doing, they're liable to be judged in a highly personal way. Whichever member of the next generation gets chosen to lead the company, that individual undoubtedly will have very real anxieties, as well. Foremost, new leaders will begin to question their own abilities. Do they have what it takes to unite the family under the new regime?

Members of the larger family may have equally deep-rooted reasons why they don't wish to confront succession planning. Founders' spouses may be reluctant to relinquish their informal control; certain norms within the family may prohibit speaking about the parent's mortality. Other family customs might prevent critically comparing the strengths of one sibling over another. As Dr. Liebowitz explains:

> From the father's point of view, to develop a succession plan can easily open all of these cans of worms. As one father said to me, "I want all the kids at my funeral," the implication being that were he to develop a succession plan and make some decisions about the successor, the equity distribution, etc., the fallout would be entirely too disruptive of the family peace and harmony.

Also, nonfamily employees are often left to worry just as much about their own future with the company. No doubt in their minds they'll have plenty of questions, Liebowitz explains, such as "Will the company be sold?" or "Will daughter *a* or son *b* want me to remain?" Or they may resist taking part in a succession plan because of their long relationship with the founder or simply out of fear of change.

Rule Number One: Formulate Rules

Despite the resistance stakeholders may have, family businesses need a succession plan if they are to survive from generation to generation, according to Bowman-Upton, just as all businesses need a strategic plan if they are to grow. (Of course, families with considerable wealth to pass on also need an estate plan to map out how assets will be passed to future generations in a tax-efficient manner.) A well-thought-out succession plan can allay many of the fears that all stakeholders in the business may face. The plan should spell out "policies for the family's role in the business." Under what circumstances can a family member enter the business, for example, and under what circumstances should that person leave? The plan should also contain some sort of mission statement that describes the family's values and how those values relate to the running of the business.

In addition, the succession plan should outline exactly how the transfer of leadership will occur and should establish the criteria that heirs must meet before being deemed ready to assume their leadership role. For an example of just how involved and personal a succession plan can become, and of its importance, the Family Business Center at the University of Massachusetts[4] points to the issue of education. A son or daughter in a family business might ask the founder whether the person being groomed for the top spot needs a college degree. If the founder is unsure, the sibling might well say, "If you do, in fact, believe that person should go to college, then you need to 'clarify the rule.'" As an alternative, the father could stop pestering the son to return to college. Failure to do either over the long haul could jeopardize the father's relationship with the son and wind up damaging the company.

Rules that form part of a succession plan can, in fact, be used to clarify many difficult issues. Another example of a rule might be for the son to first get a job with some other company before assuming a critical role with the family business. In other words, the heir should first demonstrate his acumen someplace else.

Families Must Serve the Business

Revered management guru Peter F. Drucker devised four rules that he believes family businesses need to follow to ensure their survival.[5] First, he says, family members who work in the company need to be as competent as their nonfamily peers. Those family members who don't pull their weight earn the understandable resentment of nonfamily employees but also of family members who do work hard. "It is much cheaper to pay a lazy nephew not to come to work than to keep him on the payroll," Drucker explains.

DuPont, for example, became one of history's most successful family companies, perhaps in part because it had a policy similar to one that some law and accounting firms have with respect to future partners. Under the conglomerate's policy, formulated in an earlier era, all male family members received low-level jobs at the company by decree. And they were allowed to stay with the company for a decade. After that, they were encouraged to find some other work, unless they demonstrated that they might someday be able to fill a top-management spot.

Drucker's second rule is that family businesses should look to fill vital staff positions with nonfamily members. The rationale here is that while family members are well versed in the operations and goals of the firm, they can't be up to speed on specialties such as "marketing, finance, research, or human resources," Drucker claims.

What's more, says Drucker, the company should reserve a key top spot for a nonfamily member, perhaps to serve as a kind of *consigliore,* providing the family with a much-needed outside point of view. Drucker says that the positions typically filled by outsiders, in this instance, are in finance or research, since both require considerable expertise.

And the fourth rule: Succession planning should be overseen by an outsider—that is, someone who is not a family member or an employee of the company. This is so the outsider will not be biased by the stake that person may have in the future of either the family or the company.

Even when family companies thrive by following the other three rules, Drucker says that succession planning can prove to be

their Achilles heel. This is because when power is being trans-
ferred, the needs of the business and those of the family stand a
good chance of colliding.[6]

Reconciling All Points of View

When he counsels family businesses Liebowitz tries to bring together these conflicting points of view.

> I focus on how each sees the business and what each would want
> from the business. Sometimes it is money, sometimes control, an
> equity to be sold, a monthly stipend, a memorial that would ex-
> tend through the ages, etc. My task is to reconcile all of these
> possible views. Frequently, it does boil down to money, but the
> route to a resolution can be charted through a combination of
> views. For example, "you want the business to provide you with
> a monthly stipend? Fine, but that means that the control of the
> business has to reside in the hands of your brother (whom you
> hate)." Or, "you want to be able to sell your shares in the busi-
> ness? Fine! However, since no one outside of the business will
> want to buy it, your only real choice is to sell it to your sister
> who is in the business and the only way she can buy it is in a
> 'payout' over time."

As part of his efforts to help the business, Liebowitz does
what he calls a present state analysis. This involves interviewing
many people within the organization, both family members and
regular employees. The goal of the interviews is not just to acquire lots of information but to convince all concerned that he is,
in fact, impartial.

To assemble a complete picture of the family's dynamics,
Liebowitz normally must interview family members who, though
not a part of the business's everyday affairs, do nevertheless influence its direction. "You might have an in-law who is influential on
her husband or spouse who is in the business. Unless I get access
to her, I'm missing a whole act in the drama," he says.

In a hypothetical example, Liebowitz points to one sibling who spends his time, let's say, skiing in Colorado. "The kid who's out in God's country could be the deciding vote between two brothers. Each one plays up to that person," he explains.

Goals and Visions

Although his methods derive much from talk therapy, Liebowitz says there are fundamental differences between counseling and consulting. While a psychologist might look at the past and attempt to ferret out the source of a conflict or problem, a management consultant must look toward the future to discover what the family's goals and vision for the company might be. But one thing is similar: Getting family members to bring up aching old problems can be like pulling teeth.

> For example, a family had been in therapy (individual and family) with a therapist for a long time, the precipitating reason being an ongoing conflict between the father and son. (It obviously was much more complicated then that.) Their therapist referred them to me because the son was threatening to leave the business unless he was made president. The father said the son wasn't ready. What we proceeded to do was to define "being ready." The father finally agreed that, were the son to increase sales by a certain percentage and to open up two difficult territories, that would constitute "being ready" and he would make his son president. The son in fact surpassed these criteria. The father, however, reneged on his agreement. It turned out that the father was afraid of becoming useless, cast aside—his primary buttress to his self-worth was the business. We worked out a situation whereby the son did become president but the father's role in the business was to continue making significant contributions which we defined in detail. I referred them back to therapy which proceeded rapidly from that point because the focus shifted from the son as a problem to the father who needed to take a look at himself and his marriage.

Perhaps because the problems are deeply rooted in personalities and family dynamics, when Liebowitz helps family members achieve their vision, his deliberate focus is not on personalities but on things like goals, performance measures, and criteria. All too often, in the absence of counseling, these goals become lost as a result of unfocused conflicts and accusations. For example, one family member might accuse another of not working hard enough. Perhaps the person doesn't come in to work until 10:00 each morning. Or maybe someone stands accused of spending too much money. To Liebowitz, none of these accusations are measurable, nor are they necessarily justified. Someone can come in at 10:00 and still be very productive, while money spent wisely on the business can more than pay for itself.

The All-Important Family-Business Retreat

Like other family business counselors, Liebowitz encourages families to confront their problems and devise solutions during what he calls a retreat (although the location is often a city hotel). A retreat forces families to talk and react to one another, since they're all literally confined together until they do. And indeed, the going's apt to be rough, as the questions family members must face are difficult ones.

The Small Business Administration outlines a few of the tough issues family companies must decide upon during a retreat.[7]

What Future Goals Does the Family Have?   What is the consensus? Do family members want to grow the business or keep it as it is? Do they always want to actively manage the company, or would it be best if the company reins were handed over to professional managers?

What Are the Plans of the Family's Younger Generation?   If younger members of the family don't wish to involve themselves in the company, would it be better if the family prepared now to sell?

Which Family Members Wish to Remain with the Business?   This is an opportunity for all family members to make their wishes known and for the family as a group to map out a strategy that acknowledges the desires of individual members. Something also to consider is whether the business can realistically accommodate everyone's wishes.

Which Family Member Possesses the Most Aptitude to Lead the Company?   Discussions in this area are among the most delicate. Family members are accustomed to accepting each other as they are. But as servants of the business, they must objectively evaluate the abilities of their blood relations.

What Should Happen If More Than One Member of the Family Desires to Lead the Company?   Foreseeing such conflicts early can help avoid tremendous problems later. Can the wishes of everyone be accommodated? Are there mutually acceptable alternatives to these capable members serving as head of the company?

How Should Younger Members Who Do Not Necessarily Wish to Run the Company but Seek Some Role in It Be Accommodated? Should they gain work experience within the company or seek it in another job? If they choose not to be involved in the day-to-day affairs, what role should they be allowed to play in the company's long-term direction?

How Can Family Members Who Wish No Role in the Business Be Accommodated?   Should they be encouraged to play a role nonetheless, or should the family begin looking for professional managers?

What Procedures Can Be Set Up to Groom the Company's Future Leaders?   As discussed in detail further on, this process can take several years and involves not just educating the new leader on running the business but announcing to the community that this person has been named as heir apparent.

What Would Be the Most Opportune Times to Make a Change-over of Leadership?   This must take into account when the older generation feels ready to retire and when the younger generation will be competent to take up the reins. Also important are the fiscal shape of the business and the stage of its growth. Should the business adhere to certain ratios before it's deemed ready to be turned over? Are there acquisitions or divestitures that should be enacted first? Will it be necessary to groom nonfamily members to assume new roles when the transition takes place?

How Can the Company's Current Leader(s) Best Prepare Themselves and the Business for an Eventual Smooth Transition of Power?   As will be discussed further on, older family members must make preparations in their own lives. If the business has occupied much of their time throughout their lives, they will need to find some other activities for fulfillment.

Are the Financial Implications of a Power Changeover Fully Understood by All Involved?   Older family members may wish to be "bought out" so that they will have the funds necessary to retire. Will this mean that the business needs to borrow money (perform an internal IPO) in order to make the transition workable? Should payments be made to older-generation members in a lump sum or gradually?

The Meeting Agenda

If all the previous sounds like a lot to discuss in the course of a family retreat, the SBA recommends an agenda something like the following one. Each bulleted topic would receive roughly 1½ to 2 hours, while the retreat itself would last two days. It should be held far enough from the workplace that no one is tempted to sneak away to get some work done.

Day One
Examine the business historically and operationally.
Review the roles family members currently play in the business
and examine their career goals.
Analyze goals and plans for the company's future with an eye
toward how individual family members might take part.
Ask individuals to write up goal statements for themselves and
the business, formulate or review the company mission statement and goals.

Day Two
Determine those aspects of the business that require written policy statements and create first drafts or outlines.
Determine areas of the business that would benefit from better
communications and how communications might be improved there.
Review session and preliminary agenda for subsequent
meeting.[8]

Further Considerations

Exhaustive as it might appear, even the previous agenda is not
complete. An important goal of a family retreat, for example,
might be to create rules or guidelines for future discussions on the
topic of succession. By what rules, for example, should siblings
who are rivals or otherwise be allowed to air their grievances or
differences of opinion over how the company is run?[9] How much
information should all family members receive, and when are the
appropriate times to talk about the business?

One of the most delicate but also important elements of a succession plan is to create a strategy for what to do if illness or death
strikes a key person in the company—a set of emergency procedures, if you will.[10] If the worst happens, should the company be
sold? And how—short of a costly, unproductive lawsuit—can disputes among family members be resolved?

Saying Good-bye

One of the chief reasons successions fail is because the older generation refuses to let go. The Small Business Administration has this advice for family businesses when some family members are encroaching more than they should: It essentially comes down to buying them out or easing them out. For example, you can minimize a family member's unwanted influence by offering to convert that person's investment in the corporation to preferred stock, which represents a piece of ownership but also pays a dividend. Estate planners can also devise strategies that would allow some family members to transfer ownership to younger relatives. Similarly, with expert advice from lawyers and other consultants, the business can be restructured via a new partnership agreement that redefines who has decision-making authority. Finally, retiring family members can be encouraged to devote more time to hobbies or community service.[11]

Often the business's current owners will have logical reasons for wishing to remain at the helm. Besides the personal baggage, owners may face some real financial concerns when planning for retirement. On the one hand, they can arrange a kind of leveraged buyout that will allow them to take a retirement nest egg from the firm. However, that could strap the business with debt, setting up the children to fail. The other solution—continuing to rely on the company for financial security in retirement—has drawbacks as well, because the owner may feel compelled to step in and attack the problems that are bound to spring up during the new leader's tenure.

Here once again is where a retreat can be helpful, because the family can decide how to ensure the financial well-being of the founder while smoothing the way for the new owner's success. A financial planner is essential to this process.

Enacting the Succession Plan

Assuming that an acceptable succession plan can be worked out, enacting it demands focus from all participants. Bowman-Upton says that the actual succession plays out over four stages. In the first phase, initiation, young children become aware of their parents' involvement in the business. Even at this early stage, parents can unknowingly set the stage for failure later on. If dinner table talk on many a night focuses on problems stemming from the business, the children will naturally be turned off. Just as they will be if parents are deliberately tight-lipped about what goes on at work. The children, as a result, may come to believe that their involvement in the business is unwelcome.

Noting that many parents take pains not to force involvement on their children, Bowman-Upton suggests that if you truly want them to take the reins someday, you must make that point very clearly to them. If you fail to do so, they may interpret your silence as lack of faith in their abilities. Instead, use the business as a way to share with your children. Openly discuss the positive and negative aspects of it.

Bowman-Upton calls the next stage in the succession process "selection"; during this time, the founder actually chooses a successor. "Of the entire transition process, this can be the most difficult step, especially if you must choose among a number of children," she says. Companies that fail at this stage risk greater failure later on. Selecting an heir can be especially difficult when more than one sibling wants the job. Some public companies have an easy solution to this dilemma and consider it their good fortune to have several qualified candidates to rely upon. That solution, letting the candidates openly compete for the job, would hardly work in a family business.

But another corporate model can serve family companies better, Bowman-Upton says. Here individual family members each write up a job description for the company's next president. The job description might be based on the company's strategic plan and include goals the new leader would be expected to meet.

The job description might also include the requirements for the position—such as skills, experience, and, possibly, personality attributes. For example, if a firm plans to pursue growth in the next five years, the potential successor would be required to have a thorough understanding of business valuations and financial statements, plus the ability to negotiate. Also, the person should possess a good relationship with local financial institutions.

Designing such job descriptions provides a number of benefits. First, it removes the emotional aspect from successor selection. If necessary, the successor can acquire any special training the job description outlines. Second, it provides the business with a set of future goals and objectives that have been developed by the whole family. Finally, the founder may feel more comfortable knowing objectives are in place that will ensure a growing, healthy business in the years ahead.

The third phase, which Bowman-Upton calls the education phase, is also crucial, because this is when the leader in waiting is actually groomed to take over. Often family companies fail here because parents feel awkward teaching their children about the business. If that's the case, Bowman-Upton suggests appointing someone else within the company to do the job. Whoever the trainer happens to be, Bowman-Upton suggests that the training method be objective oriented. In a variation on management by objectives, she suggests that both mentor and pupil agree beforehand what the lesson plan will be, how long it will take, and how the pupil's progress is to be evaluated. To augment the training, the pupil should have an actual critical job within the company—ideally, one that enables this individual to interact with people at all levels. This is preferable to giving the pupil a staff position, such as assistant to the president, she says, because in the latter case, the pupil only follows the president around and acts upon requests.

The pupil must master and be evaluated on many crucial areas within a short time—among them, decision-making, leadership, risk tolerance, ability to deal with others, and grace under pressure. One way to test all of these attributes is to give the pupil a problem to solve, such as how to price a product, and then discuss the thinking process used by both master and pupil in coming up with a solution.

Sometimes transitions can fail when the pupil is seemingly foisted on those with whom the firm does business. So, while this training is going on, the pupil should also be introduced to customers, bankers, suppliers, and others. And little by little, the pupil should work with them.

The New Boss

Finally comes the fourth stage, or the actual changing of the guard. Before the event takes place, some recommend that the heir get a chance to run the company for relatively brief periods, say, while the owner takes a vacation. This also helps business owners view the company from afar and, it is hoped, grow convinced that it will continue to thrive after their retirement.

However, when the actual moment of transition occurs, it's vital that this occur cleanly. Old owners should tell all concerned that they are behind the transfer of power. Then owners should step back and give newcomers the space they need. Once owners announce retirement, they must follow through. "There's no such thing as semi-retirement," Bowman-Upton says. If the children don't feel that they have free rein to run the business as they see fit, they may leave.

While prospective new leaders are adjusting to that role, owners will face adjustments of their own and may feel a tremendous reluctance to let go of the reins. Their own self-esteem is closely tied to the company, it was the source of their social life, and it structured their time and gave meaning to their existence. Losing control of the business will inevitably create a huge void. It's important for owners to develop alternatives to the company, even while grooming someone to take over.

Of course, new bosses face a whole host of challenges. While they struggle to find a place for themselves in the business, they must quickly craft the right relationships among family members. This is especially complicated when the company moves from being the strong-armed reign of the founder to a more committee-like approach, which inevitably happens in the vacuum created when the founder steps down.[12] Businesses can easily succumb to indecisiveness at this point. But one way to work around this is to create a board that includes nonfamily members who can, one hopes, act without bias, especially in sensitive areas like compensation.[13] Equally important, just as the business needs a road map through its succession plan, new bosses (or the people some call the emerging leaders) need a plan outlining their goals and strategies as well.

Families Coming Together

Despite the hassles of going through this process, there are ample rewards, says Liebowitz. "A family business gives families an opportunity to work out problems. It's a stage. If it's dealt with appropriately, there's a very positive impact. I've seen kids who have not been close to their parents come into the family and the family business. And consequently they develop an appreciation of their parents that gradually evolves into something more personal."[14]

While family businesses can succeed or fail based on their ability to transfer ownership from generation to generation, other companies are often imperiled because of ill-begotten strategy. As you'll see in the next chapter, this is especially true when the company chooses a fast-growth strategy via acquisitions.

12

Failed Synergies

How many times have we seen it on the news? Executives of two companies glad-hand each other before the TV cameras and announce either a merger or a strategic alliance. Speaking to Lou Dobbs on CNN or Neal Cavuto on Fox, the executives wax on about the incredible synergies that will spring from their union. Few engaged couples appear as excited at the prospect of their nuptials. In 2001 a breathtaking 7,500 deals totaling $819 billion were hammered together in the United States alone. The figure represented half the world's M&A (merger and acquisition) volume. And due mainly to the current economic slowdown, those numbers were down significantly from prior years.[1]

Sadly, however, no matter how much euphoria surrounds the alliance at its inception, all too often months later, when the business world's attention is focused elsewhere, a decline in the stock price of both companies will prompt a story in *Business Week* or *Forbes* about how problems between the two organizations' cultures were causing the union to fail. Business strategists can point to several high-profile alliances between companies that you might think are large enough and smart enough to get it right. Remember Taligent, the ill-fated venture between IBM and Apple Computer aimed at developing an operating system to rival Microsoft's Windows? After months of efforts by more than 100 researchers who burned through millions of dollars, a Windows-quashing OS failed to emerge. Instead, Windows faced its only real challenge from a single maverick Finnish programmer whose Linux OS was embraced by the open source movement and ultimately by Big Blue itself.

Yet even with odds stacked heavily against them, companies continue to mine for ethereal synergies by linking themselves with each other. Those linkages might be through formal mergers or through less tightly bound alliances or joint ventures. Although the two types of unions would seem to be somewhat different, in terms of how they are viewed by shareholders, at the operations level, where the merger will either succeed or fail, the distinctions are notably blurred. One company might acquire a subsidiary and take a hands-off attitude toward its management, as was the case when Dutch insurance giant AEGON acquired Transamerica. An alliance, by contrast, might receive too much attention from both parties—a possible problem with Taligent.

The Urge to Merge

Regardless of the form it takes, the current enthusiasm for strategic alliances goes back roughly 10 years. That was the era when major companies created VP-level positions charged with implementing strategic partnerships. "Before long, we were consumed by the idea that everything was strategic and nothing was tactical," one global management noted in *Forbes*. "Who would want to be vice president of tactics?"[2]

A reliance on tactics implies that companies will have an easier time developing needed assets internally, as opposed to seeking them elsewhere. To be sure, compelling arguments can be made on both sides. But the fact remains that "half or more of big mergers, acquisitions, and alliances you read about in newspapers fail to create significant shareholder value,"[3] according to an article that appeared in the *McKinsey Quarterly*. In fact, they may actually destroy value half the time.[4] That's according to an array of studies.

But it still begs the question: Why—even in the face of dire statistics pointing to the likelihood of their failing—do companies plunge ahead with so many mergers? "It's often a world of hubris and empire building," says Richard Leftwich, who teaches at the University of Chicago Graduate School of Business.[5] When the CEO is told to grow the company by 20 percent or more per year, acquisitions become the only viable option.

The urge to merge became even stronger in the light-speed dot-com world, when management realized that it was far easier to create market share by treaty than by conquest. In the summer of 2002, the Web site Orgnet.com detailed 222 alliances, most of them in the dot-com sector. The result of these unions has been a three-dimensional tangle of linkages that has seemingly borne little fruit. One management consultant remarked that if many of the highly publicized companies had focused on tactics instead of on ivory tower–devised alliances they might still be thriving today.

Shareholder Value

Yet still unanswered is the question: Why do so many mergers fail, even though they appear to make perfect sense on paper? Failure can be judged by a variety of metrics, some easily quantifiable, some not. Over the years, a group of researchers writing in the *McKinsey Quarterly* have looked at such things as shareholder value and revenue growth as leading indicators of success. What they've found is that mergers have a hard time living up to expectations in both areas.

Not surprisingly, investors favor mergers that form part of a company's overall expansionist strategy. This conclusion was reached by three *McKinsey* researchers: Hans Bieshaar, Alexander van Wassenaer, and Jeremy Knight.[6] Their study looked at stock price movements in the days before and after a merger announcement. And the three attempted to correlate stock price with the strategy that management claimed was behind the union. Expansion was defined broadly to include companies entering new geographic areas or creating new distribution channels. "The market seems to be less tolerant of 'transformative' deals," the three said. Transformative deals were simply those that attempted "to move companies into new lines of business or remove a chunk of an otherwise healthy business portfolio."

Finally, the study also found that strategies that relied on alliances and joint ventures, in place of a more formalized merger, also failed to enhance shareholder value significantly.

Revenue

Another group of *McKinsey* researchers, Matthias M. Bekier, Anna J. Bogardus, and Tim Oldham, looked at revenue growth that occurred following a merger. They discovered that mergers often fail to grow revenues to the degree their planners first envisioned. To determine this, the consulting firm studied the acquisitions made by 157 public companies between 1995 and 1996. The results: Just 12 percent grew significantly. "In fact, most sloths remained sloths, while most solid performers slowed down,"[7] the researchers noted. Overall, the study found that growth rates among acquiring firms were on average 4 percentage points below the industry norm. This finding was particularly significant because the study looked at companies within 11 different sectors, implying that it applied across the board. Moreover, the revenue-growth slowdown was likely to occur in both large and small acquisitions. Part of the reason revenue growth lagged may have been because cost-savings promised by the merger failed to appear in at least 40 percent of the cases, similar studies have shown.[8]

Yet a relatively small number—roughly 12 percent—of companies did achieve revenue growth rates that exceeded industry norms following a merger. What was their secret? According to the *McKinsey* study authors, these companies took care of business within their own organizations before embarking on a buying binge. For starters, they reined in costs. Also, they identified and worked to retain employees who were crucial to serving their existing customers. A vital task, as it turns out. Outstanding employees at all levels within merged companies typically receive headhunter inquiries five days or less following the announcement of a merger.[9]

Two business analysts, Ira T. Kay and Mike Shelton, who make that claim also say that companies adept at the merger process organized those employees into teams that could implement the company's goals and culture throughout the now-enlarged organization. This is very similar to the strategy Cisco is said to follow when it acquires a new company. At the height of the company's pre–market crash growth, it was acquiring a new company every two weeks on average. Not surprisingly, it developed highly effective procedures that allowed the company to quickly integrate its acquisitions: Months or perhaps even years before the union actually took place, analysts within Cisco were closely studying the company. Sometimes Cisco would make a first move by acquiring a small ownership position in the company—the purpose being to provide a beachhead through which to analyze the target company more closely.

Understanding the inner workings of the target company allowed Cisco to move quickly to meld its operations when the merger actually took place. A 1999 merger with the fiber optics equipment-maker Cerent Corp provides an example. Even as details of the merger were being finalized, a group of Cisco employees descended on Cerent. The team reportedly sat down with the target company's employees, outlining their new job titles and bonus plans. The preparations paid off, as very few Cerent employees chose to leave the company during the critical two months following the merger.

The Human Element

Cisco's acquisition tactics work because they emphasize the human element of the merger process. In fact, while "Plenty of attention is paid to the legal, financial, and operational elements of mergers and acquisitions," say management experts Kay and Shelton, "executives who have been through the merger process now recognize that in today's economy, the management of the human side of change is the real key to maximizing the value of the deal."[10] By the same token, the two claim, problems related to personnel tend to lie at the heart of failed deals.

People problems can result from a number of different things. Some merging companies, for example, wishing to curry favor with Wall Street, proceed headlong with integrating the two companies without proper preparation. This causes disruptions in both companies that hamper revenue growth. Indeed, if revenue growth is the goal, management would do well to hold off on integration efforts. Rather than engage in full-blown evaluations of the entire employee roster, management's first goal should be ensuring the overall stability of both companies. That means incentivizing key people within both organizations to prevent them from leaving before the merger takes place. For lower-level employees, incentives often amount to 50 percent of their pay over anywhere from a three- to nine-month period, Kay and Shelton claim. Sometimes the amounts can be paid in installments as a further inducement to staying. Senior managers may require salary increases alone, while those at the very top sometimes receive 100 percent of their entire compensation package, the analysts say.

It remains to be seen whether shareholder protests against high executive salaries will change these compensation norms. However, for now, incentive bonuses can add 5 to 10 percent to a deal's overall costs, say Kay and Shelton.

CFO magazine urges acquiring companies to scrutinize the incentive packages well. Not all companies do. Instead, "Some companies tie bonus pay to factors unrelated to the cash-flow goals in the deal, thus potentially rewarding value-destroying mergers."[11]

Vision Matters

Some of the most successful companies in the high-technology industry happen to be active dealmakers, say Kevin A. Frick and

Alberto Torres.[12] The two Silicon Valley–based management analysts called these strident deal makers gold standard companies, which grew 39 percent annually "in total returns to shareholders since 1989." In this case, having an aggressive alliance strategy may merely be the status quo. That's because in a rapidly changing industry, companies perceive that they can't keep up sufficiently just by using in-house resources. Finding partners and constantly reshuffling alliances are inevitable. The companies demonstrated expertise in four crucial areas, where conversely failing companies were found lagging: They articulated readily understood strategy for the firm, then they embarked on alliances that clearly satisfied the objectives. When they moved to acquire, they did it quickly and with minimal disruption. Finally, they learned from their mistakes and embedded their acquisition acumen into the organization's culture. In other words, they took a "programmatic approach," say Frick and Torres. Before, during, and after the deal was made, management understood, step-by-step, what it had to do to extract value from the acquisition.

Size Matters

Most tellingly, according to Frick and Torres, gold standard companies rarely sought out large deals. The cost of the average transaction amounted to less than 1 percent of the acquiring company's market cap. The industry average price paid for acquisitions was in the neighborhood of $700 million. For gold standard companies it was $400 million, despite the fact that gold standard companies, owing to their prodigious appetites, tended to be larger than their sector peers. Thinking small is especially important when companies seek to acquire technologies or other capabilities that are new to them, says Arie Lewin, who teaches at Duke's Fuqua School.[13] The risk, perhaps, is that the acquired company with the coveted technology will become dominant. Some believe this is happening as Time Warner flexes its revenue-producing muscles in an affront to its acquirer, AOL. Faced with this risk, it is far better to proceed via an alliance first.

Phase Matters

The type of acquisition strategy that gold standard companies followed was in line with their development. During a company's early development, it was more likely to focus on perfecting its own expertise and on winning a sufficient number of customers to sustain the firm's initial growth. Acquisitions during this phase tended to be limited. In a second phase, accelerated growth was the goal. Acquisitions were undertaken to add and better manage customers, scale operations, and develop collateral expertise around the company's core competencies, whereas during the slow-growth consolidation phase of a company's development, acquisitions were aimed at increasing margins by leveraging expertise and creating economies of scale.

Getting Off Track

It's during a company's second high-growth phase that management tends to be seduced by synergies that don't in fact exist. As an example, French corporate chieftain Jean-Marie Messier created a highly diversified French media conglomerate, Vivendi, from a bottled water company. The company soon embarked on a series of expensive trophy acquisitions. One of them was Seagram Co. and Pay TV group Canal+. Total cost for the two: $34 billion. Added to the stable of acquired companies was French mobile phone service provider Cegetel. The aim was to create content, while owning the platforms for its distribution. When Vivendi reported $12 billion in losses in March 2002, shareholders predictably punished the stock. "The company urgently needs to reduce its $19 billion debt and simplify its structure," commented *Business Week*.[14] "That means selling off a big pile of assets

Messier spent billions acquiring—and in effect, admitting his vision was all wrong."

High-Priced Losers

The penalties for such missteps can run into ten digits. Speculating on whether Vivendi would need to sell its stake in Cegetel, *Forbes* mused that the value of the telecom might be $7.9 billion. But because it was a fire sale, Vivendi might expect to receive only $6.4 billion.[15]

AT&T, under Mike Armstrong, pursued what appeared to be a more cohesive acquisitions strategy during the late '90s. Seeking to bypass the Baby Bells' last-mile connections to the Internet, the telecom giant wanted to create a direct-to-home wide pipe of its own, via two gargantuan cable acquisitions: TCI and MediaOne. By using coaxial cable instead of phone lines, AT&T hoped to leapfrog over the Baby Bells by offering everything from TV programs and home shopping to long-distance phone calls. The strategy's success, however, was predicated on the continued growth and profitability of AT&T's long-distance services to buttress overall cash flow. As it happened, fierce competition and monumental overcapacities in long-distance infrastructure threw a wrench into those plans.[16] Meanwhile, thanks to its buying spree, AT&T now faced a mountain of debt. Long term, it meant that AT&T's stock would likely languish. Analysts would see a steady decline in earnings per share, while growth, averaged over the entire company, would appear sluggish, even when broadband and other new services were taken into account.

Painfully expensive as it might be, the only logical course available was divestiture, along with a massive reorganization of debt. AT&T Broadband, along with other units, were thus put on the block. The fact that the company underwent its restructuring before creditors started getting antsy allowed AT&T to emerge in a far more secure position than many of its debt-ridden competitors.

AT&T's path from peril to—one hopes—salvation mirrored the motivation that led to the building of dozens upon dozens of conglomerates during the merger heydays of the '60s and '70s, according to Michael T. Jacobs, a former director of corporate finance at the U.S. Treasury Department during the first Bush administration and author of the book *Short-Term America: The Causes and Cures of Our Business Myopia.* "Companies could blend cash-generating, mature businesses with rapidly growing capital-starved business," he notes. The premise, Jacobs said, "was that corporations could allocate capital more efficiently than the markets."[17]

In fact, the concept failed. The value of U.S. companies during the conglomerate craze actually declined in real terms, he says. A reason, perhaps, is that under benign management, unproductive subsidiaries existed under a kind of benevolent socialism, administered by top-down managers whose own compensation was often not linked to performance. The leveraged buyout mania of the '80s was an inevitable result, as companies, their stock performance languishing, realized they needed to perform a good deal of pruning. Maligned as it was, Jacobs says, the rash of leveraged buyouts (LBOs) that occurred during the '80s was really an attempt to subject management to the discipline of debt.

The Private Equity Exit Strategy

As equity markets continue to flounder, making IPOs an unlikely exit strategy for any divested unit, it is indeed possible that the LBO could become the strategy of choice once again, just as it was during the '80s. Companies that suffered through intense public relations nightmares over their accounting practices might discover that the best way of preserving value is to privatize their subsidiaries, either through a sale or an internal LBO. The track record for this approach is encouraging, even when logic would seem to indicate otherwise.

Analysts were at first astounded that between 1999 and 2000, the number of chemical-firm subsidiaries taken private was roughly twice the average during the prior decade, amounting to about $20 billion, according to *McKinsey*'s London-based strategist Paul A. Butler.[18] This amused many people in the industry, Butler says. They saw no reason why financiers with no experience running a chemical company could expect to wring more money out of a subsidiary than the parent company, with years of experience, could. But, in fact, Butler claims that the privatized subsidiaries appeared to perform better than large publicly held chemical firms did, on average. The latter's shareholder returns remained relatively unchanged for 20 years. Moreover, while public chemical conglomerates have seen their share prices pummeled by institutional investors who lack faith in their management style, they are hamstrung from acquiring new high-growth subsidiaries. Often this is because the LBO firms can outbid them every time. Equally bad, from the point of view of the large chemical firms, the industry's best talent is reportedly defecting from the sector's staid giant firms and joining with the divested units. The motivation appears to be a chance to earn more by participating in an LBO-prompted consolidation.

What, then, were the private equity managers doing right that the conglomerates had failed to do? In many ways, their efforts parallel what a turnaround manager does to a firm. Just as a turnaround manager enjoys a clear mandate to fix problems, the LBO firm, no longer beholden to the overriding goals of the conglomerate, has a free rein to implement solutions as it sees fit. The advantage, of course, is that the unit it is buying often is healthy. However, the LBO firm still must move quickly if the unit is to remain that way. Namely, the LBO firm must boost cash flow in order to repay the increased debt incurred via the buyout. Presumably, it also wants a series of successive high-growth years as a prelude to a possible later IPO or sale.

Outside managers have a clear advantage because, rather than being beholden to an amorphous group of often-fickle shareholders, their own money typically is on the line if the merger fails. The Wall Street term for this is "control premium." The theory is that the share price of troubled companies is often depressed. Put another way, a value gap exists between the company's intrinsic value and its market value. This value gap results because shareholders will pay only so much for a company when they doubt management's ability to fix the problems it faces.[19] Outside private investors will pay more, because they have the will to sell off the corporate jet fleet and reduce excess layers of management—in other words, do whatever it takes to make the numbers right.

The *McKinsey* study of chemical industry LBOs bore out this conclusion: Being an established industry and part of a larger conglomerate, for example, chemical companies didn't always link compensation to results—something the LBOs could do. The LBOed companies also achieved cost savings in insurance and legal bills by becoming more environmentally friendly.

But less obvious were the negotiating tactics used by LBO firms. "Financial buyers pay less on average not only because of their dispassionate approach to acquisitions but also because they tend to negotiate downward during the due-diligence phase from a price that had earlier been accepted in principle," according to the study. Then, when it came time to sell, presuming the LBO firm was able to squeeze more value from the company, it had the luxury of waiting for optimal marketing conditions. Here again, the buyout firm benefited from not belonging to a larger conglomerate. That is, it could time its sale unhindered by any pressure from Wall Street analysts or from the parent firm wishing to improve its overall numbers via the sale.

One implication of the study, according to the authors, is that companies faced with failed synergies can emulate the tactics of LBO firms. If it works in the staid chemical industry, long out of favor with investors, it should work in other, less cyclical, sectors.

The Nissan Turnaround

None of this is to suggest that mergers are ill advised. *Fortune* magazine recounts[20] how Renault's surprise purchase of a minority interest in Nissan during the '90s succeeded in reining in the

Japanese company's gargantuan debt. After a tumultuous period, it succeeded in turning around Nissan's operations, while providing the parent company with a high-quality additional entrée into both U.S. and European auto markets. That success came despite the vast cultural differences that existed between the French management team and its Japanese counterparts. The *Fortune* article credits the success to Nissan's charismatic manager Carlos Ghosn and the tightrope strategy he devised to save the company. Ever mindful of the need to observe Japanese customs, he refrained from laying off employees. Instead, downsizing occurred through attrition and reassignment.

Ghosn also "created nine cross-functional teams." Each was charged with deconstructing facets of the Japanese automaker. Japanese employees at all levels of the company served on the teams, along with Renault executives, the latter lending an outsider's perspective. The team's official language became English, to make sure everyone could communicate, according to a *Business Week* article. One of Ghosn's more radical changes was to start the very un-Japanese practice of paying for performance—often via stock options—instead of for seniority. Engineers were given more freedom to experiment, while, in another affront to the consensus-minded Japanese, all managers were given clearly defined areas of authority.

Some say that Ghosn succeeded because Nissan employees knew full well that he was the company's last best chance at survival. And while Ghosn encountered much resistance at first, the successful turnaround gave the Brazilian-born Ghosn demigod status in Japan. With the company no longer on the ropes, the next phase presumably is to create joint ventures with other auto firms.

Back to School

Companies value M&A skills so much, they support no less than seven executive programs at major universities devoted to the practice.[21] Most of these programs take the form of intense multiday seminars, costing $8,000 or more per participant. Those attending simulate actual mergers, according to *CFO* magazine. Role-playing executives reenact major deals of the past, meeting in small groups to decide on a strategy. Professors, meanwhile, reveal the results of executives' decisions and barrage them with tough questions. "You need to understand what is captured and what is not when you forecast the bottom line," one professor at Pennsylvania's Wharton School tells his class. "If the company is the low-cost provider in its industry, for example, does that show up in its financials?" Other advice is more prosaic: Once a manager falls in love with the company being targeted, he loses his required discipline, a professor warns.

The Wharton School emphasizes that mergers often fail because responsibility for scrutinizing the deal falls upon several individuals. One executive may perform the due diligence, another may be charged with strategy, while a third executive focuses on valuation. Ideally, these tasks should be integrated to make sure the findings mesh with each other and with the strategy making up the deal.

Knowledge gained from such seminars may be sorely needed in the months ahead, as companies embroiled in accounting scandals are forced to divest their assets or risk failing. The reasons companies were faced with this sad dilemma often have far more to do with basic failures in human nature than with any objectively arrived-at strategy.

13

Greed and Arrogance

On the very good chance that its readers were confused by keeping track of the long list of U.S. companies that toppled in 2001 and 2002, the *Economist* ran an article entitled "A Guide to Corporate Scandals."[1] Of Enron, the *Economist* wrote, "Tops the list of America's biggest corporate collapse." And as for Andersen, the magazine dryly said, "They were destroyed as a firm, even before being found guilty of obstruction of justice in June [2002]."

Only news of a major war could have drowned out the nightly deluge of stories devoted to corporate malfeasance. For months we've heard the accounts of questionable accounting practices, deliberate earnings misstatements, and shareholder assets pillaged as if they were medieval city-states. This chapter will add little to these accounts. Instead, it focuses on a more important issue that has received much less attention—the underlying reasons for the disgrace of so many respected companies. Along with this, we will look at another, even less understood, topic: how to prevent the same abuses from occurring again.

Plenty of ideas have been suggested for what caused so many good companies to run amuck, but they all basically boil down to greed and arrogance. *New York Times* commentator Paul Krugman hinted at how both came into play: "As people, corporate leaders are no worse (and no better) than they've always been.

What changed were the incentives."[2] These became huge. When CEOs are able to command compensation packages in the tens and even hundreds of millions of dollars, it's quite natural that some will go to extraordinary lengths to keep the money flowing.

Yet that leaves unanswered the question of how CEOs came to control so much money in the first place. An article in *Fortune,* entitled "The Great CEO Pay Heist,"[3] offers this answer. It argues that the roots of America's corporate scandals actually go back more than half a century, specifically to the Revenue Act of 1950. Hidden within the measure signed by President Truman was a provision making stock options both legal and practical. Although it took a while for momentum to build, compensation packages on the order of nine digits became inevitable from that moment on. "A big reason for its [stock options] runaway popularity is the insane way accounting authorities let companies treat options in financial statements—a way that's great for executives and awful for shareholders," according to *Fortune.*

Lean and Mean

For his part, Krugman gives another reason why the great compensation "land grab" got started: The greed that so appalled the American public was an inevitable outcome of what he calls a "hard-nosed" corporate culture that has evolved over roughly the last 20 years. So, what exactly happened? Some years before actor Michael Douglas, playing the infamous stock manipulator Gordon Gekko, coined the phrase "Greed is good," in the movie *Wall Street,* corporations operated in a paternalistic fashion, akin to "socialist republics," Krugman writes. Moreover, many companies also benignly looked out for their various stakeholders. A company might therefore feel some loyalty toward the community in which its factory was located. Larger corporations also exercised benevolent care over employees. Lifetime employment, though not a matter of policy, was often the norm. Workers who met the company's standards could expect a comfortable—if perhaps unexciting—

career. And in exchange for that, they gave the company their undying loyalty. Some larger companies, IBM being one example, went even further and maintained lavish country clubs for employee use. During the '50s and '60s, perks like these attested to the fact that corporate America had built the kind of workers' paradise that Communists failed to deliver. And such perks were a considerable step up from the Friday beer busts that were said to typify Silicon Valley's worker-friendly culture.

What threw a wrench in this system, says Krugman, were the takeover wars of the '80s. Their aim, supposedly, was to wring hidden value out of companies. Out of this movement, an emphasis on earnings growth emerged. That emphasis justified plant closings and mass layoffs, which have become normal corporate behavior ever since.

One could argue that fierce global competition would have forced the very same changes on the cozy corporate world of decades past. Thus, the corporate culture that resulted would still be the same. Top management would have eschewed benevolent socialism, in favor of generous financial incentives that rarely flowed to any great extent beyond the first few layers of command. From there, it can be a very short leap to cooking the books in order to realize still greater rewards. In top management's eyes, the company and its mission ceased being an end in itself and became a means to an end. In the very worst cases, management ceased being caretakers and became robbers instead.

Inbred Boards

If the ranks of top management had any loyalty, it was to each other. As a group, its members were bent on self-preservation. And one way to safeguard their interests was to stack company boards to ensure that the interests of management, rather than of shareholders, were protected.

Commenting on that, *Business Week* online notes that being on a corporate board can be quite lucrative—all the more so, if you acquiesce to the desires of management. "In addition to money, perks, and prestige, directors frequently enjoy an array of side deals that may include millions of dollars in consulting and legal fees, leases, and contracts," the article said.[4] And the article went on to say that some corporate boards gave the appearance of being private clubs whose members could "dip into the corporate coffers at will." Indeed, a group called Executive Compensation Advisory Services notes that 25 percent of U.S. corporations have board members who present some sort of conflict of interest, the article said.

A separate *New York Times* article alleges that boardrooms in Silicon Valley are among the most incestuous: "With scandals and tumbling stock prices putting corporate America under pressure to mend its ways, stiff resistance to change is coming from the epicenter of the excess during the boom years: Silicon Valley."[5] Specifically, it appeared that company board members continued to act as they had throughout the '90s boom. While the NASDAQ and the New York Stock Exchange developed reform proposals that might force companies to diversify their boards and make a better accounting of stock options, the boards of Silicon Valley companies were said to remain beholden to management. And, in fact, board members and managers have strongly resisted change, according to the article.

Among other things, they continued to rely on stock options. And their argument, the *Times* article alluded, was that tech companies need the kind of direct compensation that stock options provide.

Stock options are the life blood of an entrepreneurial culture, so the argument goes, because start-ups require an inordinate amount of human commitment in order to succeed. In their take-no-prisoners competitive world, an innovation must move quickly from an engineer's garage to the marketplace. The only way for this to happen is if venture capitalists enter the picture early on with the necessary capital. Skilled managers, likewise, must be quickly brought on board to move the innovation to market. All of this demands that incentives be both large and easily graspable upon success.

Those Who Forget the Past Are Doomed to Repeat It

With competition becoming ever fiercer in every area of business—not just in technology—it could be argued that all companies must eventually adopt this model. There are, however, some serious flaws with this argument, beyond the fact that it is self-serving.

For starters, an exit strategy built on stock options demands, obviously, that the public be willing to purchase the shares and pay a premium price for them. This has hardly been the case since the 2000 crash. But even if the public were willing, it would still be necessary to create a story about a stock in order for it to sell. The temptation to exaggerate the details would be all too great, given the huge sums involved. Furthermore, because of the lucrative rewards that stock options provide and the small, tenuous window in which those rewards remain available, there is a strong tendency to rush companies to market before they're ready. Certainly, that was the case with many high-profile dot-com IPOs during the '90s. This may have contributed to their early demise. In fact, any time fleets of companies are launched mainly for the purpose of scoring big on an IPO, they stand a very good chance of failing. Merely look at history and you can confirm this.

Analysts say that the new issues associated with each boom are always pegged to current market fads. Just as, during the '90s, people saw the Internet as the invincible new medium, in the '60s investors couldn't get enough of stocks in companies that had even the remotest connection to aerospace and electronics. This was the era when NASA led the Free World's race to the moon. (One example of the space-race fad inadvertently benefiting a firm was the meteoric rise of Welch Scientific Company, detailed in chapter 4.)

There is yet another consequence of pegging a company's future on its IPO: the temptation to control the stock's sale in a way that will cause it to rise. When Ross Perot took his infant computer firm Electronic Data Systems Corp. public in 1968, he used a Texas cattlemen's analogy to describe the process. "If you have 20,000 head and bring them to market all at once," he said, "the buyers know you have to sell, and you won't get much. But if you bring in a few head at a time, you get more per pound."[6]

Throughout the decade, shares of new computer companies had flooded the over-the-counter market. As a result, some 16 investment banking firms made the trip from Lower Manhattan to the wide plains of Texas, urging Perot to let them manage the EDS IPO. Various offering share prices were reportedly discussed, ranging from 30 to 70 times earnings. The 17th banker to visit Perot, Kenneth Langoene of R. W. Pressprich and Company, dangled an offering share price that was roughly 100 times EDS's $1.5 million per year earnings—a multiple worthy of any dot-com.[7]

Shrewdly, however, Perot allowed only 10 percent of EDS stock to trade publicly. He himself retained 72 percent ownership in the company. The shares hit the market at $16.50. By 1970 they had risen to $160—which put Perot's net worth in excess of a billion.

Perot's EDS was different, however. Unlike many start-ups of that day, EDS could show solid earnings. But many companies whose shares debuted at the time were not on such solid ground, and the tactics they used were refined a few decades later, as investment banks and venture capitalists sought to capitalize on the Internet.

Examining the tactics of investment banks during the '50s and early '60s, the Securities and Exchange Commission completed an exhaustive study. What became known as the SEC *Special Study* vilified some new issue underwriters, saying, "A number of public offerings appear to have been the result not of any genuine corporate need for funds, but rather of calculations by promoters that a large profit could be made by satisfying investors' demand for new issues."[8] Like the '90s-era spin-doctors, molding the image of freshly formed Internet companies, the buzz-meisters of the '60s knew the importance of a good name. As the SEC charged:

> Some companies with prosaic names were rechristened in order to give the impression, correct or not, that they had some connection with electronics, in much the same way Hollywood starlets are renamed and glamorized to satisfy the public's craving for romance.[9]

Substitute *dot-com* for *space* and you have the essence of the '90s boom. Just as real space was infinite, cyberspace was limited only by the human imagination's ability to colonize it. Moreover, it could seemingly be exploited with near-infinite speed. Using off-the-shelf software or, more likely, a series of virtual online partners, it was possible to create an online store or a service operation—*a virtual company* was the popular term—literally within days. As one National Public Radio columnist, commenting on the launch of the online political magazine *Slate.com* by Microsoft Corp., cynically explained: The Web allowed an entrepreneur to take the most mundane idea and make it sound ingenious simply by adding the words "on the Internet." So if you said, why don't we start a cigar store, everyone would think the idea unoriginal. But if you added the words "on the Internet," you could get millions in venture capital. Hindsight reveals that these companies and the millions that went into funding them were destined to disappear.

But amid the boom-era psychology, dot-com cheerleaders needed ways to justify why their companies were worth the huge price of their shares. Accordingly, a common theme among many Internet stock cheerleaders was that dot-com companies were really in the business of creating an entirely new species of economy—cutting out the middleman, speeding the flow of information, aggregating buyers and sellers into groups that would have been impossible in the pre-Net era. Priceline.com was often held up as an example of how Internet companies were said to be changing the very dynamics of commerce. Priceline operates a kind of reverse auction for airline tickets. It's even succeeded in getting a patent on the process. Users input a price they're willing to pay for, let's say, a New York–London flight. Priceline finds an airline willing to sell you a ticket at or near that price. The company devised plans to expand its reverse-auction concept into other areas, such as mortgages, insurance, and auto sales.

Because of companies like Priceline, all the stuffy old rules of investing were said to be no longer applicable. Traditional measures had no meaning, it was claimed, when the very nature of capitalism was mutating before the world's eyes. Still, it was a tough argument to make, because the numbers posted by even the most solid Internet players blew out the normal measures used by fundamental analysts. Amazon.com, even after the August–September '98 crash, was selling for about 16 times sales. Again, that's sales—not profits. Amazon had yet to generate profits. If every business enjoyed valuations like that, the corner magazine store, with a yearly gross of, say, $100,000, would be worth $1.6 million, even if it consistently lost money!

So the real question to Internet stock pundits became this: If the traditional measures are too scary to use, how else could you determine Amazon's value? Buyout value was one method used. Still other analysts sought to redefine the price sales ratio, a traditional fundamentalist measure. This valuation method was based on the idea that all Internet companies were brand new. Most new companies lose money. Ergo, the important thing to focus on was not earnings but sales. How much had sales grown over the years? Amazon.com provides an illustration. At one point during the late '90s, it had a sales growth rate of something like 838 percent— which meant that maybe the stock wasn't such a bad buy after all, even if it was selling for 16 times sales. Indeed, in 1998 when star analyst Henry Blodgett, who was working for CIBC Oppenheimer at the time, said that Amazon's price might hit $400, the announcement set off a fevered buying frenzy.[10]

Another popular method used to predict an Internet's stock value was called *discounted future price*. Here, the financial software–maker Intuit, selling at a pre-crash price of $39 or 32 times earnings, provides an example. Let's suppose analysts predicted that Intuit would grow by 20 percent annually over the next several years. Current earnings were something like $1.21 per share. Compound that amount by 20 percent annually. Result: By 2004, Intuit should earn about $3.12 per share. Now multiply that figure by 32 (the accepted pre-crash Street multiple). By that reckoning, Intuit should sell for just under $100 per share by 2004. Reason enough to buy the stock at $39. Use a more conservative multiple—say, 22 times earnings—and the price comes out to around $69 per share. That still makes $39 look like a bargain.

Thanks to these justifications, the market rose daily to unsustainable new heights, and the pundits continued to paint an even brighter picture of its future. Mob psychology ruled, analysts later said. Everyone seemed mesmerized by the madness of crowds. "The individuals composing the crowd lose their conscious personality under the influence of emotion and are ready to act as one, directed by the low, crowd intelligence," wrote Thomas Templeton Hoyne,[11] author of the classic book *Speculation: Its Sound Principals and Rules for Its Practice*.

What Hoyne suggests is that greed and arrogance will arise out of a mob. It's easy for companies to get caught up in the popular delusion—to their peril.

Taking Risks

A boom period will also prompt individuals to stray. The fabulous rewards available during boom times require that fabulous risks be taken. And some believe that successful managers—indeed, successful people in all walks of life—by their very makeup, can become addicted to risks. Risks-taking after all, is a skill successful people must cultivate. Without taking risks they would not have reached their current station in life. But a run of good luck in the executive suite, just like a run of good luck at the casino, can lead to feelings of invulnerability. And even a string of failures alternated by successes can create the seeds of addiction. The rewards feel so good in the wake of the failures.

Industrial psychologist Mortimer R. Feinberg, who advises CEOs of Fortune 500 companies, says that the high intelligence and other skills needed to reach the top enhance this penchant for risk taking. Feinberg is coauthor, along with consultant John Tarrant, of the book *Why Smart People Do Dumb Things*.[12] In some ways, he believes that managers are great risk takers: they're natural salesmen, so good that they can even sell themselves on the idea that the risks are minimal, which makes them charge forward.

Moreover, he says, successful people are able to compartmentalize. They can operate effectively in a high-risk environment, all the while brushing aside the dangers.

Former President Bill Clinton is an all-too-obvious example. Why would he risk having an affair with a much-younger subordinate, while his enemies and the media are lurking around? Feinberg says that these seemingly foolish, if not irrational, actions may arise from a kind of operant conditioning. Risks have rewarded these people in the past; so it becomes only natural for them to seek out the same. People involved in sports and many other endeavors exhibit similar behaviors. There are stories, for example, of scuba divers who descend to dangerous depths in order to experience the euphoric effects of nitrogen saturation in their systems, a condition known as nitrogen narcosis. The deeper they go, the more pronounced the feeling, and the lesser the chance that they'll be able to surface safely.

Some who have studied risk taking in individuals say that the ability or lack of it can be tied directly to how people operate in the world. Engineers are said to be poor risk takers because their professional ethics quite appropriately mandate that they make decisions only when they're certain of the outcomes. Pilots, on the other hand, are natural risk takers. They're often said to make good stock traders. And, indeed, the two are similar. While trading stocks or flying an airplane, people must follow a mind-numbing list of variables. Whatever the outcome, they are prepared to act, because, whether flying a plane or holding a stock position, the greatest risk is often doing nothing.

"Catch Me If You Can"

Yet another school of thought suggests that people engage in illegal behavior, ruining companies in the process, because the risks aren't really so great after all, not when measured against the rewards. A *Business Week* article[13] looked at just how difficult it is to catch and then prosecute corporate criminals. For one thing, the boundaries governing what constitutes illegal behavior are fluid and at times easily circumvented. A company, for example, can misstate its numbers and still comply with generally accepted accounting principles. Likewise, "The laws regulating companies are ambiguous, juries have a hard time grasping abstract financial concepts, and well-counseled executives have plenty of tricks for distancing themselves from responsibility." Although a typical jury might readily understand what's going on when a prosecutor paints a picture of a murder or robbery, the details surrounding corporate crime are difficult enough for experts to grasp, let alone prove beyond a reasonable doubt.

Don M. Svendson, a Turnaround Management Association member who works for Deloitte & Touche, believes that the culture of some companies encourages thievery. Internal controls in such companies are typically weak or unmonitored, he says. The company or the department might be dominated by just one or two powerful managers, whom others are afraid to question.

The temptation to push the envelope, whether via accounting methods or through outright stealing, becomes especially great when a key "manager's compensation is linked to short-term results," Svendson explains. If a boss approaches that manager and says, "You've got six months to increase your sales or you're fired," the manager might create a stack of false invoices, if only for self-preservation.

Oftentimes, the guilty parties decide that they will transgress "just this one time." If they secretly borrow money from the company to pay off a gambling debt, for example, they vow to pay it back. "The bottom line is that opportunity exists and [they] can rationalize their way through this and there are pressures—they do it," Svendson says. To help track down the culprits, he uses forensic accounting. Little known or understood before the huge corporate scandals of 2001 and 2002, forensic accounting basically involves following the money, even following it out the door, if that's where it's going. The discipline combines a detective's insights with an accountant's mathematical acumen. Svendson describes a possible situation: "People say sales are up, fixed costs are unchanged. But profits are down. You do some work and find that inventory is down, because somebody is selling it out the back door."

Closing the Door on Arrogance and Greed

So, how can companies protect themselves from thieving management? Throughout 2002, industry analysts put forth solutions that you've no doubt heard before: Eliminating conflicts of interest between boards and management and between accounting firms and the companies they're charged with auditing will help, to a point. Increasing regulatory scrutiny may help, too. Yet the number of potential culprits and hence the schemes they devise will always outpace the resources of regulators.

Some also suggest that the market will exercise its discipline. People will refuse to do business with companies caught in the act; traders will sorely punish the offending company's stock price. But these market mechanisms have long been in place, and the malfeasance continues. The fact is, the market also handsomely rewards falsified results until they are discovered. And by that time, the chief culprits may well have cashed in their chips.

In theory, the market can encourage companies to toe the line, but not in a way most think. Often, in the periods following booms and scandalous stock downfalls, equity prices remain depressed, to the extent that companies turn to other means to raise funds. Some opt to privatize. Others turn to the debt market for cash.

The dividend tax exemption, whether it succeeds in passing now or at some point in the future, may well prove to be another method of keeping companies on the straight and narrow. And that's because it will focus management and investor attention on a stock's yield and not as much on its earnings growth. This will effectively lower expectations, allowing management to focus on the long term, rather than on quarterly results—just so long as these provide a predictable dividend yield.

In fact, dividend yield has been the reason to buy stocks during the duller periods in-between stock market booms and the excess and subsequent busts that often follow. Throughout much of the 1920s, for example, dividends always managed to hold stock prices in check. Back then, stocks of large companies were often primarily seen as dividend investments. That is, people bought stocks for the dividend income these provided and not—as is largely the case today—because they expected the share price to rise. Dividend income tended to put a natural cap on a stock's value for a simple reason. As the stock grew pricier, its dividend yield actually *decreased,* as a percentage of its purchase price. A lower yield made other competing investments more attractive. Put simply, if a dividend stock grew too pricey, no one would buy it.

With any luck, an emphasis on dividends could return some sanity to the world's still arrhythmic markets. Companies will desperately need this stability to face much larger challenges ahead.

14

Future Challenges

Wired magazine specializes in forecasting the future, but an article in its November 2002 issue, entitled the "Hot Zone,"[1] presented a vision that seemed particularly fascinating and frightening—at least, for companies intent on doing business as usual. The article focused on China's Delta River Valley, known locally as Dongguan. Like the Maquilladora region along Mexico's border with the United States, the Chinese industrial center just miles inland from Hong Kong has become a hotbed of ultra-fast-turnaround manufacturing. Indeed, companies thrive here in a kind of Wild West laissez-faire atmosphere, in which ad hoc trade associations hold more sway than local government officials do, and companies spring in and out of existence like fireflies.

Because it offers unbridled economic opportunity, the Dongguan draws untold numbers of immigrants from impoverished regions elsewhere in China, as well as some of the best entrepreneurial talent from Mainland China, Taiwan, and other nations. Many Taiwanese are said to arrive with little more than suitcases full of cash with which to fund new companies. And many of these Taiwanese reportedly leave as rich men.

As factories, ramshackle houses, and karaoke bars spring up along the muddy streets outside traditional Chinese feudal-style villages, the region's Communist bosses have prospered, too, handing out land and permits to those able to work the system. What in an ancient era might have resembled a kind of sprawling bazaar of tinsmiths, jewelers, and rug makers has become in this high-tech age a vast conglomeration of factories devoted to making electronic circuit boards, cables, plugs, and disk drives, as well as more familiar goods. Exports from the region total an astonishing $19 billion per year—more than what many entire nations sell abroad.

And while the Dongguan's free-wheeling atmosphere and sorry lack of infrastructure would seemingly make it difficult to get anything done, as the *Wired* article points out, the area functions with unrivaled efficiency: "Dongguan makes everything—shoes, shirts, office furniture, wristwatches—more cheaply and efficiently than anywhere else on earth." In fact, business thrives, thanks to a finely melded network of relationships between suppliers and manufacturers that outsiders might find impossible to fathom, let alone penetrate. With margins forever razor thin, factories within each supply chain must be close to one another to save on transportation costs—a phenomenon called cluster manufacturing, which takes the Japanese idea of just-in-time manufacturing to the extreme. And so goods are produced in an ever-faster melee within the teeming region, and as those "goods move from factory to factory in Dongguan, the money that pays for them flows from account to account in Taipei."

Wired isn't the only magazine to see the emergence of China's new wave manufacturing sector as a fundamental paradigm shift—one that business leaders everywhere must take note of, and, if they are to survive, one they must learn to compete against. A *Business Week* cover story, in October 2002,[2] claims that fast-growing Chinese companies could one day challenge the likes of Cisco and other giant U.S. firms, in the same way that Japanese car makers and electronics firms gave their American counterparts a rude awakening a generation ago. But this time the inroads by foreigners won't be confined to consumer goods. Instead, Chinese companies are making vast strides producing everything from satellites to sophisticated network routers to genetically modified rice and bioengineered drugs. In fact, Chinese executives now reportedly journey to Silicon Valley to lure back recent immigrants from their homeland to take up the lucrative managerial jobs that await there.

As American companies discovered during the previous century, emerging Chinese industrial giants know they can turn to their nation's immense home market to develop economies of scale that will later enable them to compete with devastating effectiveness throughout the world.

And yet in a fast-changing world, China, too, will one day have to face its share of up-and-coming supercompetitors as part of yet another paradigm shift—just as Japan, the original miracle-economy exporter, has been forced to contend with the other Asian tiger economies in Thailand, Taiwan, Singapore, and elsewhere over the past 20 years. A BBC article in the fall of 2002[3] notes that the Bangladeshi region known as Sylhet is fast building out its wireless network infrastructure so that it may someday form the bedrock of a nascent high-tech manufacturing industry.

Changing Dynamics Everywhere

The rapid growth of global high-tech manufacturing centers able to thrive within an atmosphere of libertarian lawlessness is just one challenge that companies in the rest of the world must face in coming years. Terrorism, civil unrest, and the threat of deadly disease are other examples of accelerated changes in dynamics that have already greatly affected how we work and travel. Terrorism, in particular—high on everybody's list of fears—presents perhaps the most visible challenge to how businesses operate. Although terrorist acts are despicable and able to inflict enormous damage, the aftershocks of these attacks are the most devastating to businesses. Witness the airlines, hotels, and airport service providers that suffered as a result of September 11.

The very unpredictability of terrorism and the fear and uncertainty that this provokes within the business community will become permanent components of the economic environment throughout the foreseeable future. Companies cannot predict whether terrorist acts will close off potentially valuable markets, as has occurred in Bali, Indonesia, following the Al Qaeda nightclub bombing. Nor can companies predict whether they themselves will be targets of terrorism. Up until September 11, that fear was largely confined to companies with extensive operations overseas. But now, an office, a bank, a railroad, or an oil refinery have all become potential targets. Worse, to defend against a terrorist attack, companies must add costly security measures that only lessen productivity, while doing nothing to enhance the bottom line. And surely all bets would be off, should the unthinkable happen and terrorists resort to biological, chemical, or radiological weapons of mass destruction.

Doom and Gloom Scenarios

If you examine closely trends that are occurring now, you will see that other foreboding changes are far easier to predict than terrorism, although anticipating all of their consequences may not be. With the idea of playing devil's advocate, let us look at some worst-case scenarios of a world that may not be many years off. For example, estimates vary, but in coming years, the UN and other relief agencies foresee that immense portions of the globe will suffer from chronic water shortages, and that water might even become the cause of future wars. What will be the effect of these conflicts on the global business environment?

Similarly, AIDS will wreak havoc with many nations that are least equipped to deal with the epidemic. A report prepared by the CIA[4] reveals that Russia, China, India, and Ethiopia are among the nations most likely to suffer. Although wealthier nations will possess the resources to provide the expensive medicines needed to treat AIDS victims and, it is hoped, the educational capabilities to slow the disease's spread, nations such as Russia will find their resources sorely stretched to their limits. Unable to afford adequate treatment for their populations, the poorer nations could face crippling social unrest. Millions of orphans growing up in the plague will face a life with little opportunity, as the nations' leaders and resources are consumed by the disease. This cruel phenomenon is already playing out in Central Africa. Meanwhile, health-care workers, whose services are sorely needed in their own nations, will leave AIDS-afflicted areas en masse for better-paying jobs and better working conditions in the industrialized nations.

It is quite possible that this combination of AIDS and severe shortages of water and other resources will cause the virtual disintegration of governments throughout large areas of the globe. Again, this phenomenon can already be seen in parts of Africa, rural South America, and Central Asia. Afghanistan, before the U.S.-led invasion, is a prime example. Within the ensuing power vacuum following the Soviet troop withdrawal, power reverted to feudal-style warlords and merchants employing mercenary armies that even the Taliban, who eventually came to rule, could not control.

Just as now there are many locales on earth where most of us would as soon not go, entire regions and subcontinents may soon be cordoned off from the rest of civilization, essentially devolving into the kind of feudal barbarism we see in parts of Pakistan, Colombia, and Africa.

The Future Belongs to the Quick

These possible disasters represent a worst-case scenario. Fortunately, gloom and doom predictions have a way of being proved wrong. Not long ago, for instance, many predicted the demise of democracy. But the logarithmic growth of information technologies made democracy, with its free exchange of ideas, the only viable form of government for nations that wished to effectively compete.

Likewise, not long ago doomsayers were predicting that massive famines would result in mass starvation. But improvements in agriculture, forming part of the so-called green revolution, mean that today it is possible to produce more than enough food for everyone on the planet. Only politics and wars prevent this food from reaching those most in need of it. While the earth's population continues to grow at an uncontrollable rate, in the years to come miraculous discoveries in genetic engineering may make it possible to grow food in many parts of the globe where it is now impossible, again greatly increasing the food supply. Similarly, a breakthrough in the energy field—harnessing nuclear fusion or creating a sustainable hydrogen economy, for example—may lead to an unprecedented economic boon. And fantastical advances in medicine may wipe out all the plagues of our day in a single stroke.

Jack Be Nimble, Jack Be Quick

Regardless of whether the future turns out to be bountiful or bleak, in the interim business will surely face an environment in which the only constant is change and the only certainty is uncertainty. Thus the only way to compete is to be nimble and quick and ready to pounce on opportunity when and where it happens.

One sector that aptly illustrates just how powerful the forces of change are in the world is the Internet service providers, or ISPs. Though all but nonexistent before the early '90s, ISPs have progressed from a cottage industry of local services, some managed by a single individual, to multibillion-dollar satellite, cable, DSL, and wireless providers. A relatively recent entry, so-called Wi-Fi (broadband wireless), promises to make the Net available to laptop and handheld users everywhere from coffee houses to airports to commuter trains, creating yet another paradigm shift within the sector. The low cost of setting up Wi-Fi infrastructure has favored smaller players that can quickly install networks in public areas of their own communities. This has basically caused a rebirth of the early form of mom-and-pop ISPs. Inevitably, the low cost of entry will lead to an overabundance of competition, falling margins, and the resulting creation of a few large networked providers, just as occurred with wired ISPs. Meanwhile, another technology waiting in the wings, ultra-wideband, could supplant Wi-Fi. So the sector will undergo a fourth evolution in less than two decades.

Incorrect bets on these sorts of wrenching changes have been the wreck of the telecom industry, as well as of grandiose schemes such as the Teledesic network of satellites. Yet despite the carnage, a white paper by the U.S. Internet Industry Association[5] notes that the original wired ISPs—the small, now mature operations—will still find a niche. While the major companies wrestle for 80 percent of the market, the most adaptable ISPs will find opportunities serving rural areas or providing value-added services to those working at home.

The lesson here is that small, nimble players are the ones best adapted in the short run to manage change. This is particularly true of those smaller companies that have learned to use lightning-fast Internet connections to create the same kind of relationships that the Chinese entrepreneurs of the Dongguan have created through close personal ties. These smaller, highly focused, and tightly connected companies pose a huge challenge to old-style monolithic organizations and may perhaps lead to the latter's demise.

But What About Large Companies?

In their book *Reengineering the Corporation*,[6] Michael Hammer, former professor at MIT and now head of the consulting firm Hammer and Company, and James Champy, head of the consulting firm CSC Index, Inc., say that nothing short of a total revamp of a monolithic company's organizational structure will permit its survival in the highly competitive times ahead. In fact, the two allude that radical change is long overdue. The typical large corporation today is still modeled after precepts outlined by the economist Adam Smith in the late 1700s. Likewise radical at the time, Smith foresaw how specialization of labor would lead to quantum leaps in productivity. This formula was uniquely suited to a period in history when masses of customers eagerly clamored for whatever products and services a company cared to provide.

Quality, customer service, and timely delivery were less important in an era when customers believed that any manufactured product, even when it was of poor quality, was preferable to no product at all. That's because in many cases the products allowed customers hitherto unimagined changes in productivity and lifestyle. Using a motorized washing machine was infinitely better than hand-washing clothes, even if it broke down frequently. By the same token, a car that required constant tinkering was still faster than a horse-pulled wagon.

The ability of American corporations, in particular, to deliver massive quantities of affordable manufactured goods peaked in the years following World War II, the authors claim, creating an era of unprecedented prosperity. But subsequently, as we all know, foreign companies with access to far cheaper labor were fast learning how to equal, if not surpass, American goods in terms of quality. A new competitive paradigm emerged, as a result, one in which the old bureaucratic model was shown to be sorely ill-equipped to compete. Top-down decision making, management by the numbers, and bureaucratic malaise couldn't produce high-quality products as quickly as the consensus-managed Japanese firms that American companies suddenly found themselves at war against. Although it took more than a decade, American companies adapted, perhaps faster than their Japanese counterparts did. And now, companies from both nations face yet another paradigm shift and fresh challenges such as those posed by cluster manufacturers of China's Dongguan.

Taking a Fresh Look

To reiterate, in a world where "faster, cheaper, better" constitutes nothing more than business as usual, the bureaucratic model appears hopelessly out of place.

Hammer and Champy give one example of why this is true: Within many companies, product order processing might involve individuals from multiple departments all reporting to different supervisors who have differing priorities—from the sales force that initiates the order reporting, ultimately to the vice president of sales, to the customer service representative who actually processes the order, to the credit department that's attached to the company's finance division, to the warehouse employees who actually locate the product, to the shipping department that sends it off. As the authors note, such a system is inherently inflexible and incapable of responding to inquiries or special requests.[7]

Such problems, according to management visionaries like Peter Drucker and others, reveal that we are evolving past the era of monolithic, self-perpetuating, steadfastly bureaucratic organizations. Indeed, the very idea of an organization as the centerpiece of the work environment is somewhat recent and potentially fleeting. Before 1900, people didn't think of themselves as working for organizations, Drucker asserts.[8] Rather, they worked on farms or in family-owned factories, which is to say, they worked for individuals. The idea of working for an organization reached its zenith in the 1950s, the era of the so-called company man, an American moniker that interestingly enough the Japanese adopted with zeal. Half a century later, as more and more people now work from home and find themselves only peripherally linked to an organization, the very idea of an organization being the center of work may in turn wane.

What this means for companies is that they must manage by example and not by coercion. That is because the organization's very legitimacy and efficacy will be called into question. Drucker suggests that CEOs study the way Native American tribal leaders presided over the amorphous bands that made up their nations. They were able to lead, in other words, because they were afforded everyone's respect. They were advisers or counselors, as opposed to being generals.

A radical shift to be sure. And it begs the question: How can companies reform themselves so fundamentally? To begin the process of radical change within the organization, Hammer and Champy recommend first stepping back to view the company as if for the first time: "It means asking this question," they say, "'if I were recreating this company today, given what I know and given current technology, what would it look like?"[9] Some of the ideas that might be conjured up would depend only on the imaginations of the company's visionaries: for example, the market niche the company serves, its size, and its mission. Still other facets of the company by necessity would be dictated by prevailing trends.

Elder Wisdom

Chances are, the company would look a lot older, since virtually everywhere in the industrialized world the workforce is aging rapidly. Standing before a small group of Japanese human resources executives some years ago, Drucker asked them a single question that rocked the room: "How will you run a company in 15 years when the retirement age will be 75?"[10] Those listening to Drucker were reportedly taken aback, since the current retirement age in Japan was 60. But peering into the future, Drucker saw the demographic handwriting on the wall. There was no getting around the fact that in the coming years Japan would become the industrialized nation with the oldest population, and it would be unable to support such a large percentage of retirees. Hence, the government would be compelled to raise the retirement age. Similar trends may well occur here, as boomers postpone retirement, voluntarily or otherwise.

Just as Drucker was able to predict the future with reasonable certainty for the Japanese, former White House adviser Todd G. Buchholz believes—and he's hardly alone—that the hordes of baby boomers in this country set to retire over the next two decades will sorely tax Medicare, social security, and the other programs and systems we use to care for the elderly. And this at a time when the average family has just $10,000 in savings, he says. In his book *Market Shock,* Buchholz says that younger generations will surely balk at the high taxes needed to support such a large nonworking segment of the population.[11] Those younger people who do assist their elders conceivably could face the all-but-impossible task of caring for three generations in addition to themselves: that is, their own children, plus their parents, and even perhaps their 90-something grandparents.

Companies, meanwhile, will face increasing pressures to keep older workers on the payroll, as many people find that it's impossible to retire, if only because in retirement they'll be forced to shoulder a larger share of ever-increasing health-care costs. Conflicts within the workplace might arise between older and younger workers, stymieing workflow.

Diversity and Outsourcing

While businesses struggle to thrive as their workforce ages, they will be further challenged to create a productive work environment as the U.S. population becomes more diverse. Companies that succeed at this, of course, will garner an overwhelming advantage.

It may well be that the most dynamic organizations in the future evolve into small, tightly knit, like-minded worker groups. However, membership in these groups might consist of employees, contract workers, and consultants, Drucker and others say. And that membership might well change from week to week. In effect, the groups will self-create their own autonomous divisions within the protective umbrella of the larger organization. And they will be highly focused and specialized. This is already taking shape in the form of outsourcing, as IT, billing, and the like are contracted through outside firms. Even employees today are contracted through a service firm.

What we may be left with is what *Business Week* once called the virtual company: Examples may be readily found in the apparel industry. There, freelance designers provide the coming year's line of clothing, which is manufactured by the lowest-bidder factories located anywhere from Guatemala to Malaysia, while the clothes are promoted via an outsourced advertising agency. Meanwhile, only a handful of people would be needed to run the core operations. Companies hoping to compete with such ultra-lean operations will have about as much success as a sailing vessel with a crew of 100 competing against a supertanker with less than a dozen sailors onboard.

The outsourced economy carries with it other implications as well. As companies tightly integrate their operations with partners via the Net, they must learn to hone in on their specialty, whether that means providing human resource outsourcing, transportation, or communications. At the same time they must be able to adapt that service rapidly to any number of different clients and to thrive in an environment where they are interchangeable pieces in a puzzle that itself is constantly changing.

Net-Speed Changes

While diverse work groups will find that they can unite quickly, thanks to the Internet, the medium itself will pose enormous challenges to companies. In addition to fostering an environment where components of a supply chain become readily interchangeable, the Internet will greatly accelerate the commoditization of all types of products and services. As an example, a Web shopper can go to any number of sites to instantly find the best price on everything from cars to cameras. And in the future, reverse auctions such as Priceline will no doubt accelerate the pressure to price things lower—or even to give them away.

Nowhere is this more true than with information products. The same information some companies charge for can be gotten for free with only a few additional mouse clicks. Commoditization opens the possibility that companies in the future may be locked into wars of attrition far more vicious than those described in chapter 8. That is, unless they succeed in segmenting their market, according to Buchholz. He uses Bloomberg as an example. The diverse financial-media company provides basic information about the financial markets free to customers via its Web site. But it also charges customers with more specialized needs. Such a strategy, Buchholz says, involves broadcasting to reach large groups of potential customers, then narrow-casting to those customers who have particular interests.[12]

IBM adopted a similar strategy. In an effort to undercut archrival Microsoft, the company embraced the open-source Linux operating system, a product that is essentially free to all. But it sought to add value by providing a full array of consulting services. And to augment its ability in that area, it purchased PriceWaterhouseCoopers.

Enter the Change Masters

IBM is a good example of a large organization that has been able to reformulate itself—albeit not always easily—to rapid changes. And, in fact, more and more companies are attempting to predict the consequences of change and even quantify what is unforeseeable—the goal, of course, being to change themselves as necessary. This effort has led to the growth of a new management specialty, so-called risk managers. Their job is to lead efforts aimed at identifying and then mitigating the risks inherent with company activities. And this small but growing field has devised numerous methods for doing just that.

Typically, risk managers focus on a single project. An example might be the development of a new product or a facility. As a first step, categories of potential risk areas are identified. The risks of developing a new product might break down as follows:

Market risks. The market forecasted for the planned product or service may simply not be there; a paradigm shift or incremental change may have prompted customers to buy elsewhere.
Financial risks. Economic uncertainty stemming from the possibilities of new wars or terrorist actions might cause a further erosion of people's spending power. As a result, the company's market for the new product could shrink.

Competitive risks. Other companies might steal market share by better leveraging their borrowing capacity. Or, they could develop a product with superior features.

Political risks. The product might anger consumer or environmental groups, or its use could be voided by government action. As an example: The airport security companies put out of business when government workers took over their jobs following September 11.

Environmental risks. The product or the manufacture of it might be seen to cause unforeseen harm to the environment.[13]

The actual list would in each case depend on the project at hand. And in all likelihood, many more items could be added. In fact, the list is liable to grow as it is passed around and commented upon by all those involved with the project. To identify still other, more specific risks, some companies conduct brainstorming sessions with those involved with a project. Another technique favored by Carnegie Mellon is to conduct group interviews. In this case, a team of, say, four interviewers would question four project members.

As a result of these discussions, probabilities may be assigned to each item on the list. Other risk-assessment methodologies call for trying to discern patterns or relationships between individual items on the list. A lack of funding, for example, might lead to shortcuts in research, which might create shoddy workmanship and thus increase the product's liability risk.

Wheel of Fortune

Finally, specific methods would be assigned to further evaluate some of the more pressing risks. For example, strict testing procedures could quantify engineering risks, while surveys and other market research techniques could evaluate market risks, and economic modeling on a macro and an organizational level could adjudge the financial risks. Still another technique is to use something called Monte Carlo analysis. This is a complex statistical evaluation program first developed for the financial services industry. The program looks at prevailing trends—such as the historical performance of a group of stocks. Then it creates, at times, hundreds of different scenarios. Again, using finance as an example, the stock market might race ahead, remain sluggish, or continue to decline drastically within the assigned timeframe. Hundreds of variations within these extremes are also possible. Monte Carlo analysis permits risk managers to see each possibility and—more important—the statistical likelihood that it will occur.

Armed with a true sense of what the risks of an undertaking are, risk managers can then devise a strategy to mitigate all those that seriously threaten the project. At this point, some risk managers may in effect go back to square one and reevaluate all the risks of the project now that the mitigating strategies are in place, to see if the overall dynamic has improved sufficiently.[14]

The Risk-Aware Organization

The ultimate extension of risk management is to use it as a framework for setting and evaluating all corporate strategy. Lowell L. Bryan, writing in the *McKinsey Quarterly*,[15] outlines such a strategy, which he says is uniquely suited to an environment where change is a constant. Under those circumstances, there is no choice but to create a strategy that is able to change, one in which an obligation to deliver shareholder value remains one of the few constants.

Bryan's proposed solution is analogous to how Allied commanders handled the problem of transporting supplies across the Pacific Ocean during World War II. Because the actions of the enemy were entirely unpredictable, the Allied commanders resorted to convoys containing both warships and cargo vessels. By fielding many ships together, it was reasonably assured that some would evade the enemy.

Similarly, companies need to think of themselves not in the static terms of a diversified portfolio of assets, Bryan says, but rather as a portfolio of initiatives. And like the convoys that helped win World War II, these initiatives can be synergistically grouped together, he says.

The pharmaceutical industry operates in this way, according to Bryan.[16] Larger pharmaceutical companies have several drugs "in the pipeline," all of which may be undergoing different stages of testing, as mandated by the FDA. Should testing results prove unsatisfactory, further development on the drug is normally suspended. Similarly, venture capital firms provide funding to a portfolio of companies, normally at similar stages of development. Continued funding is contingent on satisfying certain objectives, and the goal is always to create a profitable exit strategy.

Larger companies likewise can grow a portfolio of businesses internally, all aimed at satisfying certain overall corporate objectives. In doing this, the company functions like venture funds by seeding the new ventures with start-up cash and funneling progressively greater resources to those that warrant it. Because numerous initiatives are continually in the process of formation, the company achieves a mentality of being able to change directions and adapt as needed, while constantly affirming its commitment to innovation.

Appendix: In Search of a Failure-Proof Strategy

While this book was being written, almost-daily headlines chronicled AOL Time Warner's growing misfortunes. The world's largest communications conglomerate is perhaps a classic example of why companies fail, or, more specifically, why seemingly good companies fail. Indeed, few companies possess more talent within their ranks than AOL Time Warner does, from the crack reporters on CNN, to the pioneering software engineers who tweak new applications for AOL, to the product-development and marketing teams that fight daily battles in the cutthroat world of magazines. Moreover, few companies have embodied grander visions. AOL Time Warner sought to harness beneath one roof its library of quality media content and to deliver it via streamlined pipes directly to the homes of millions of consumers.

And yet the dream has proven painfully elusive. A *Business Week* article brought up a laundry list of problems the media conglomerate faced at the start of 2003. Its analysis, like most others, focused on the company's ubiquitous online service as the reason behind the company's ills. (And so will this appendix.)

For starters, the article said, AOL subscribers—upward of 200,000 per month—continue to defect from the safe but pokey dial-up world of AOL's proprietary content. In its place, those customers are opting for the "fat pipes" of broadband, where they can enjoy always-on connections and ultra-fast online gaming and music downloading. Marketing efforts to replenish what amounts to a small city's worth of defections each month were forecasted to cost AOL $2.2 billion by 2005. Meanwhile, cash flow for the company has withered by roughly $900 million, the article said, and AOL Time Warner needed to pay out $666 million annually to service its $10 billion debt.[1]

By some accounts, these problems had not arisen as a result of management miscalculations or shortsightedness. And while some business analysts expressed reservations at the onset whether AOL Time Warner would be able to pull off its merger, the consensus among many was that the union would succeed. All too well, in fact. Many in the industry feared how the merged media giant might affect their business. Rival Internet service providers, for example, were afraid that after the merger, they would be shut out of the cable systems owned by Time Warner, in favor of AOL. Those fears prompted unprecedented efforts by federal regulators to require AOL to open up its broadband pipes to competing service providers.

At the same time, many analysts reflected that the AOL Time Warner union might positively change the nature of both computing and communications for years to come. Some said that AOL's rise to prominence proved that Microsoft's monopoly in operating systems was vulnerable. AOL's online interface was already a de facto competitor to Windows. And with a user base that would eventually grow to 35 million, AOL truly had become the first online mass medium. At certain times of the day, the number of AOL subscribers logged onto the network was greater than the number viewing some cable TV stations. Significantly, those subscribers weren't just passively viewing AOL's content; they were interacting with it. Around the world, millions hooked up to AOL to research stocks, comment on the latest films or books in chat rooms, play games, and research products they hoped to buy. AOL offered a hint of an online experience that would become the digital alternative to reading a stack of magazines on a rainy afternoon.

Over time, AOL became better known than the conglomerate it had created with Time Warner. In fact, the online service's name recognition was such that Hollywood executives launched the movie *You've Got Mail,* confident that American moviegoers would know that the title referred to the AOL voice that spoke when users logged on. And yet, within months of reaching these heights in public awareness, many were calling AOL a dinosaur and a millstone around the neck of Time Warner.

The Roots of the Problem

So where, then, did AOL go wrong? Can any of this book's 10 reasons for why companies fail be applied to AOL's predicament? It's easier to name the areas that don't apply.

Did AOL Time Warner allow stock price to dictate its strategy, a deadly sin discussed in chapter 4? The acquisition benefited from AOL's pre-crash stock price, giving the online upstart inordinate leverage in the deal. Since the merger with Time Warner has punished shareholders severely, it can't be said that the company's stock price overwhelmingly dictates its operations. Moreover, the fall of the conglomerate's stock price can, in large part, be explained by the stock's high price when the Time Warner merger was first consummated near the height of the Internet boom.

The company did experience growing pains—the problem explored in chapter 5—during the mid-'90s. If anything, these growing pains stemmed from AOL's success. And rather than building capacity in advance of growth, as a retail or a restaurant chain must do, AOL allowed its infrastructure to lag—though too much, as it turned out. By the time the company made the needed expensive upgrades, the customers were already signed on and paying their monthly fees.

Finally, AOL doesn't appear to have ignored customers, another sin delved into in chapter 7. The proof of this might be that several million customers are willing to pay for a broadband connection, plus an additional monthly fee to access AOL's content.

One area where AOL is likely guilty is in failing to achieve synergies, the topic of chapter 12. True, on the one hand, the company has made impressive attempts to integrate its marketing operations. The conglomerate's popular publications, like *Time, People, Sports Illustrated,* and *Fortune,* are co-branded with CNN news shows. Also, advertisements for the AOL online service seemingly appear at 10-minute intervals.

On the other hand, the company's short marriage to Time Warner has so far been fraught with tales of boardroom squabbling and resentment, on the part of Time Warner employees for their erstwhile new owner. Those fights culminated in the announced resignation of AOL's chairman, Steve Case, which was preceded by the exodus of several other key company executives. These top-level struggles naturally increased analysts' uncertainty about the company. So it could be said that AOL, though still a young company, has not handled its succession planning properly, a subject covered in chapter 11.

Some analysts say that AOL was a victim of a paradigm shift—see chapter 6. Specifically, it rose to prominence in the Internet's earliest days. And it did so by providing an unintimidating interface to first-time users of the Net. AOL, in fact, really rose to dominate a pre–World Wide Web version of the online realm, the world of dial-in computer bulletin boards. These were proprietary networks that people dialed into. In AOL's earliest days, its chief competitors were companies we hardly think of now, such as Prodigy or CompuServe, plus hundreds of other dial-in networks that have since ceased to exist. And while AOL—thanks to its famous and colorful user-friendly interface—grew into the largest bulletin board service of all, the still-new World Wide Web offered relatively sparse and crude content to compete with it. That would change, of course. Gradually, the online world became a dichotomy. There was AOL, and there was the World Wide Web. Significant content providers felt that they needed a space on both.

But, gradually, the Web matured. And the number of its users grew logarithmically. Content providers encountered relatively few hassles when they set up shop on the Web. An army of fiercely competing Web-hosting companies brought the monthly price of maintaining a Web site to less than the cost of owning a telephone, in some cases. Little wonder that the number of Web sites also mushroomed. For that reason, some people fault AOL for not developing enough proprietary, must-have content—of under-innovating, in other words (see chapter 10).

The "Reinvent the World Syndrome" and Other Lessons from Peers

In that sense, AOL's struggle is similar to that of another PC-era company that had its ups and downs over the years. And, significantly, that company also rose to a dominant position because it emphasized a no-hassle user experience. The company was Apple Computer. Like AOL, Apple built a veritable wall around itself, in order to preserve its unique user experience: the Apple OS user interface. If Windows seems awkward by comparison, it is in part because the Microsoft OS's design must work with an endless array of third-party PCs, all of which differ somewhat in design. Apple PCs, by contrast, are tweaked to work with the Apple OS. Even for the brief period when Apple allowed third-party manufacturers to sell so-called Apple clones, the design of those machines was rigorously controlled by Apple itself. Apple's business model, like that of the early online service providers and their viewdata service, described in chapter 10, had opted to reinvent the world. The company was intensely *vertically integrated,* to use a better-known term, and this proved to be an expensive, nearly company-killing, option. Thus, ultimately, Apple's market share slipped for reasons that are similar to the problems facing AOL. Software manufacturers were reluctant to adapt their software to Apple machines. The finite Apple universe of machines, OS design, and applications was a world unto itself that existed in parallel to the much-faster-growing world centered around Windows PCs.

Just as in the battle between AOL and the Internet, the PC industry enjoyed certain huge advantages over Apple. Namely, thousands of companies were building machines and writing applications. And, collectively, they poured enormous sums into making their products better, cheaper, and faster. By contrast, the Apple business model had locked the company into paying for much of its own research and development expenses for future machines and versions of its operating system—a fact that explains why Apple products tend to be more expensive than their Windows competitors.

Analogously, this is the same reason why AOL has been unable to develop enough proprietary content with the sizzle sufficient to make it a must-have for the online service's subscribers. It is an impossible task, notwithstanding the fact that part of the rationale for acquiring Time Warner was undoubtedly to harness its vast library of movies, books, and magazine content. Like Apple Computer, AOL carried a huge burden. It needed to provide both the onramp to the Net and masses of proprietary content capable of rivaling what the Net had to offer. Competing Internet service providers, by contrast, are able to content themselves with furnishing just the onramp. At the same time they offer a vast universe of content available on the World Wide Web, with the sole exception of AOL's proprietary content. After all, literally millions of individuals and companies around the world are working night and day to create alluring content. How could AOL ever dream of competing?

Perhaps it could compete by taking a cue from how Apple has managed to survive thus far. The computer maker took advantage of the fierce loyalty of its customers and focused on particular niches. Many of Apple's customers work in creative fields such as desktop publishing, graphic design, and video production. Being creative thinkers, these customers likely appreciated the Apple interface because it allowed them to focus on their craft. Apple recently appealed directly to this group with its line of large-screen notebook computers that allowed filmmakers, graphic designers, and others to see their work in large format, wherever they happened to be.

Apple has long sought to build upon its reputation for user-friendliness by expanding its niche to include at-home customers who want to use their computers for creative ends. And in doing so, they have successfully expanded their product franchise. The company's lower-end computers are now touted as digital hubs that allow users to capture photos from digital cameras or to download tunes for playing on its iPod music recorders. Apple would seemingly be perfectly positioned to capitalize on the newest convergence trend, which is the linking of computers with TV viewing and recording. Here, too, its reputation for user-friendliness would serve it well, since customers are far less tolerant of TV system crashes than they are of freeze-ups on their home computer. Navigational ease is also of primary importance.

Future AOL Scenarios

Somewhere at the heart of AOL's enormous customer base is a core group of subscribers that is likewise fiercely loyal to the product. Many of those can be found among subscribers who pay a premium for a broadband connection, in addition to a fee for access to AOL's proprietary content. But whoever this core group turns out to be, the task at AOL entails discovering what product attributes or specific content will keep them on as subscribers.

Perhaps, like Apple's core customers, they want to access particular bits of content via a friendly interface that doesn't get in the way of their search. Or perhaps they seek certain applications within the framework of the AOL interface that are likewise easy to use. With AOL, as with Apple, the company's greatest asset is likely to be that interface.

Some say that in order to fully exploit the potential of that customer base, AOL should be divested from its parent so that it can exist unhindered by demands from the conglomerate's management. The same *Business Week* issue that offered a damning assessment of AOL's problems also provided a second opinion of sorts, via a second article.[2] In that article, two analysts, Catherine

Yang and Timothy J. Mullaney, said that AOL needed to develop proprietary "sticky" content. However, "This shouldn't be the glitzy HBO-type stuff that AOL Time Warner has been pushing." Instead, the two suggested applications like online loan services, dating services, and e-mail that allowed users to easily send photos and videos.

More basic changes might also improve the online service's chances of survival. AOL built its reputation on a user-friendly interface; it should back that up with unparalleled customer service. The company also rose to prominence on the strength of its innovative spirit. When other online bulletin boards were unappealing text-based libraries, AOL offered color images and sound, providing a unique online experience at the time.

As Harvard Business School professor Clayton Christensen points out in chapter 10, so many companies that succeeded thanks to their earlier innovative efforts, later allowed those innovations to become sustaining technologies that they are content to simply tweak in order to continue serving their customer base in the manner to which people have become accustomed. Meanwhile, competitors may be hard at work creating disruptive technologies that will displace the old standards. Improvements made to the sustaining technologies will eventually become futile, like fine-tuning a steam-powered car after the world has moved to gasoline engines. Only companies that continue to harness that spirit of innovation will survive long term.

In AOL's case, Yang and Mullaney said that survival may mean unequivocally embracing broadband. To do that, AOL must work through partners—which means that it will likely be forced to cut painful revenue-sharing agreements with cable systems. The company could also develop applications that enhance the cable experience, similar to but far better than the crude TV programming guides that now appear on many systems or the TiVo recording feature that's become outrageously popular.

Extrapolating from this idea, an AOL remote, modeled after a personal digital assistant (PDA), could provide an online experience that complements the larger screen's programming. Once again, AOL's ability to create a smooth user interface will prove its most important asset. In yet another scenario, numerous home and small business applications—everything from home security to accounting—could be provided by AOL, using an ASP (application service provider) model.

However, even these innovations may not be enough to save AOL (and many other portal sites that compete with it) from yet another upcoming paradigm shift in online interfaces. Web sites like the Sims Online and There.com offer a glimpse of what surfing the Web and interacting with others online will be like in the years, if not the months, ahead. Instead of interacting via a two-dimensional display of text and graphics, users will be able to immerse themselves in a virtual 3D world. While there, they can assume identities and physically explore an artistically rendered series of locales that emphasizes games and the unexpected. Compared to that interface, AOL's once-innovative graphic appearance may seem as primitive as the text-based bulletin boards that AOL itself supplanted.

Survival Restructuring

Unlike some of the companies serving as examples in this book, AOL and Apple Computer remain viable businesses. Their reputations are such that armies of customers and even hardened analysts continue to root for their survival. In that way, however, they illustrate a frightening aspect of business failure alluded to at the start of this chapter—the fact that good companies can be struck down perhaps just as readily as bad ones. And sometimes through no fault of their own. Such failures are more common than you might think.

Technology executives speak with fear about being *Betamaxed.* The term refers to Sony's pioneering videotaping format that reputedly surpassed VHS cassette tapes in quality. Betamax failed because it was outmarketed by its competitors. Similarly, some say that Apple's OS has been Betamaxed by Windows. Betamaxing has become a fact of life in the ongoing war over standards for new audio and video formats. Sadly, the company with the best technology doesn't always win. More often, the company with the best marketing or political muscle does. If there's a lesson from the Betamax phenomenon, it's that companies can't simply rely on good products; they must market them as aggressively as their scrappiest competitors do. Though this doesn't mean that they, too, should resort to scrappy methods. Apple proves that companies can prevail when they are outgunned on the marketing front. Instead of being the ubiquitous computer standard, as the company might have hoped, Apple occupies a high-end niche with consumers and serves professionals working in a few select fields.

However, IBM provides an even more illustrative example of how a company whose products have been eclipsed by aggressive marketing can retake the high ground.

From DOS to Open Source

It has been said that very high on the list of world-class business blunders was IBM's original licensing of the disk operating system (DOS) from a then-fledgling Microsoft. Had IBM bought or licensed the operating system outright from Bill Gates and company, Microsoft might not have existed, and IBM presumably would have ruled the personal computer universe. This, of course, is not how things turned out. As the familiar story goes, IBM—an old-line, highly confident maker of mainframe computers and expensive office automation equipment—belatedly saw the need to enter the more consumer-oriented microcomputer arena. At the time, the personal computer market was highly fragmented. Different computers ran on different, incompatible operating systems. And networking—still a distant dream in most offices—was something you needed mainframes to achieve. Perhaps for that reason, IBM may have seen little value in actually owning the operating system it chose to run its PC. It may even have suited the company to have many incompatible operating systems. Because if that were the case, IBM could sell everyone the software needed to link those incompatible systems. In any event, as we all know, IBM allowed Microsoft to retain the rights to DOS. And in the process, the computer giant was eventually dealt a staggering blow. Here was a company expert at serving customers, with its notably superior sustaining technologies, that was in danger of being outgunned by Microsoft's skilled marketing. Microsoft, while growing exponentially, was uniquely positioned to take on Big Blue. By focusing exclusively on software, its operations could be kept far leaner, while its margins widened coincident with the growth of the PC market as a whole. IBM, by contrast, was in the business of producing hardware and software—a model that forced it to absorb relatively higher fixed costs.

Suddenly, however, Big Blue found itself thrust into the consumer market, likely with full knowledge that its future depended on claiming a viable stake there. It turned out to be a huge challenge. With its first attempts, IBM proved sorely unable to adopt a consumer focus. Its ads and product packaging appeared awkward in those early years.

That is perhaps one reason why the company failed to stop Windows with the IBM operating system, called OS2. And it found itself being Betamaxed in the process. One version of Windows that OS2 competed with was Windows 95, groundbreaking at the time but clunky in comparison to later Windows generations. By some accounts OS2 was superior to mid-'90s-generation Windows products, even quite innovative in comparison to today's Windows versions. The IBM product featured, for example, built-in voice dictation and peer-to-peer networking, increasingly popular ideas among power users now that have yet to spread to the PC-using population as a whole. Still, despite an expensive ad campaign and aggressive pricing, IBM failed to overcome the entrenched lead enjoyed by Windows.

After losing the OS battle, IBM suffered an even more humiliating defeat in office-suite software. Applications, after all, were at the heart of Big Blue's strength. And the company had pioneered the development of word processing and database programs. To gain entry into the consumer and business market in 1995, IBM paid the then unheard of price of $3.5 billion for Lotus. The company owned the de facto standard in spreadsheet applications, namely, Lotus 1-2-3. Some called spreadsheets the killer app (application) that compelled customers to purchase personal computers in the first place. Yet Microsoft was extremely successful at linking its Microsoft Office suite of programs to its Windows operating system, at least in customers' minds. Over time, MS Office became the standard at enough companies that users concerned about document interoperability were reluctant to switch. In the course of losing this battle, too, Lotus's office suite eventually commanded a fraction of the market and of Microsoft Office's price. In some cases, versions were bundled free with IBM PCs, where they resided unused. Meanwhile, Microsoft made inroads into high-margin specialized software areas, such as Net server and Web development tools. For IBM, this must have seemed like a painful round of stomach punches.

IBM finally got a chance to regain its advantage, though that chance didn't come until the turn of the century. And, ironically, it came about directly as a result of Microsoft's increasing domination of all aspects of the software market. IBM's core business customers wanted an alternative to Microsoft's products, which some claimed now compelled them to continually purchase upgrades. That escape route proved to be Linux. For the software industry, the fledgling operating system—first designed, supposedly on a whim, by Finnish university student Linus Torvalds—represented a paradigm shift and, at the same time, the intrusion of a disruptive technology. The paradigm shift resulted because, rather than being controlled by a single company, Linux came to be run by a committee of users. This open-source platform—in something as fundamental as operating systems—threatened Microsoft in the same way that AOL had been threatened by the Internet at large or that Apple had been threatened by the PC market. Suddenly, with Linux, hundreds of companies the world over were working to make it better, spending billions of dollars doing so. Just like Apple and AOL, Microsoft, by contrast, was forced to shoulder development costs itself and also to rely on its massive but still finite talent pool to compete.

IBM, owing to its own experiences, likely understood the quandary that Microsoft now faced as a result of Linux. Its singular great contribution to the PC revolution was to create an industry standard platform: the IBM PC. And that standard permitted untold thousands of companies to provide both hardware and software refinements, ultimately at the expense of IBM's own market share.

The sticky problem with any revolution (and disruptive technology), however, is that things tend to be messy at the outset. The Linux revolution proved no exception. It was intimidating to many inexpert computer users. Compared to it, the Windows world is downright staid. What was needed was a reliable company that could help its large-scale customers transition safely to what was otherwise a Wild West environment. IBM, with its long-time emphasis on consultative sales, uniquely fit the bill. If IBM could impose the PC architecture as the de facto standard for microcomputers, it could bestow the same honor on Linux.

Microsoft, meanwhile, certainly possessed the capacity to reinvent itself to play a similar role. It had managed to brilliantly do just that during the '90s, when it became apparent that the Internet would dominate computing from thence on. In a remarkably short time, Microsoft reversed course and became a company organized around the Internet. During a lengthy marketing battle, its Internet Explorer Web browser eventually edged out Netscape Navigator. (Some would say that Navigator was Betamaxed by Explorer.) And Microsoft mimicked the logic of open-source marketing by giving Explorer away. But the Linux revolution seemingly had the company trapped. And IBM, by any reckoning, knew it. If Microsoft supported Linux, it would be at the expense of its own high-margin products. The result is that not since the advent of the IBM PC has Big Blue been presented with such a significant market-dominating opportunity.

Becoming Bullet Proof

Not all companies are lucky enough to be given the kind of opportunity that IBM received. And even fewer companies have the ability to grasp a product when the opportune time arrives to exploit it. But in lieu of that, companies can create a climate that allows them to adapt, claims one analyst in *Fortune*.[3] According to Gary Hamel, that effort involves not so much a direction at the top as it does a leadership style, which sets the tone for a culture of adaptability and nimble response to change. To illustrate, Hamel compares today's large, far-flung corporations to flocks of geese that relentlessly pursue a general goal—that is, migration south—without overt leadership. By contrast, he says, "Too many executives try to design flight plans for their far-flung flock, rather than work to create conditions that would help their brood get off the ground and on their way to new shores." In his view, strategy is less important than "creating conditions out of which wealth-creating strategies are likely to emerge." And he proposes several ways of doing that, among them (with comments):

Set high goals. Achieving goals, Hamel says, largely depends on expectations among those in the company. If they believe that they can do great things, they well might. And the reverse is also true.

Turn the business into a cause. People naturally strive for great things when they're working for a higher purpose. Yahoo became successful because its founders saw their mission as helping people navigate the Web. Its original group of academic-oriented employees became personally dedicated to that mission. In another example, a new generation of online brokers saw themselves challenging the Wall Street establishment on the part of their clients.

Create a team of young up-and-comers and have them brainstorm new ideas. This encourages out-of-the-box thinking and helps the select group upon whom the firm's future may depend to develop valuable working relationships.

Seek low-risk innovations. Here Hamel takes a cue from venture capitalists, who in effect run highly unhierarchical and diverse organizations—in other words, the companies they choose to fund. Venture capitalists' value added service is that they wield inordinately high leverage. Which is to say, they hand over relatively small amounts of seed capital and allow the business to bootstrap itself. In contrast to that, large companies tend to prefer buying established organizations. And they're willing to pay dearly for them.

Finally, Hamel advises companies to generously reward their innovators. In doing so, they send a clear message throughout the organization about the kinds of change they wish to embrace.

The Wartime Metaphor

While allowing for a culture of adaptability, some companies are adopting quite a different organizational, project-centered mode of operations that harks back directly to the military. It's a mode that promotes speed and focus almost to the extreme. And in that sense, it's an information-oriented economy's equivalent to the relationship-oriented, "extreme manufacturing" methods employed in the Chinese Delta River Valley, discussed in chapter 14.

Just as the armed forces have long relied on "war rooms" or nerve centers to bring together the myriad pieces of information related to a military campaign, companies are taking a highly focused approach to their new projects. Some refer to it as a "war room" approach. The name conjures up images of darkened rooms replete with glowing maps, with commanders hunched over computer screens. But, in fact, extreme project management in some circles has moved beyond the concept of a war room per se.

A war room implies that the place where planning gets done is distinct from where work is actually accomplished. And the current thinking is to combine the two.

This approach involves concentrating workers in a location specifically devoted to the project at hand. Continually updated graphs on the wall depict a project's progress for all to see. All the workers know what elements of the project are due from their teammates, as well as what's expected of them. And if a change is needed, it can be easily communicated to all concerned. Such focused work environments are designed to keep everyone in the loop. A prerequisite is that all members have access to all the needed information. Stand-up meetings, when absolutely required, keep everyone keyed into the task at hand, quickly. And all the while, project leaders function more as facilitators, smoothing communication and workflow.

One of the first private companies to make successful use of the concept was Lockheed (now Lockheed Martin) with its Skunk Works. The crack division within the firm developed some of the Cold War's most successful aviation breakthroughs—most notably, the U2 spy plane. According to *Wired* magazine, the Skunk Work's motto was "Be quick, be quiet, and be on time." In keeping with that mission, the number of Skunk Work employees was kept deliberately low, presumably so that everyone depended on everyone else to succeed. Reports were required to be less than 20 pages. And Skunk Workers performed their tasks in a "window-less blockhouse,"[4] devoid of any distractions.

For years, few companies besides Lockheed used the approach. However, in recent times it has reportedly became popular with companies involved with large-scale IT projects. It is being used by companies that must routinely create new products, as well as by small modern manufacturing firms the world over, whether consciously or otherwise. These firms often focus on a single component, one of perhaps thousands used in the eventual construction of a complex product such as a motorcycle or a computer. The approach is eons removed from the vertical integration that was often the norm for companies engaged in the manufacture of these same products. Because the outsourced manufacturing operation is relatively small, the plant supervisor can see all aspects at a glance and can communicate directly with individual workers.

Many companies have made the shift from bringing together team members in a real war room environment to uniting them in a virtual environment—that is, a Web site. Here again, the military provides a model.

An article by the Associated Press describes a high-tech war room in a tent on the frontlines in Afghanistan.

> Inside, tables are lined with soldiers bent over laptops. They look up at computer maps of Afghanistan projected on large screens illuminating the dim interior. All are logged onto the Tactical Web Page, a secret, secure website being used in combat for the first time.[5]

The newsroom of a big city newspaper is a perfect metaphor for the virtual war room approach, combined with one or more actual war rooms. Correspondents and bureaus throughout the world file their stories electronically to the main newsroom. Wire services also constantly stream in information, while within the newsroom itself, editors monitor TV news reports. In the process of manufacturing their product, different reporters, editors, and artists within the newsroom all contribute. And the manufacturing process essentially begins fresh each new day.

Currency trading and stock-trading operations have also long functioned this way. Many of the trading rooms used by large financial firms are arranged like a newsroom, with rows of computer monitors set atop desks facing giant screens that depict vital world market information. In specialized trading, such as bond trading or energy trading, a smaller group of experts might sit around a horseshoe desk. Individuals at the table, interacting with clients around the world, are also within easy speaking distance of their colleagues in the room, in an environment that functions round the clock.

Indeed, some global financial institutions maintain offices on three continents. Like tag teams in a wrestling match, their traders hand over responsibilities for buying and selling as the sun tracks over the earth. Thus, these institutions can protect themselves if an international crisis in the Middle East occurs at 1 A.M. New York time and sends markets toppling in Asia. The operations work something like this: After trading shuts down in New York, these large trading firms may quickly pass their work on to an affiliate trading room in Asia. Hours later, the European exchanges open their doors, and trading in Asia is handed over to yet another affiliate trading room on the Continent. Later, the action shifts to New York once again.

Similarly, computer software firms have created 24-hour virtual rooms, manned by teams in two or more parts of the world. While the U.S. team might work on a project during the day, at night they'll pass the work to their colleagues in India, who will pass it back in time for the U.S. morning shift.

In operations such as this, teleconferencing can be of enormous help in bridging the geographic gap between two locations. Some have also suggested using a large flat-panel video screen that would provide an always-on telelink to a sister facility, which would likewise have a screen on its wall. That way, colleagues at both sites could simply call each other to the display and discuss the project as if they were standing just feet apart.

Business at Hyperspeed

Interestingly enough, in order to function in this rapid, information-critical environment, news production, stock trading, and software manufacture firms have found that they must incorporate a culture that allows workers to exercise considerable discretion in how they operate within the larger framework. Just as the aforementioned leaderless flock of geese relentlessly pursues the overall goal of migration, reporters on newspapers are responsible for finding, developing, and writing stories that will enhance the paper, often with little direct oversight. Similarly, the individual traders packed into a trading room must scan the continual array of buy and sell orders and themselves find matches that will further the firm. Finally, individual programmers must devise creative solutions to each small piece of the puzzle that crosses their screens.

If we look at these extreme examples of product manufacture, in the case of a newspaper and a software firm, or of process, in the case of a trading firm, it is impossible to overstate the integral role played by information and its seamless communication in their operations. Where would the newsroom or the trading be, for example, without an always-on connection to wire service or market reports? Where would the software firm be without its computer network, capable of assembling all the pieces of a larger program that are constantly being churned out?

Quite possibly, the innovations these industries have devised will spread by necessity to other sectors. Variations on the virtual war room, for example, are already proving invaluable to companies that actively work with their suppliers to quickly usher through products from design to manufacture to the customer.

Writing in the *McKinsey Quarterly,* Remo Hacki and Julian Lighton describe these firms as networked companies, the best known and the most successful of which is Cisco Systems. "As Cisco morphed into a virtual corporation during the 1990s, it . . . created a 'gated network' of contract manufacturers and suppliers connected to one another and to itself by a powerful set of network applications running on its proprietary extranet," the authors say.

With large companies like Cisco, this networked organization is akin to the Japanese *kieritsu,* they claim. But where the *kieritsu*—which may be loosely defined as a conglomerate or family of businesses—is bound together by overlapping debt and stock ownership, the networked company is linked by information.

Will all companies be forced to radically redesign themselves in order to compete within this tightly integrated informational web? The remedy might appear extreme. But you only have to consider the effect of previous communications paradigm shifts. How would a business have fared 70 years ago without telephones? What will happen to businesses currently whose employees don't have access to e-mail? Moreover, the chasm that companies must cross to be successful is no larger than the one retailers have been forced to reckon with: going from smalltown stores to 24/7 supercenters in the course of a generation. In either case, the one constant, sadly, is that companies that either can't adapt or refuse to adapt will fail. And in an ever more closely entwined global economy, there will be hundreds, if not thousands, of companies standing in line to take their place.

Notes

Preface

1. David A. Ricks, *Blunders in International Business*, Third Edition (St. Louis, MI: University of Missouri/Blackwell, 2000), pp. 20, 22.

2. Tim Carvell, Adam Horowitz, and Thomas Mucha, "The 101 Dumbest Moments in Business," by *Business 2.0*, April 2002, accessed online at: www.business20.com/articles/mag/print/0,1643 ,38604,FF.html.

3. David W. Hendon, *Classic Failures in Product Marketing: Marketing Principles Violations and How to Avoid Them* (New York: Quorum Books, 1989).

4. Joann Muller, "Commentary: Kmart's Shopping List for Survival," *BusinessWeek* online (March 25, 2002).

5. Ram Charan and Jerry Useem, "Why Companies Fail," *Fortune* (May 27, 2002), accessed online.

6. Siliwa, "IT Troubles Helped Take Kmart Down," CNN.com (January 29, 2002).

7. James C. Collins, *Good to Great: Why Some Companies Make the Leap and Others Don't* (New York: HarperCollins 2001), cited in "Why Companies Fail."

8. "Learn from Failure? Losing Really Stinks," from the *Wall Street Journal* online www.startupjournal.com/runbusiness/failure/2001 0628-lancaster.html.

9. Margaret Popper, "Maytag: Stuck in the Spin Cycle," *BusinessWeek* online (November 27, 2000).

10. Heesun Wee, "Maytag Is Cleaning up Its Act," *BusinessWeek* online (May 17, 2002).

11. Carvell, Horowitz, and Mucha, "The 101 Dumbest Moments in Business."

Chapter 1

1. Jean Scheidnes, "Gap Shares Slide After CEO's Resignation," Reuters, Wednesday, May 22, 2002. http://biz.yahoo.com/rb/020522/retail_gap_stocks_7.html.

2. This is a pseudonym.

3. Robin D. Schatz, "You'd Better Sit Down, Kids," *BusinessWeek* online (April 23, 2001).

4. "What Every Investor Should Know . . . Corporate Bankruptcy," online document published by the SEC, available at www.sec.gov/investor/pubs/bankrupt.htm.

5. Brian O'Keefe, "Fallen Companies: Gold Out of Garbage," *Fortune* (March 4, 2002).

6. David Shook, "The Empty Truth About Bankruptcy Stocks," *BusinessWeek* online (May 9, 2002).

7. Jennifer Keeney, "Just-in-Time Financing," *Fortune Small Business* (February 8, 2002), accessed online.

8. Linda Himelstein, "Dead Dot-Com? Marty's Your Man," *BusinessWeek* online (April 1, 2002).

9. "Options and Alternatives for Troubled Internet Companies: Bankruptcy Options," online document available at www.webmergers.com.

10. O'Keefe, "Fallen Companies."

11. Keith H. Hammonds, "Big Bets, Fast Failures," *Fast Company* (July 2001).

12. Mike McNamee and Joseph Weber, "Bloodied but Rich," *Business Week* (June 3, 2002): 74.

13. Hillary Rosenberg, *The Vulture Investors* (New York: John Wiley & Sons, 2000), pp. 1–20.

14. Hammonds, "Big Bets, Fast Failures."

15. Personal interview.

Chapter 2

1. Mark Lewis, "Will AOL Go the Way of the Model T?" *Forbes* (April, 19, 2002), accessed online.

2. Julie Creswell, "Gap Got Junked, Now What?" *Fortune* (March 18, 2002), accessed online.

3. Helmut K. Anheier, editor, *When Things Go Wrong: Organizational Failures and Breakdowns* (Thousand Oaks, CA: Sage Publications, 1999), p. 4.

4. *The Phoenix Forecast: Bankruptcies and Restructurings, 2002,* Price-WaterhouseCoopers, prepared by Carter Pate, March 2002.

5. Ram Charan and Jerry Useem, "Why Companies Fail," *Fortune* (May 27, 2002), accessed online.

6. "Corporate Renewal Professionals Have More Realistic View of Troubled Companies, TMA Survey Reveals," Turnaround Management Association press release, March 30, 2001.

7. Personal interview with Randall Patterson.

8. Bruce G. Posner, "Why Companies Fail," *Inc. Magazine,* June 1993.

9. Kevin Scott and Greg Grand, AMR Research, "Failed Dot-Coms Fell Victim to Their Own Lack of Focus," *Outlook* (December 12, 2000).

10. Cited in "The Great Internet Money Game: How America's Top Financial Firms Reaped Billions from the Net Boom, While Investors Got Burned," by Peter Elstrom, *Business Week* (April 16, 2001): EB16.

11. Troy A. Festervand and Jack E. Forrest, "Small Business Failures: A Framework for Analysis," paper available at www.sbaer.uca.edu/Research/1991/SBIDA/91sbi271.txt.

12. Festervand and Forrest, "Small Business Failures: A Framework for Analysis," p. 2.

13. Ibid.

14. Dominic DiNapoli, editor, *Workouts & Turnarounds II, Global Restructuring Strategies for the Next Century,* PriceWaterhouse-Coopers, p. 3.

15. Ibid., p. 4.

16. Mortimer Feinberg, Ph.D., and John J. Tarrant, *Why Smart People Do Dumb Things: The Greatest Business Blunders—How They Happened, and How They Could Have Been Prevented* (New York: Simon & Schuster, 1995).

17. Stewart Alsop, "The Tragedy of Webvan," *Fortune* (August 13, 2001), accessed online.

18. Katherine Catlin and Jana Matthews, *Building the Awesome Organization: Six Essential Components that Drive Business Growth,* (New York: John Wiley & Sons, 2002).

19. Raymond E. Miles and Charles C. Snow, *Fit, Failure & the Hall of Fame: How Companies Succeed or Fail* (New York: Free Press, 1994), pp. 84–86.

Chapter 3

1. Alex Berenson, "From Dream Team at Tyco to a Refrain of Dennis, Who?" *New York Times,* June 6, 2002.

2. William O'Neil, *How to Make Money in Stocks* (New York: McGraw-Hill, 1995), pp. 5, 9, 10.

3. Ibid., p. 22.

4. Ibid., p. 11.

5. Peter F. Drucker, "The Shape of Things to Come: An Interview with Peter F. Drucker," *Leader to Leader,* Peter F. Drucker Foundation for Nonprofit Management, no. 1 (Summer 1996).

6. Ram Charan and Jerry Useem, "Why Companies Fail," *Fortune* (May 27, 2002), accessed online.

7. "The Phoenix Forecast: Bankruptcies and Restructurings 2002," PriceWaterhouseCoopers, prepared by Carter Pate, March 2002.

8. "Woe Is Worldcom," *Business Week* (May 6, 2002).

9. "Creditors Miffed at Kmart Exec Payments," UPI, June 20, 2002.

10. John Balzar, "The Business of America Is Out of Control," *LA Times,* June 5, 2002.

11. "How to Fix Corporate Governance," *Business Week* (May 6, 2002): 69–78.

12. Nina Munk, "In the Final Analysis," *Vanity Fair,* (August 2001): 100-113.

13. Nina Munk, "Power Failure," *Vanity Fair* (July 2002).

14. Vicky Ward, The Battle for Hewlett-Packard," *Vanity Fair* (June 2002).

15. Michael Arndt, "Q&A: The Repairman in Charge of Fixing Maytag," *BusinessWeek* online, November 19, 2001.

16. Martin J. Pring, *Investment Psychology Explained* (New York: Wiley, 1993), pp. 120–124.

17. "How to Fix Corporate Governance," *Business Week* (May 6, 2002): 69–78.

18. *The Wall Street Journal Guide to Who's Who and What's What on Wall Street,* the editors of the *Wall Street Journal* (New York: Ballantine Books, 1998), p. 390.

19. "How to Fix Corporate Governance," *Business Week* (May 6, 2002): 69–78.

Chapter 4

1. Robert H. Hayes and William J. Abernathy "Managing Our Way to Economic Decline," *Harvard Business Review,* July-August 1980.

2. Securities and Exchange Commission, *Special Study of the Securities Markets* (Washington, D.C.: SEC, 1963).

3. "The Street Won't Be the Same Again," *Business Week,* May 23, 1970.

4. Gary Rivlin, *The Plot to Get Bill Gates: An Irreverent Investigation of the World's Richest Man . . . And the People Who Hate Him* (New York: Three Rivers Press, 1999 and 2000), pp. 224–227.

5. Robert X. Cringely, *Accidental Empires, How the Boys of Silicon Valley Make Their Millions, Battle Foreign Competition and Still Can't Get a Date* (Reading, MA: Addison-Wesley Publishing, Inc., 1992), pp. 171–172.

6. "The Rise and Rise of the Redmond Empire," *Wired,* December 1998.

7. Peter Elstrom, "The Great Internet Money Game, How America's Top Financial Firms Reaped Billions from the Net Boom, While Investors Got Burned," *Business Week*, June 18, 2001.

8. Ibid.

9. Ibid.

Chapter 5

1. "This Spotcom Is Now a Notcom," *CIO Magazine* (March 15, 2001).

2. Davide Dukcevich, "Funeral Industry: Back from the Dead?" *Forbes* (January 11, 2002).

3. Stuart C. Gilson, *Creating Value Through Corporate Restructuring: Case Studies in Bankruptcies, Buyouts, and Breakups* (New York: John Wiley & Sons, 2001), pp. 25–34.

4. Herb Greenberg, "Against the Grain: The Buy-'Em-Up Boondoggle," *Fortune* (July 22, 2002).

5. Geoffrey Colvin, "J. Peterman Company," *Fortune* (February 25, 1999).

6. "A Slippery Slope Made of Plastic," *Business Week* (May 6, 2002).

7. Robert Stowe England, "Where Credit Is Due: Companies Lending to Hard-Pressed Consumers Can Learn a Few Lessons from Sears," *CFO Magazine* (November 1, 1997).

8. Ashish Singh and James L. Gilber, "The Limits of Scale: Pharmas Need to Successfully Restructure Around a Few Therapeutic Franchises to Grow," (Bain & Company, 2002).

9. Bruce Orwall and Martin Peers, "Facing Crisis, Media Giants Scrounge for Fresh Strategies," *Wall Street Journal*, January 14, 2003, accessed online.

Chapter 6

1. Marshall E. Blume, Jeremy J. Siegel, and Dan Rottenberg, *Revolution on Wall Street: The Rise and Decline of the New York Stock Exchange* (New York: W.W. Norton & Company, 1993), p. 147.

2. General Accounting Office, "Financial Crisis Management: Four Financial Crises in the 1980s," May 1997.

3. Hal Lux and Jack Willoughby, "May Day II," *Institutional Investor,* February 1, 1999.

4. John Greenwald, "The Secret Money Machine," *Time,* April 11, 1994, accessed online.

5. Ibid.

6. National Center for Policy Analysis, "Bad Policies Triggered 1987 Market Crash."

7. General Accounting Office, "Financial Crisis Management."

8. "Research that breaks the mold," *Technology Review,* December 2002/January 2003, accessed online.

Chapter 7

1. Robert Sobel, *When Giants Stumble: Classic Business Blunders and How to Avoid Them* (Englewood Cliffs, NJ: Prentice Hall, 1999), p. 257.

2. Geoffrey Colvin, "Greyhound Returns," *Fortune* (Wednesday, April 21, 1999).

3. *Fortune* (September 1998).

4. William Christie and Paul H. Schultz, "Why Do NASDAQ Market Makers Avoid Odd-Eighth Quotes?" *Journal of Finance,* vol. XLIX, no. 5 (December 1994): 1813.

5. Remembering, of course, that their study preceded decimalization by a decade. The postdecimalization equivalent is $0.25.

6. Christie and Schultz, p. 1814.

7. *Securities Week* (May 30, 1994), cited by Christie-Schultz.

8. Ibid.

9. "Why Did NASDAQ Stop Avoiding Odd-Eighth Quotes?" (follow-up article), *Journal of Finance* (December 1994): 1853.

10. *Investment Dealers Digest,* May 22, 1995.

11. Federal Reserve Bank of Atlanta, "The NASDAQ Investigation: A Chronology," *Economic Review,* Third Quarter 1998.

12. Ibid.

13. *The Wall Street Journal Guide to Who's Who and What's What on Wall Street,* the editors of the *Wall Street Journal* (New York: Ballantine Books, 1998), p. 390.

14. Ibid., p. 415.

15. NASD bio.

16. SEC, "Order Instituting Public Proceedings Pursuant to Section 19(h)(1) of the Securities Exchange Act of 1934, Making Findings and Imposing Remedial Sanctions, Release No. 37538, August 8, 1996.

17. Paula Dwyer, "Tough Love at NASDAQ," *Business Week* (November 3, 1997).

18. "NASD Announces Plan for Restructuring Boards to Streamline Decision Making," NASD press release, June 26, 1997.

19. *Customer Service: Extraordinary Results at Southwest Airlines, Charles Schwab, Lands' End, American Express, Staples, and USAA,* edited by Fred Wiersema (New York: HarperBusiness, 1998), p. 6.

20. David Kushner, "It's a Mod, Mod World," *IEEE Spectrum* (February 2003): 56.

Chapter 8

1. Michael Schrage, "The Dell Curve," *Wired* (July 2002).

2. Ken Belson, "Asia's Fiber-Optical Illusion," *Fortune* (October 15, 2001).

3. Stephanie N. Mehta, "Why Telecom Crashed," *Fortune* (November, 27, 2000).

4. Michael T. Jacobs, *Short-Term America: The Causes and Cures of Our Business Myopia* (Boston: Harvard Business School Press, 1991), pp. 31–57.

5. Joe Connolly, "How to Succeed Despite Competitors' Low Prices," Startupjournal.com, date unknown, accessed online.

6. Robert J. Dolan and Hermann Simon, *Power Pricing: How Managing Price Transforms the Bottom Line* (New York: The Free Press, 1996).

Chapter 10

1. James Martin, *Telematic Society: A Challenge for Tomorrow,* (Englewood Cliffs, NJ: Prentice Hall, 1978 & 1981), p. 5.

2. Ibid., pp. 31–32.

3. Christine Y. Chen, "Ricochet, R.I.P.," Fortune.com (August 15, 2001), accessed online.

4. Stephen Baker, "Yes, It Really Is the Next Big Thing," *Business Week* International Edition (May 22, 2000), accessed online.

5. Hilary Stout, "Internet Hotshots End Up Too Far Ahead of the Market," *Wall Street Journal* online, date unknown, accessed online.

6. "Marketing Decisions Are the Most Important," *Business Week* online (June 18, 2001), accessed online, author unknown.

7. Clayton Christensen, *The Innovator's Dilemma: When New Technologies Cause Great Firms to Fail* (Boston: Harvard Business School Press, 1997), p. xv.

8. Jonathan D. Day, Paul Y. Mang, Ansgar Richter, and John Roberts, "The Innovative Organization: Why New Ventures Need More Than a Room of Their Own," *McKinsey Quarterly,* special edition, "Strategy = Structure" (2001), pp. 17–27.

9. *The Innovator's Dilemma,* p. 101.

10. Ibid., p. 125.

11. Geoffrey A. Moore, Paul Johnson and Tom Kipola, *The Gorilla Game: Picking Winners in High Technology* (New York, HarperBusiness, 1998), p. 219.

Chapter 11

1. Shel Horowitz, "Training for Successful Succession," *Related Matters Newsletter* (undated), University of Massachusetts Family Business Center (www.umas.edu/fambiz/successful_succession.htm).

2. "Transferring Management in the Family-Owned Business," by Professor Nancy Bowman-Upton, director, Institute for Family Business, Hankamer School of Business, John F. Baugh Center for Entrepreneurship, Baylor University, Waco, Texas, Small Business Administration, Emerging Business Series, 1991, unpaginated.

3. Bowman-Upton, "Transferring Management in the Family-Owned Business."

4. Drs. Paul and Pat Frishkoff, "Defining Opportunities for Involvement For Younger Family Members," Umass Family Business Center, date unknown, accessed online.

5. Peter F. Drucker, "How to Save the Family Business," www.umass.edu/fambiz/drucker_how_to_save_fambiz.htm.

6. Peter F. Drucker, "How to Save the Family Business."

7. "Challenges in Managing a Family Business," Management and Planning Series, U.S. Small Business Administration (author unknown), accessed online at http://www.sba.gov.

8. Bowman-Upton, "Transferring Management in the Family-Owned Business."

9. Ibid.

10. Shel Horowitz, "Succession Can Cause an Identity Crisis," University of Massachusetts Family Business Center (undated), accessed online.

11. "Challenges in Managing a Family Business."

12. Horowitz, "Training for Successful Succession."

13. Horowitz, "Succession Can Cause an Identity Crisis."

14. Personal interview.

Chapter 12

1. Roy Harris, "A Lesson Before Buying," *CFO* (May 2002): 58–65.

2. Bill Robinson, "Why Strategic Alliances Don't Work," *Forbes* online (July 1, 2002).

3. Hans Bieshaar, Jeremy Knight, and Alexander van Wassenaer, "Deals That Create Value," *McKinsey Quarterly*, no. 1 (2001): 65.

4. Kevin A. Frick and Alberto Torres, "Learning from High-Tech Deals," *McKinsey Quarterly*, no. 2 (2002): 113.

5. Roy Harris, "A Lesson Before Buying," pp. 58–65.

6. Bieshaar, Knight, and van Wassenaer, "Deals That Create Value."

7. Matthias M. Bekier, Anna J. Bogardus, and Tim Oldham, "Why Mergers Fail," *McKinsey Quarterly*, no. 4 (2001): 6–9.

8. Haarmann Hemmelrath Management Consultants, *Stahl und Reisen,* vol. 119, no. 8, p. 131, cited in "Why Mergers Fail."

9. Ira T. Kay and Mike Shelton, "The People Problem in Mergers," *McKinsey Quarterly,* no. 4 (2000): 27.

10. Ibid., pp. 27–28.

11. Roy Harris, "A Lesson Before Buying," pp. 58–65.

12. Frick and Torres, "Learning from High-Tech Deals."

13. Roy Harris, "A Lesson Before Buying," pp. 58–65.

14. Carol Matlack, "How Vivendi Should Clean up Messier's Mess," *Business Week* (July 8, 2002): 50.

15. Penelope Patsuris, "Vivendi's Real Problem," *Forbes* (July 2, 2002), accessed online.

16. "Deconstructing AT&T" (author unknown), *CFO* (July 2002): 47–52.

17. Michael T. Jacobs, *Short-Term America: The Causes and Cures of Our Business Myopia* (Boston: Harvard Business School Press, 1991), p. 106.

18. Paul A. Butler, "The Alchemy of LBOs," *Strategy = Structure, A McKinsey Quarterly Reader* (2001), pp. 4–15.

19. Jacobs, *Short-Term America,* p. 112.

20. Alex Taylor III, "Nissan's Turnaround Artist," *Fortune* (February 18, 2002), accessed online.

21. Roy Harris, "A Lesson Before Buying," pp. 58–65.

Chapter 13

1. "A Guide to Corporate Scandals," authors not listed, Economist.com (July 11, 2002), accessed online.

2. Paul Krugman, "Greed Is Bad," *New York Times,* June 4, 2002, accessed online.

3. Geoffrey Colvin, "The Great CEO Pay Heist," *Fortune* (June 25, 2001), accessed online.

4. Louis Lavelle, "When Directors Join CEOs at the Trough," *Business Week* (June 17, 2002), accessed online.

5. Matt Richtel, "On Its Boards, Silicon Valley Tends to Stand By Its Culture," *New York Times,* July 8, 2002, accessed online.

6. "The Poker Game That Ross Perot Won," *Business Week* (March 27, 1971): 74.

7. John Brooks, *The Go-Go Years: The Drama and Crashing Finale of Wall Street's Bullish 60s* (New York: John Wiley & Sons, 1973, 1999) p. 17.

8. Securities and Exchange Commission, *Special Study of the Securities Markets* (Washington, D.C.: SEC, 1963), p. 499.

9. Ibid., p. 498.

10. Nina Munk, "In the Final Analysis," *Vanity Fair,* August 2001, p. 102.

11. Martin Pring, *Investment Psychology Explained* (New York: John Wiley & Sons, Inc., 1993), p. 109.

12. Mortimer Feinberg, Ph.D., and John J. Tarrant, *Why Smart People Do Dumb Things: The Greatest Business Blunders—How They Happened, and How They Could Have Been Prevented* (New York: Simon & Schuster, 1995).

13. Mike France and Dan Carney, with Mike McNamee and Amy Borrus, "Why Corporate Crooks Are Tough to Nail," *BusinessWeek online,* July 1, 2002, accessed online.

Chapter 14

1. Arthur Kroeber, "The Hot Zone," *Wired* (November 2002).

2. "High Tech in China: Is It a Threat to Silicon Valley?" *Business Week* (October 28, 2002): 80–91.

3. Ahmed Janaid, "Watery Region Hides Hi-Tech Hothouse," BBC News, November 1, 2002.

4. *The Next Wave of HIV/AIDS: Nigeria, Ethiopia, Russia, India, and China,* report by the National Intelligence Council, September 2002 (www.cia.gov/nic/pubs/other_products/ICA%20HIV-AIDS%20unclassified%20092302POSTGERBER.htm).

5. "Internet Service Providers in the 21st Century," white paper produced by the U.S. Internet Industry Association, June 2002.

6. Michael Hammer and James Champy, *Reengineering the Corporation: A Manifesto for Business Revolution* (New York: Harper Business, 1993), pp. 7–30.

7. Ibid., p. 26.

8. Peter F. Drucker, "The Shape of Things to Come: An Interview with Peter F. Drucker," *Leader to Leader,* no. 1 (Summer 1996), accessed online.

9. Hammer and Champy, *Reengineering,* p. 31.

10. Drucker, "The Shape of Things to Come."

11. Todd G. Buchholz, *Market Shock* (New York: Harper Business, 1999), p. 3.

12. Ibid., pp. 62–64.

13. Adapted from "The Risk Breakdown Structure As an Aid to Effective Risk Management," Dr. David Hillson, paper presented at PMI Europe 2002 conference, Cannes, France, June 2002.

14. Personal interview with Dr. David Hillson.

15. Lowel L. Bryan, "Just-in-Time Strategy for a Turbulent World," *McKinsey Quarterly,* no. 2 (2002).

16. Ibid., p. 21.

Appendix

1. Tom Lowry, "AOL Has No Future," *Business Week* (January 27, 2003): 36.

2. Catherine Yang and Timothy J. Mullaney, ". . . Yes It Does," *Business Week* (January 27): 37.

3. Gary Hamel, "Reinvent Your Company, *Fortune* (June 12, 2000), accessed online.

4. Bruce Sterling, "Silent but Deadly," *Wired* (March 2003), accessed online.

5. Associated Press via *Wired News,* "The War in All Its Glory," May 30, 2002.

6. Remo Hacki and Julian Lighton, "The Future of the Networked Company," *McKinsey Quarterly,* no. 3, (2001): 29.

Index